ELEMENTARY SCHOOL COUNSELING

A Blueprint for Today and Tomorrow

John C. Worzbyt, Ed.D.
Department of Counselor Education
Indiana University of Pennsylvania
Indiana, PA

Kathleen O'Rourke, Ed.D.
Director of Guidance
Altoona Area School District
Altoona, PA

ACCELERATED DEVELOPMENT INC.
Publishers
Muncie, Indiana

ELEMENTARY SCHOOL COUNSELING
A Blueprint for Today and Tomorrow

Technical Development: Tanya Dalton
                              Delores Kellogg
                              Marguerite Mader
                              Sheila Sheward

Cover Illustration: Lisa Dedek

Library of Congress Cataloging-in-Publication Data

Worzbyt, John C.
    Elementary school counseling : a blueprint for today and tomorrow
/ John C. Worzbyt, Kathleen O'Rourke.
      p.   cm.
    Includes bibliographical references.
    ISBN 0-915202-69-7
    1. Personnel service in elementary education--Vocational guidance-
-United States.   2. Elementary school counselors--Training of-
—United States   3. Child development--United States.   I. O'Rourke,
Kathleen, 1941-   .   II. Title
LB1027.5.W674   1989
372.14--dc20   89-36793
                                         CIP

LCN: 87-70345

ACCELERATED DEVELOPMENT INC.
PUBLISHERS
3808 West Kilgore Avenue
Muncie, Indiana 47304-4896
Toll Free Order Number 1-800-222-1166

PREFACE

Elementary School Counseling: A Blueprint for Today and Tomorrow was prepared for elementary school counselors, teachers, and administrators to assist them with the development and management of new elementary school counseling programs and with the renewal and revitalization of existing programs. Counselor educators will likewise find the book useful in preparing counselors in training for their role as future managers, leaders, and service providers in elementary school counseling programs.

Elementary school counselors in today's dynamic and ever-changing world are challenged to help schools and those who work in the school environment to make worthwhile performance contributions to that system which will help enable children to become all they are capable of being. *Elementary School Counseling: A Blueprint for Today and Tomorrow* was written with that goal in mind.

Counselors are characterized as leaders and managers who, with the appropriate skills, can get extraordinary things done in the schools. They are people with the potential for turning challenging opportunities into remarkable successes. They are the people who can seize these opportunities and lead their programs and the children they serve to greatness. While the potential exists for these statements to reflect reality, a gap seems to be widening between what is possible and the struggle that many counselors face in trying to keep their programs viable.

We believe that elementary school counselors, in their determination and struggle to provide services to administrators, parents, teachers, and children, become so enveloped in their service role that they often lose sight of their management and leadership responsibilities. In so doing, they also lose a sense of perspective regarding program philosophy and mission. When counselors lose sight of program philosophy and mission, they begin to function as the sole providers of counseling services and become buried in the morass of duties and responsibilities that comes with trying to be all things to all people.

The fundamental purpose of *Elementary School Counseling: A Blueprint for Today and Tomorrow* is to assist counselors and Counseling Program Committees to view themselves as managers and leaders of a program that is deeply rooted in and supports all educational programs. Part I (Chapters 1 through 6) introduces the reader to a comprehensive management plan which highlights the goals of education, the philosophy of elementary school counseling programs, and the role of the elementary school counselor in the educative process. With these understandings firmly established, the elementary school counselor and Counseling Program Committee are led through a comprehensive, sequentially organized, and detailed step-by-step management process which builds on the four management functions of planning, organizing, actuating, and controlling.

Counselors follow a detailed six step process which focuses on

1. identifying and clarifying desired counseling program goals,

2. conducting a three phase needs assessment,

3. establishing counseling program goal priorities,

4. developing program strategies and activities,

5. actuating the counseling program utilizing a two-stage process, and

6. controlling the counseling program in relation to expected outcomes.

The last chapter in Part I (Chapter 6) contains a number of ideas that counselors can use in breathing new life into an existing elementary school counseling program. Using a format of things to think about, people with whom to talk, things to do, and suggested activities, counselors are provided with a blueprint for success in developing and implementing program energizers.

Part II (Chapters 7 through 11) carries the counseling program management process into curriculum design. The elementary school counseling program is organized around the tripartite of the child (child development), the behaviors to be learned, and the conditions of the learning environment (physical and psychological factors which contribute to effective learning). These three determinants represent the key to successful counseling program development. Counselors are provided with a learning model; curriculum design ideas pertaining to child development needs (physical development, social development, self-concept development, cognitive development, and career development); and a number of activities that support the five dimensions of child development.

Counselors are shown how they can meet children's developmental and societal needs through curriculum design using a five stage learning model. The same care is demonstrated in providing for the management of the school counseling curriculum as is detailed in the management of the total school counseling program.

Part III (Chapters 12 & 13) helps counselors and Counseling Program Committees plan for and manage the future by introducing them to the concept of futurism. Counselors are presented with five leadership practices and ten behavioral commitments designed to help them create the future. Several practical ideas are provided to guide counselors through the leadership challenge of searching for new ideas, experimenting and taking risks, creating challenging visions, breaking routines, enabling others to act, modeling the way, and celebrating contributions and accomplishments along the way.

With a plan for creating the future, counselors and Counseling Program Committee members are acquainted with a number of future issues and possible directions that elementary school counseling programs might take in maximizing the effectiveness of computer applications in counseling and human development; in exploring multicultural issues and directions; in addressing the needs of children living in a nuclear age; in helping children understand, secure, and practice their rights; and in developing wellness lifestyle curriculums that comprehensively address children's needs. Counselors also are challenged to look at their future roles regarding the leadership and management processes of school counseling and the effects of power and politics in shaping counseling programs of the future.

Successful elementary school counseling programs represent many people, with a unified direction and purpose. If the people perform well, then school counseling performs well; if the people don't, the school counseling program can't. The school counseling program thus represents a collection of people who work together to achieve a common purpose. That purpose can be achieved to the extent that elementary school counselors see themselves first as managers and leaders and secondly as human service providers. *Elementary School Counseling: A Blueprint for Today and Tomorrow* provides for the creation and implementation of a program designed to meet the needs of all children because it involves the support of all people who care about what happens to children.

John C. Worzbyt

John C. Worzbyt

Kathleen O'Rourke

Kathleen O'Rourke

ACKNOWLEDGEMENTS

Many persons have influenced the development of *Elementary School Counseling: A Blueprint for Today and Tomorrow.* To all those persons, counselors, co-workers, friends, and students, we express our gratitude. They shared with us their knowledge, suggestions, support, time, patience, and experience in helping us to create a book that is simply written and full of practical ideas. For that we are deeply grateful.

The many details and stages of development that are involved in the production of a manuscript are numerous. Without the invaluable support of several key persons, we would not have been able to turn our dream into reality. To those people, we owe a special thank you.

To Dr. Joseph Hollis, our publisher, who provided invaluable suggestions, direction, and support throughout the many drafts of the manuscript.

To Mrs. Linda Butler, Counselor Education Department Secretary, for her continuous assistance in typing, in coordinating the typing efforts of work-study students, and in humoring the authors during the past two years.

To Debbie Yesilonis, student and principal typist, for her energetic, supportive, and cheerful disposition throughout her typing of numerous drafts during the book's evolution. We also would like to extend a special thanks to Amy Shrock, student, who also assisted with the typing.

To David Roush and Daria Wargo, Counselor Education graduate students, for the many hours they spent in gathering data for the manuscript and the significant contributions they made in helping to develop the futures chapters (Chapters 12 & 13).

To Dr. David Lynch, Dean of the Graduate School at Indiana University of Pennsylvania (IUP), for providing typing resources, for arranging work release time for one of the authors to do research and to write, and for his personal support and interest in advancing scholarly activity at IUP.

With all of the special people that we have recognized, the manuscript could not have materialized without the love and support of our families. To those persons, we dedicate this book.

CONTENTS

LIST OF FIGURES

LIST OF ACTIVITIES

Physical Development Activities

Social Development Activities

Social Development Activities (Continued)

Self-Concept Activities

Cognitive Development Activities

Career Development Activities

Career Development Activities (Continued)

PART I

MANAGING AN EFFECTIVE SCHOOL COUNSELING PROGRAM

PART I

MANAGING AN EFFECTIVE ELEMENTARY SCHOOL COUNSELING PROGRAM

Elementary school counseling has met with many successes during the past twenty-five years as an important support service in our schools. However, as we embark on a new decade and soon a new century, we need to revitalize our efforts and make new commitments to elementary school counseling programs. The time is right for school counseling reform.

The following six chapters are designed to assist and guide the reader in either developing a new elementary school counseling program or in redesigning an existing program. These chapters are unique in that they spotlight the elementary school counseling program from a management perspective. Management is an exciting process which focuses on seeking, setting, and achieving goals. In many ways, we are all managers in that we direct our own lives. The practice of management is found in every dimension of human activity: schools, businesses, churches, government, unions, armed forces, and families (Terry & Franklin, 1982). Regardless of the nature or scope of our management activities, the process is similar, as are the pitfalls.

The level of success that an elementary school counseling program attains or that people attain personally in their lives can be attributed to the manager's ability to manage. "A manager's role is to set goals and amass and mobilize the resources of men and women, materials, machines, methods, money, and markets to accomplish the desired results within predetermined constraints of time, effort, and cost" (Terry & Franklin, 1982, p. 4).

If elementary school counseling programs are to make a significant contribution in meeting children's developmental and societal needs and are to create and maintain the kind of supportive teaching/learning environment which will be needed, elementary school counseling programs will require effective management. Effective management is a process consisting of activities of planning, organizing, actuating, and controlling for the purpose of accomplishing the desired goals through people and resources.

Chapter 1: *Elementary School Counseling Program* presents a philosophy and rationale for elementary school counseling programs. In this chapter are discussed the components of a model elementary school counseling program and an overview of components of program development and management.

Chapter 2: *Planning for Program Effectiveness* stresses the importance of planning as a fundamental function of management. Steps in the planning process are outlined and include identifying desired program goals, conducting a three stage needs assessment, establishing goal priorities, and developing the elementary school counseling program offerings.

Chapter 3: *Organizing the Elementary School Counseling Program* explains how an effective organizational structure is both necessary and critical to actuating a successful elementary school counseling program. The organizing function of management provides the structural design through which people, resources, and program plans unite in meeting the elementary school counseling program goals.

Chapter 4: *Actuating the Elementary School Counseling Program* promotes a two step process which moves the elementary school counseling program to action. Parents, teachers, administrators, school staff, children, and community volunteers are first oriented to the school counseling program, are introduced to the goals and benefits of the program, and are shown how they can access program services. The second phase of actuating teaches the same program recipients how they can contribute to the success of the program as providers of services.

Chapter 5: *Controlling Elementary School Counseling Program* emphasizes the importance of the controlling function of management in monitoring, guiding, and implementing corrective action, when necessary, in keeping the elementary school counseling program "on target." The controlling function helps answer the question: How well are we doing in progressing towards and meeting our planned program goals?

Chapter 6: *Breathing New Life Into an Existing Program* presents six (6) ways in which elementary school counseling programs can be energized. The topics are Parent Volunteer Support; Networking: A Spiderweb of Support; Environmental Connectiveness; Pupil Service Interfacing; School and Community Partnerships; and Public Relations. Things to think about, people to talk to, things to do, and suggested activities are provided for each topic in helping the reader breathe new life into the elementary school counseling program.

These six chapters will provide the reader with a wealth of information, skills, and confidence necessary to plan, organize, actuate, and control an effective counseling program which will be sensitive to the needs of children and in tune with values of the larger community.

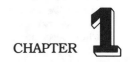
ELEMENTARY SCHOOL COUNSELING PROGRAM

What is elementary school counseling? To answer this question by outlining counseling activities or listing counseling services would be an endless task. Rather what makes more sense is to examine elementary school counseling not as an entity unto itself, but as a support service designed to enhance the educational value of the school system, since that is how it will be judged.

GOAL OF EDUCATION

Elementary school counseling, as with other programs, takes on meaning in a school system which recognizes the counseling program's purpose for being and has a clearly stated mission which it strives to attain. The school's mission and what the school views as the central goal of education should be synonomous. Van Hoose (1975) stated some years ago that "The goal of education in a free society is to enable youth to acquire the skills and understandings to be competent and responsible people" (p. 27). Participants of the 1970 White House Conference on Children stated the goal of education in yet another way when they said:

> The right to learn is the goal that we seek for the twenty-first century.
> We want for our children a range of learning opportunities as broad as

the unknown range of their talents. We want our children to know themselves and, secure in that knowledge, to open themselves to others. We want to have freedom, and the order, justice, and peace that the preservation of their freedom demands. (US Dept of HEW, Office of Child Development, 1970, p. 75)

While the 1970 White House statement was written nearly two decades ago, its message is as much on target today as then. Our educational system seeks to develop moral beings with purposes and loyalties which are valuable to the individual and society. Herr (1984) stated it best when he said that ". . .educational reform of any kind must be mindful that at the center of attention are the individual needs for knowledge and skills having general currency in the society that students will occupy" (p. 219).

If these educational goals, or ones like them, are to be realized, schools will need to

1. provide opportunities for every child to grow, learn, and live creatively; and

2. redesign education to achieve individualized, humanized, child-centered learning.

While the order is a big one, it can be filled by an educational team whose members have diversified backgrounds and skills which complement each other. The elementary school counselor, as a member of the team composed of parents, teachers, educational specialists, administrators, and community representatives, can help meet the challenge of educational excellence in the schools.

PHILOSOPHY OF ELEMENTARY SCHOOL COUNSELING

A developmental elementary school counseling program is concerned with assisting the school to achieve its educational goals. Elementary school counseling programs strive to build educational systems that will develop moral beings with purposes and loyalties which are valuable to the individual and society. Such counseling programs recognize the unique nature of children; the necessity of meeting their individual needs; and the importance of providing a humanized, child-centered learning climate. While elementary school counseling programs are committed to and support the teaching of academic skills such as reading, writing, and arithmetic, equally important they also support the contention that children need to acquire skills of self understanding, values clarification, self-esteem enhancement, interacting with others, learning to perform within the context of a work environment, developing positive attitudes, and desiring to participate in lifelong learning. Developing an understanding and utilization of self is a lifelong learning process and is a prerequisite in effective functioning in the schooling process and in the work force.

Counseling programs strive to help children accomplish tasks that will lead to cognitive, affective, and psychomotor development. The program recognizes the need for children to become critical thinkers, to be able to communicate their wants and needs to others, to become skilled at processing information, and to develop the capacity for making responsible decisions for self and society. While these skills and processes develop and mature over many years, they continue to serve each of us and the environment at every stage in our development. *Counseling is, therefore, a now process with lifelong continuous benefits that will be utilized over a lifetime.*

RATIONALE FOR
ELEMENTARY SCHOOL COUNSELING

Research supports the contention that what happens to elementary school children during their early years of development will have a marked effect on their coping behaviors in later life. If we want to provide children with opportunities to grow, learn, and live creatively, we must pay attention to the full range of developmental, environmental, and hereditary factors affecting the teaching-learning process.

Benjamin Bloom's (1956) longitudinal research on intelligence indicated that the environment, in addition to heredity, is a significant factor in determining the educational achievement of children. He stated that approximately 80% of a child's intellectual growth takes place during the first eight years of life, with the remaining growth being completed by age seventeen. Since the period of most rapid growth takes place during a child's early years of development, environmental experiences during those years are most critical and should not evolve by circumstance alone.

The historical and long standing research of Havighurst (1952, 1953) and Maslow (1954) further supports the contention that what happens or fails to happen to children developmentally during their early years will more than likely determine lifelong attitudes toward learning and assist or deter children in the acquisition of skills, attainment of goals, and evolvement of satisfactory attitudes toward self and society. Thus, children's perceptions, experiences, and interactions with others, when added together, will either contribute to the development of adequate, success oriented individuals, or will produce ones who will come to view themselves as failures and worthless human beings.

Knowing what we do about the complex nature of children, a school system which purports to meet the needs of children through a strictly academically oriented program, gearing all learning around curriculum packages which have not changed with the times, is restricting the world of the child to a less than adequate experiencing of self. If the school is to contribute to the growth and development of children, school personnel must view children as children; they must be able to identify what behaviors children need to develop; and they must recognize what effect environmental conditions (physical and psychological) have on the teaching/learning process.

One of the major criticisms of the many reports on the need for national educational reform is that the curriculum revisions called for are elitist in focus in that they emphasize the importance of content primarily appropriate for the college bound. They de-emphasize, by omission, the need for addressing those skills and understandings which are central to life and living. The issue is not whether we need to increase the availability of more science, math, and foreign languages in the curriculum, but whether we do this at the expense of ignoring the emotional side of learning.

Herr (1984) stated that the collective reports on educational reform failed to address the importance of recognizing the difference in learning styles and the importance of cultivating the multiple forms of human ability which are required in our society. The reports likewise failed to point out the necessity of recognizing and responding to the emotional life of children and youth and the importance of such activity in enhancing the teaching/learning process. In addition to these omissions, many of the reports chose not to address the social problems confronting children and their families, the emotional problems associated with the abuse of drugs and alcohol, escalating juvenile delinquency and violence in the schools, problems created by the changing family structure, the increased numbers of school drop-outs, the rise in child and teen depression and suicide, and the list continues. While the educational reform reports failed to address these issues, the schools cannot.

In times past when the family was intact and people experienced a sense of community in their neighborhoods, all shared in the responsibility of child rearing and nurturing. Perhaps during those times, the school was able to place more emphasis on academic learning and intellectual pursuits. However, times have changed. Children and families are experiencing many new problems brought forth by a changing society and have nowhere to turn but to schools.

The school has no choice but to recognize and address the impact that such issues as poverty, unemployment, hunger, single parent families, and child psychological neglect have on the teaching/learning process. Whether or not addressing these issues ought to be the prime mission of our schools is a debatable topic. However, to ignore such realities is to deny many children an education which will ultimately result in a nation at risk.

An elementary school counseling program is designed to assist the school and community in addressing the full range of variables affecting the teaching/learning process, from meeting children's needs to creating new growth producing learning environments for them. Elementary school counselors have knowledge and understanding in such areas as child growth and development, human learning, group dynamics, and self-concept development. And they have the necessary skills and expertise to assist teachers, parents, administrators, and educational specialists in managing the broad range of the teaching/learning spectrum. Elementary school counselors also can be of assistance to school personnel in coordinating team planning efforts which utilize the capabilities and strengths of other school specialists and community resource people in tackling those situations which call for their collective participation.

With all that has been said about the impact of a complex society on education and the importance of providing the right kind of education for children, is it any wonder that the ever expanding research, educational technology, increasing body of knowledge about human growth and development, and new teaching approaches have far surpassed the capacity of any one educational generalist to keep abreast of all that is new pertaining to the teaching/learning process? The day of the educational generalist is in the past. We have moved into an age of specialization. Elementary school counseling, as a specialized field in education, has a place in today's schools and will remain there for as long as that program contributes to the provision of quality education for all children.

School counselors and effective counseling programs have achieved a record of empirical successes in assisting the school and community in helping children to acquire knowledge, positive attitudes, skills related to academic achievement, mental health, interpersonal relations, career awareness, decision making, climatic adjustments to school involvement, stress management, and increased self-esteem (Herr, 1983; Herr & Pinson, 1982). In so doing, elementary school counselors have been instrumental in encouraging and developing successful school-community partnerships which have begun to encourage the participation of people from many divergent and variant fields of study in responding to the physical, social, and ego needs of children.

THE ELEMENTARY SCHOOL COUNSELOR AND THE EDUCATIVE PROCESS

The central function of an elementary school counseling program is to enhance and improve the learning environment of the school so that each child in the elementary school has an opportunity to learn to the best of his/her capacity. An effective elementary school counseling program seeks to create learning environments and develop programs which encourage children to understand themselves, to develop satisfying peer relationships, to accept personal responsibility for their own behavior, to understand the world of work and education, to make decisions, and to develop sound values and high ideals.

In helping to create effective learning environments, one role of the elementary school counselor is to identify school practices and obstacles which inhibit the freedom to learn and to devise ways of removing them. This person acts as a catalyst in helping teachers critically evaluate the teaching/learning process. Teachers, for example, are encouraged to de-emphasize memorization in their teaching practice in lieu of discovery; to move away from educational methods that promote conformity and help children understand and treasure their differences and cultivate their talents; and to promote an educational system which assists children in learning what they need to learn when they need to learn it.

One of the counselor's most important functions is to intervene in the lives of children and to intervene in the learning environment of the school in order to help children to learn through experience the meaning of freedom and responsibility so that they can become free and responsible persons. In order to accomplish this end, the elementary school counselor who becomes an effective functionary in the educative process will need to invest more time in aiding human development than in the tedium of record keeping, testing, and adjustive guidance.

The child's classroom is as expansive or narrow as the environment which is utilized in the teaching/learning process. That classroom, if it is to meet children's needs, must cultivate their independence, individuality, freedom, spontaneity, and originality. These efforts can be accomplished through comprehensive elementary school counseling programs which deliniate counseling functions similar to those proposed in recent state legislation mandating elementary school counseling (West Virginia, Arkansas, and Tennessee) and in the 1984 American School Counselor Association (ASCA) Counseling Role Statement.

Further substantiating recent national commitment to elementary school counseling is Resolution 4.1.26 drafted by the National School Boards Association (NSBA, 1986) on Guidance and Counseling and adopted by its general assembly in April 1986. The resolution stated that NSBA encourages local school districts to support comprehensive counseling programs kindergarten through grade twelve and staffed by trained counseling personnel. "A counselor in every elementary school" is the recommendation of the National Foundation for the improvement of Education in the recent publication *Blueprint For Success* (NEA, 1986) sponsored by the National Education Association. Also the College Entrance Examination Board report, *Keeping the Options Open* (1986) urged school districts to begin counseling programs in elementary school. The authors of that report further stated that the unfortunate omission of the topic of counseling by the educational reform movement has serious consequences for children.

The current practice of providing large amounts of local, state, and federal dollars for remedial and crisis intervention programs related to such issues as school failure, dropouts, juvenile delinquency, and drug and alcohol abuse may be a case of "too little too late." In the long run, early counseling intervention, prevention, and developmentally focused school counseling programs make more sense. While funding school counseling programs represent an added expense to already overburdened school district budgets, not to address this issue now may prove to be even more costly to our communities, states, and nation in addressing societal ills which are expanding not decreasing in size.

An effective elementary school counseling program led by a well trained school counselor can make a significant difference in promoting the educational welfare and developmental growth (physical and psychological) of children by seeking to

1. recognize early indicators of social maladjustment, child abuse, and neglect, and other physical and emotional problems requiring immediate attention and referral services.

2. provide information and an understanding of the world of work; the value of a work oriented society; career awareness; career development; and the interactions of business, industry and government.

3. coordinate and assist school personnel in conducting classroom activity sessions for developing thinking, decision making, and interpersonal skills; physical coordination and dexterity functions; self understanding and utilization of self abilities; and developing and practicing coping and management strategies designed to benefit self and society.

4. provide information and coordinate positive home/school/community relations designed to recognize and support cooperation among and between all people regardless of color, religion, ethnic origin, age, sex, and belief.

5. conduct teacher preservice and inservice training sessions on such diverse topics as individualized learning styles, child growth and development, classroom management, group dynamics, child self-management techniques, and curriculum design using counseling strategies, for the purpose of enhancing the teaching/learning environment.

6. contribute to the growth and development of positive and productive family living environments by providing information and conducting parent groups that focus on such topics as child rearing strategies, child discipline, raising your child's self-esteem, improving family communications, sex education, home/school networking, and life in a non-traditional family setting.

7. coordinate the counseling program and develop the necessary networking linkages between the counseling

program and all those who must understand and contribute to its success (Administrators, board members, parents, teachers, school specialists, and community supporters).

8. coordinate and manage a comprehensive counseling program that not only provides a depth of service, but is also longitudinally sound in that the program delivers services that cut across all grade levels K-12.

9. infuse the total counseling program into every aspect and dimension of the learning environment, so that program concepts and understandings become a way of life and contribute significantly to helping each child become all he/she is capable of becoming.

DEVELOPING AN
ELEMENTARY SCHOOL COUNSELING PROGRAM

Some twenty-five years have passed since the beginning of the elementary school counseling movement and during that time a constant theme has occurred regarding the lack of consensus with respect to the programatic nature of elementary school counseling. While we have come a long way since our inception, no one to date has developed a counseling program which all other counseling programs now model. Variations in pupil personnel organizations, school philosophy and mission, and community needs by their very nature will serve to dictate variations in elementary school counseling programs and methods. *Strong counseling programs are strong not because they mirror programs that are respected elsewhere, but because the role of the counselor and the elementary school counseling program elements are based on the educational philosophy and goals of the school, the needs of children, and values of the school community.* This point of view supports the need for elementary school counseling programs to be planned and managed effectively if they are to make a strong impact on enhancing the educational process in ways described in this chapter.

Program Development

The management of elementary school counseling programs is of major concern to school districts, the recipients of counseling program services, the counselor, and the community. A counseling program that is not managed effectively will become a costly disappointment to all who are left to pick up the pieces. Whether a school district plans to update an existing program or take the time to establish a new program, facing the challenge of management is a must. The management process can be defined as consisting of four steps: (1) making a plan to develop a counseling program which personalizes and humanizes the educational process for all children, (2) organizing the people and resources in the school and community needed to implement the plan, (3) assisting the people who will be involved in performing the tasks necessary to implement the program, and (4) evaluating the counseling program in relationship to goal attainment (Ivancevich & Matteson, 1987).

What follows is a program development process which can be used to create new elementary school counseling programs or to revise existing programs. For the purpose of providing direction, the process will be presented as though a new program is being developed. Figure 1.1 depicts the management stages necessary for program planning, organizing, actuating, and controlling.

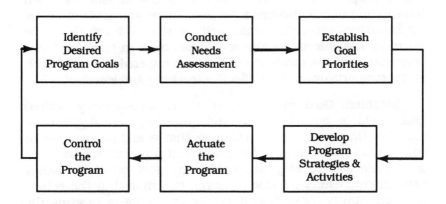

Figure 1.1. Elementary School Counseling Management Plan.

Identify Desired Program Goals. In order to be effective, the school district and community need to first determine what goals their elementary school counseling program should be addressing. The elementary school counseling program proposed in this book is organized according to five major dimensions of child development and a number of societal issues which effect children's lives.

The first step in developing a new program or revising an existing one is to explore a variety of possible goals for each dimension the counseling program wishes to address. This can be accomplished by reviewing the school district's philosophy and mission statement; reading books on elementary school counseling programs; reviewing national educational reform reports; securing school and community ideas; and conferring with local, state, and national school counseling associations. This list of goals will give the Counseling Program Committee direction and focus when developing the needs assessment process.

Conduct Needs Assessment. Only with clear and comprehensive goals which are responsible to the given realities of the school and community can a school district develop an elementary school counseling program which will best serve the needs of the children and the community. A comprehensive needs assessment is an activity designed to determine the problems, wants, and needs of a given school community in relationship to its children. The needs assessment will yield information about children's developmental and societal needs, the behaviors which the school believes that children should be learning, how successful the school has been in teaching those behaviors, and the condition of the learning environment which either supports or disrupts effective teaching and learning.

Establish Goal Priorities. To try to satisfy every desired goal would be both foolhardy and quite impractical given the available time and needed resources that would be required to complete the task. The needs assessment process thus becomes a valuable second step in establishing goal priorities. Needs assessment results provide a means for informing the school and community about how well they are doing in meeting the desired goals that they hoped to achieve. By comparing the *desired goals list* with the *needs assessment goals list,* the

Counseling Program Committee can identify those goals which are being met and those which are not. From this information, goals can be prioritized based on their *importance* and *need* as determined by the assessment process. Since some goals will require more attention than others, the resources can then be strategically allocated according to priorities that have been established.

Develop Program Strategies and Activities. Elementary school counseling program strategies and activities are needed to implement and satisfy goal attainment of the various program goals. The strategies (methodology) and activities need to be designed and infused into the regular academic curriculum, developed in accordance with sound learning theory, result in the behaviors to be learned, and satisfy the developmental and societal needs of children for whom they were developed. The strategies and activities also must promote positive teaching/learning climates designed to foster high self-esteem and stimulate the desire for continued lifelong learning in children. Of a more pragmatic nature, strategies and activities are to be designed so as to make use of the full range of resources (people, materials, equipment, budget) available to the school and community in addressing the program goals. A sound elementary school counseling program demands the input and collective cooperation of many people with diversified skills and talents, if the school district is to be successful in meeting the identified needs of the children it serves.

Actuate the Program. Many otherwise successful elementary school counseling programs have failed because the school district and counselor did not have an implementation plan. For a program to succeed, it must have an organizational structure which enhances the delivery and reception of program services to those who will benefit from them. The management process requires knowing how to get things done through people. The counselor, using the organizational structure and the goal priorities list as a guide, will need to successfully communicate the nature of elementary school counseling as a cooperative school and community program designed to meet the developmental and societal needs of children.

Control the Program. While the final stage of the management process is control (evaluation), it is really an on-going process. A monitoring system is required to determine the degree to which program strategies and activities are meeting program goals.

Effective controlling systems provide readily available and continuous feedback which is used to keep the counseling program on target as it moves toward goal satisfaction and attainment. Responsible controlling efforts save money, improve resource utilization, and foster elementary school counseling programs which get desired results (Albanese, 1988). Elementary school counseling programs which make use of on-going evaluations help to insure program wellness by being in tune with and paying attention to their programatic needs.

COUNSELING PROGRAM COMMITTEE

An elementary school counselor cannot plan a new counseling program or make changes in an existing one by working in isolation. In order to insure that the elementary school counseling program is an integral part of the total school system and community, a committee, representing various segments of the school and community needs to be involved.

The Counseling Program Committee will become actively involved in all facets of the management process as delineated in Figure 1.1. The committee will participate in planning, organizing, actuating, and controlling the program and will function under the leadership of the school counselor. School districts, which involve the total participation of the school and community, add breadth and depth to the elementary school counseling program which radiates beyond the role of the school counselor as the sole provider of services (Worzbyt, 1978).

Membership on the Counseling Program Committee should be broad enough in scope to touch all dimensions of the system, but small enough in number to accomplish its mission. Key people to consider are teachers (primary and intermediate grades), administrators, health personnel, pupil personnel staff, specialized instructional staff, and community representatives (school board member, parents, business/industry representative). The Committee membership probably should not exceed ten (10) to twelve (12) people.

Committee membership can be secured in a variety of ways. The key consideration is that members should be informed in advance of their participation as to the role, function, and time commitment of the Committee. They then can decide if they choose to participate.

Developing a team approach to elementary school counseling is critical to the management process. When staff members are involved in the design and implementation of the elementary school counseling program, they are inclined to support it. The committee process, while time consuming, provides an excellent vehicle for promoting the role of the elementary school counselor and involving the entire school community in the delivery of services.

In keeping with this philosophy, the elementary school counseling program described in this book reflects the four priority counseling recommendations for action in the schools as delineated in the 1986 College Entrance Examination Board Report, *Keeping the Options Open.*

1. Establish a broad based process in each local school district for determining the particular guidance and counseling needs of the students within each school and for planning how best to meet these needs.

2. Develop a program under the leadership of each school principal that emphasizes the importance of the guidance counselor as a monitor and promoter of student potential, as well as coordinator of the school's guidance plan.

3. Mount programs to inform and involve parents and other members of the family influential in the choices, plans, decisions, and learning activities of the student.

4. Provide a program of guidance and counseling during the early and middle years of schooling especially for students who traditionally have not been well served by the schools. (pp. 5-6)

Schools must develop caring environments in which children are viewed and supported both as learners and as human beings. All children deserve no less than the very best which schools can provide in meeting their developmental and societal needs. Yet we have not heard from educational leaders about the importance of attending to children's needs as much as we have heard about new academic requirements, more tests, and longer school hours (College Entrance Examination Board, 1986).

The Study Commission of the College Entrance Examination Board (1986) stated that many children have become discouraged in today's schools because their needs are not being met and that improved school counseling programs could contribute significantly to reducing the considerable waste of human talent which currently exists. By addressing the four priority recommendations stated earlier and outlined in the 1986 College Entrance Examination Board Report, *Keeping the Options Open*, school counseling programs can help to make a significant difference in fulfilling the promise of meeting children's needs and providing equal educational opportunities for all.

The fulfillment of the College Board's four recommendations will surely result in a positive future for children in which they hopefully will be able to attain those attributes envisioned at the 1970 White House Conference on Children.

> We would like him [her] to be a man [woman] with a sense of himself [herself] and his[her] own humaness, with awareness of his [her] thoughts and feelings, with the capacity to feel and express love and joy and to recognize tragedy and grief. We would have him [her] be a man [woman] who, with a strong realistic sense of his [her] own worth is able to relate openly with others, to cooperate effectively with them toward common ends, and to view mankind [womankind] as one while respecting diversity and difference. We would want him [her] to be a being who, even while very young, somehow senses that he [she] has the capacity for lifelong spiritual and intellectual growth. We would want him [her] to cherish that vision of the man [woman] he [she] is capable of becoming and to cherish the development of the same potential in others. (U.S. Dept of HEW, Office of Child Development, 1970, p. 78)

BIBLIOGRAPHY

Albanese, R. (1988). *Management.* Cincinnati: Southwestern Publishing.

American Association for Counseling and Development and ERIC/CAPS Clearinghouse. (1985). *Counselors: Agents for educational excellence.* Conference Proceedings: January 13-15, 1985. Orlando, FL. Falls Church, VA: Author.

American Association for Counseling and Development. (1987). *The future of school counseling: Bibliography of materials.* Alexandria, VA: Author.

American School Counselor Association (1984). *Role statement on the elementary counselor.* Alexandria, VA: AACD

Bloom, B.S. (Ed.) (1956). *Taxonomy of educational objectives handbook 1: Cognitive domain.* New York: David McKay.

College Entrance Examination Board (1986). *Keeping the options open recommendations: Final report of the commission on precollege guidance and counseling.* New York: College Board Publications.

Goodlad, J. (1983). *A place called school: Prospects for the future.* New York: McGraw Hill.

Havighurst, R.J. (1952). *Developmental tasks and education.* New York: Macmillan.

Havighurst, R.J. (1953). *Human development in education.* New York: Longmans, Green.

Herr, E.L. (1983). *Why counseling?* Falls Church, VA: American Personnel and Guidance Association.

Herr, E.L. (1984). "The national reports on reform in schooling: Some missing ingredients." *Journal of Counseling and Development 63,* 4, 217-220.

Herr, E.L., & Pinson, N. (1982). "The effects of guidance and counseling: Three domains. In E.L. Herr and N. Pinson (Eds) *Foundation for policy in guidance and counseling* (pp. 155-184) Falls Church, VA: American Personnel and Guidance Association.

Ivancevich, J.M., & Matteson, M.T. (1987). *Organizational behavior and management.* Plano, TX: Business Publications.

Maslow, H.A. (1954). *Motivation and personality.* New York: Harper & Row.

National Education Association (1986). *Blueprint for success.* Washington, DC: NEA Publications.

National School Boards Association (Adopted 1986). *Resolution 4.1.26.* Washington, DC: NSBA.

Terry, G.R., & Franklin, S.G. (1982). *Principles of management,* 8th Ed. Illinois: Richard D. Irwin.

United States Department of Health, Education, and Welfare, Office of Child Development. (1970). *Report to the President: White house conference on children.* Washington, DC: Government Printing Office.

Van Hoose, W.H. (1975). "Overview: The elementary counselor in the 1970's." *Virginia Personnel and Guidance Journal, 3,* 1, 17-30.

Worzbyt, J.C. (1978). *Elementary school guidance: Program planning, organization and implementation.* (Title III ESEA Report). Harrisburg, PA: Pennsylvania Department of Education.

PLANNING FOR PROGRAM EFFECTIVENESS

Planning is a necessary management function for any program to survive, grow, and develop. The planning process not only determines the program goals and objectives, but also specifies the resources that will be needed to implement the program and achieve goal satisfaction in a cost effective manner. The planning process shapes the organizational structure of the program; determines the most effective methods for implementation, program maintenance, and enhancement; and establishes appropriate methods for conducting on-going evaluations. Planning answers the questions: Where are we now? Where do we want to go? How do we get there? How are we doing (Terry & Franklin, 1982)?

While planning an effective elementary school counseling program designed to meet the physical, social, self-concept, cognitive, and career development needs of children is important, action is the key to success, not planning. Planning provides the Counseling Program Committee with a sense of direction and should be thought of as a means to an end and not as an end in itself. "Planning is selecting information and making assumptions regarding the future to formulate activities necessary to achieve organizational (program) objectives" (Terry & Franklin, 1982, p. 148). The process is continuous and serves to provide the elementary school Counseling Program Committee with numerous decisions to be made so that the Committee can best serve children both now and in the future.

STEPS IN PLANNING

The elementary school counselor and the Counseling Program Committee will need to become involved in many different planning activities associated with developing an effective counseling program. One such planning process relates to reviewing the philosophy and mission of the elementary school and then establishing a philosophy and mission statement for the elementary school counseling program which supports the school's position. In Chapter 1, *Elementary School Counseling Program* is discussed the importance of establishing a philosophy and mission statement prior to developing a new elementary school counseling program or revising an existing one. With that in mind, in Chapter 2, *Planning for Program Effectiveness*, we will be covering those steps necessary in developing an elementary school counseling program which supports the philosophy and mission of the school system and that of the elementary school counseling program.

The first four steps in establishing or revising an elementary school counseling program are

1. identifying desired program goals,

2. conducting a needs assessment,

3. selecting goal priorities based on need, and

4. developing program offerings through linking program activities and strategies to priority goals (Szilagyi, 1984).

Developing program organization, implementation, and evaluation activities also need to be a part of any planning process. They will be discussed in Chapters 3, 4, and 5 respectively.

IDENTIFYING DESIRED PROGRAM GOALS

Desired program goals are those priority goals that an elementary school counseling program hopes to achieve in meeting the developmental and societal needs of children. The goals that are selected are ones that the school and community feel strongly about and want included in the educational program of the school. This goal list will serve as a guide in developing the needs assessment process which is the next step in program development.

The Counseling Program Committee need not be concerned at this stage with whether or not the selected goals are being addressed, the conditions of the learning environment, or whether or not the needed resources are available to meet the goals. These factors will be reviewed during the needs assessment. The Committee's primary function is to determine what children's developmental and societal needs are in relationship to enhancing the teaching/learning process and then to formulate goal statements which will provide direction in establishing an effective program.

Literature Review

The developmental needs of children can be reviewed by reading books by such people as Elkind (1978 & 1981), Maslow (1954), Havighurst (1953), Dinkmeyer and Caldwell (1970), Gesell and Ilg, (1946) and McCandless (1967). *The develop-mental needs of children can be categorized according to five dimensions of development: physical, social, self–concept, cognitive, and career.* As child development books are studied, the Committee should be asking itself, what are the developmental needs of children in each of these areas and what behavioral outcomes are most important for them to achieve in order to be contributing members of society?

Educational Philosophy Statement

In addition to reading child development texts, the Committee will find the school's educational and counseling philosophy and mission statements useful to review. These statements embrace a point of view subscribed to by the school and counseling program and can give direction to program development as well.

School and Community

Another source of useful information in establishing direction for the elementary school counseling program is to talk with school personnel. They have daily contact with children and can provide insightful information about the developmental needs of children and what goals to establish in achieving the desired outcomes.

Likewise, the community in which the school resides has a perception of its own about what children need to learn and understand about themselves and the environment (societal needs) in order to "make it in this world." A variety of environmental issues (economical, sociological, medical, demographics, multi-cultural/ethnic, political, legal, technological, and educational) do impact upon children by creating needs which also must be addressed if children are to take full advantage of the teaching/learning process both in and out of school.

Educational Reform and Counseling Program Statements

If the Counseling Program Committee members are not already familiar with the following educational reports, books, and bibliographies they should consider reviewing these printed resources, as well as others, in preparing the desired elementary school counseling program goals list.

1. *A Place Called School* (Goodlad, 1984)

2. *Keeping The Options Open* (College Entrance Examination Board, 1986)

3. *Counselors: Agents For Educational Excellence* (AACD, 1985)

4. *Role Statement on The Elementary Counselor* (ASCA, 1984)

5. *The Future of School Counseling: AACD Bibliography Materials* (AACD, 1987)

Counseling Program Goal Statements

Once Counseling Program Committee members have reviewed the available data on the developmental and societal needs of children, they are ready to create a counseling program goals list. The list should be organized according to the five dimensions of development (physical, social, self-concept, cognitive, and career) and those societal issues in the community which have created specific child needs that must be addressed if children are to grow and develop in self-enhancing ways. What follows is a sample list of counseling program goals arranged according to the suggested headings.

1. Physical

    a. Assist children in understanding their own personal growth and development (physical and emotional changes).

    b. Assist children with hand-eye coordination, balance, body in space, and laterality.

    c. Assist children with small and large muscle development.

2. Social

    a. Assist children in developing peer relationships.

    b. Assist children in learning to work effectively in groups.

    c. Assist children in developing interpersonal skills.

3. Self-Concept

    a. Assist children in developing an understanding and utilization of self.

    b. Assist children in developing a positive self-esteem/ self-concept.

    c. Assist children in developing life management self-help skills (stress management, assertiveness management, values clarification, and communication skills).

4. Cognitive

   a. Assist children with decision making, goal setting, risk taking, and life planning experiences.

   b. Assist children with developing rational cognition skills.

   c. Assist children with developing thinking skills and operations.

5. Career

   a. Assist children in developing pride in their work.

   b. Assist children in understanding and appreciating the values of a work oriented society.

   c. Assist children in exploring and more fully appreciating the use of their leisure time.

6. Societal Issues

   a. **Economical:** Rising unemployment, high taxes, and low income levels may require special school programs to combat family stress, hunger, and child abuse.

   b. **Sociological:** Family problems, differing family constellations, and varying child rearing practices may require effective parenting programs, latchkey safety programs, and situational adjustment programs to respond to such issues as divorce, separation, depression, weight control, drug and alcohol abuse, and step parenting.

   c. **Medical:** Threatening community problems and changing health practices may require counselors to address issues like AIDS, death education, and creating wellness programs to meet society's changing interest in promoting total health.

   d. **Demographics:** Demographic changes to include population shifts, declining birth rates, increased aging of the population, and rising divorce rates have led to a significant increase in the number of United States citizens not directly involved in schools. A direct relationship appears to exist between these demographics and the growing difficulty of securing top dollars to support public schools. While many schools are closing down, America's need for education will not diminish. For America's schools to survive, not to mention attaining good health, the support of America's citizenery is imperative. Counseling programs that bring children and adults together will help to emphasize the importance of schools and the significance of citizen support in protecting America's future.

e. **Multi-Cultural/Ethnic:** America has always been a multi-cultural society. However with shifting birth rates, population mobility, and ever-increasing interests in world trade and travel, all Americans must learn to appreciate and cherish multi-cultural and ethnic diversity. School counseling and academic programs must model respect, cooperation, self-worth, and accomplishment for all children representing diverse cultures, religious backgrounds, and educational needs. Such programs need to create a sense of unity and appreciation for both children and adults and their unique cultural contributions.

f. **Political:** Negotiation, arbitration, mediation, and persuasion are all political processes that people use to support and promote a particular view or cause. As human beings, people both effect and are affected by politics. Counselors and educators must be evermindful of the societal issues which children must be prepared to address, such as those created by political reform. Children also must be taught how to be political in a world, which by its very nature, is political in scope.

g. **Legal.** Modern day societies are governed by laws. Laws represent a binding custom or practice of a community. Such enforceable rules of conduct are meant to redress possible wrongs and represent advisable actions taken by a society to instill fairness and order. Laws require people to modify their behaviors for the good of all. Children's lives are as much affected by law as are adult lives. Counseling and educational programs must be designed to protect the legal rights of children and to teach children how to live in a society governed by laws, ethics, and morality.

h. **Technological:** The twentieth century has brought with it many technical changes and advances. Many of these changes also have resulted in legal and moral dilemmas. Children need to be exposed to and experience technical advances as well as to participate in the discussions which establish the moral and legal application of their uses.

i. **Educational:** Education is under a microscope at the close of the twentieth century as educators study its problems and prospects for the future. As changes are made, children's lives will be affected. Counselors, teachers, educational specialists, parents, and community leaders will need to be ever mindful in addressing the needs of all children created by those educational changes.

The elementary school counseling program goals list provides the counselor and the Counseling Program Committee with a set of important goals which they support and which specifies what they believe the elementary school counseling program should be doing. Parents, teachers, administrators, school board members, and community supporters have all had a hand in setting the initial direction of the program which is sensitive to the developmental and societal needs of children unique to the surrounding community.

CONDUCTING A NEEDS ASSESSMENT

Having developed the desired program goals, the Counseling Program Committee has established a solid sense of direction from which to create and implement the needs assessment process. Asking the right questions is a critical first step in creating a needs assessment plan which will yield the appropriate corrective and developmental measures needed in designing an effective elementary school counseling program. Needs assessment refers to those sets of activities which will assist the Counseling Program Committee in determining the gaps that exist between where the elementary school counseling program is now versus where that program needs to be if it is to deliver services needed by children (Gannon, 1977). By comparing the *desired program goals list* with those goals that will eventually evolve from the needs assessment process, the Counseling Program Committee will be able to identify the *priority program goals* and be able to estimate the extent of the resources necessary to achieve goal attainment.

Process

The effectiveness of any educational program is in its ability to foster meaningful learning experiences which enable children to become all they are capable of becoming. Learning may be characterized as a process which enables children and adults to behave in ways which will satisfy their developmental and societal needs. Therefore, determining what should be learned and how best to impart those learnings are significant factors to be addressed in any needs assessment. With these points in mind, the focus of the self study should be threefold: (1) to evaluate the needs of children in relation to what is being learned, (2) to assess the curriculum and the teaching/learning process, and their capabilities to deliver needed services, and (3) to make a thorough study of the environment and those climatic conditions which affect the teaching/learning process (Worzbyt, 1978).

Assessing Children's Needs. Children are first and foremost complex individuals with developmental and societal needs. Developmental needs imply that children grow and develop in sequentially ordered stages. Within each stage of development are specific, identifiable needs and tasks that must be met through the teaching-learning process in order to guarantee successful developmental progress through the remaining stages of development.

In addition to the generally predictable nature of development are the not so predictable situational variations in children's needs which are attributed to societal issues and hereditary differences in children's backgrounds. These needs also must be addressed. Consequently, the assessment process must evaluate children's developmental and societal needs in order to provide purposeful, meaningful, and relevant learning experiences.

The Counseling Program Committee, using its knowledge of child growth and development and its understanding of the school and community environment, are encouraged to develop assessment instruments designed to ascertain the needs of children in the same five dimensions of development mentioned earlier in the chapter. With an understanding of what counseling goals the Committee wishes to meet, they must now ascertain to what degree those goals are actually being met.

1. **Physical Development Goals:** To what extent are children's developmental similarities and differences being addressed as they affect the teaching/learning process? Does the elementary school counseling program work with children and parents in responding to variances in physical maturation, hereditary conditions, and environmental factors, which require individualized attention in meeting children's needs?

2. **Social Development Goals:** To what extent are children learning to work together in groups, developing skills of social living, developing positive and healthy peer relationships, and understanding the nature of group dynamics in a world which demands learning to belong and adjusting to continuously shifting peer groups?

3. **Self-Concept Development Goals:** What evidence exists that children are developing a positive view of self: are learning self-assessment and self-management skills: are learning self-trust, self-confidence, and developing feelings of self-acceptance?

4. **Cognitive Development Goals:** To what degree have children developed those cognitive skills related to thinking, decision making, goal setting, communicating, processing information, and cognitive management

(positive thinking, cognitive planning, using imagery, moral development)?

5. **Career Development Goals:** To what extent do children understand the world of work, the nature of a work oriented society, their place in the family and other groups to which they belong, how to effectively make use of their leisure time, and the meaning of work as it applies to them in the here-and-now?

6. **Societal Issues Goals:** To what extent do economical, sociological, medical, demographic, multi cultural/ethnic, political, legal, technological, and educational issues in the community influence and determine children's needs? How successful are the school's existing academic and counseling programs in meeting those needs? Depending on the nature of societal issues impacting on any given community, a school may need to establish specific program goals designed to address community health needs, multi-cultural and ethnic influences, and recent technological advances about which children must learn and understand.

While the nature and impact of societal issues will vary from community to community, every community will be affected by a number of societal issues which will impact significantly on children's growth process. Societal issues must be recognized and school program goals established to meet the critical needs of children which they have created. In so doing, children will become better equipped having learned the necessary behaviors (skills) to live and grow in today's ever-changing, and fast-paced society.

As the assessment process is planned, the Counseling Program Committee will need to discuss the specific tasks that children should be able to perform or demonstrate at various stages in their development. The degree to which the children are attaining the expected range of behavioral competencies (goal criteria) will be indicative of the range of success enjoyed by the elementary school counseling and academic programs. When determining expected levels of child performance, the best procedure is to consult a variety of recognized child development texts, authorities on child growth and development, and respected commercial assessment instruments.

In addition to devising their own evaluation instruments, school districts are encouraged to make use of commerically prepared measurement devices; parent, teacher, and counselor observations; cumulative folder data (physical examination reports, anecdotal records, samples of student work, pupil self-report data, standardized test results, previous academic records, parent conference records, sociometric data, and case studies); psychological data; and classroom performance information. School board members, representatives from business and industry, and social service agency representatives also can provide useful data regarding their assessment of the product which schools turn out. What deficiencies, if any, do these people recognize in the developmental and societal areas which the schools should be addressing?

When the needs assessment has been completed, the Counseling Program Committee will be able to identify the full range of successes and deficiencies that exist within the current elementary school system. With that information in hand, the Counseling Program Committee will be ready to evaluate the curriculum in terms of what is being taught, how it is being taught, and the purpose served by the various curriculum offerings and requirements in meeting the developmental and societal needs of children.

Assessing the Curriculum. Elementary schools that are not in tune with the developmental and societal needs of children may very well be creating curricula which run counter to their needs. Therefore, what is to be learned and the patterning and sequencing of the learning experience must be tailored to the maturational development of children and the various needs which must be addressed.

In assessing the curriculum, not only is an examination to be made of what is being taught, but also when it is being taught, and how it is being taught. The Counseling Program Committee should be concerned with the adequacy of the existing elementary school counseling and academic programs to meet the developmental and societal needs of children as defined by the needs assessment.

One way in which school and community participants can be involved in assessing the school curriculum is to respond to a questionnaire. Participants can be given a descriptive, graphic rating instrument containing randomly ordered goal statements representing the developmental and societal goal areas selected for study. Each goal statement is designed to specify the expected outcome behavior(s) to be learned. Participants are then given an opportunity to rate the extent to which they believe the curriculum is teaching those behaviors. Figure 2.1 is an illustration of a goal statement and scale that would be an example of a questionnaire and format that could be used to assess the curriculum.

Upon completion of the survey, the scores for each goal can be averaged so that separate mean scores for every goal statement can be obtained for each of the various community school sub-groups represented. Once the scoring has been completed, the goal statements can be arranged in sequence according to the needs as perceived by the sub-groups. Goals with mean scores of six (6) or below have the greatest need for attention, while goals with mean scores in the ten (10) to twelve (12) range are thought to be adequately met and, therefore, would not necessarily require additional emphasis. Goals with average score ranges of 13 or above are thought to be receiving more attention than is warranted.

While the survey results will specify the perceptions of school and community survey participants, and that is important information to have, those data do not necessarily reflect what is actually happening. The Counseling Program Committee needs to compare children's developmental and societal needs as determined by the needs assessment with the curriculum survey results and then conduct an actual evaluation of the curriculum.

The degree to which children's needs are met through the curriculum is as much due to perception of people as it is to curriculum design and content. The Counseling Program Committee needs both sets of data. When evaluating the

To: Parents, School Board Members, and Community Representatives

Directions: Read the goal statement and then answer the question by circling a number on the scale that best expresses your response.

Goal: Children understand and practice skills in effective decision making.

Question: In *my opinion,* how well are current school programs meeting this goal?"

Extremely Poor	Poor	Fair, but more needs to be done	Leave as is	Too much is being done
1 2 3	4 5 6	7 8 9	10 11 12	12 14 15

The same questionnaire could be given to school personnel by changing the persons identified after "To:" and the "Question" is illustrated by the following:

To: Teacher, Administrators, and Special Service Personnel

Directions: Same as above

Goal: Same as above

Question: *"How well" are my school's current programs meeting this goal?*

Figure 2.1. Illustration of one goal statement and related question for needs assessment questionnaire.

curriculum, recognition must be made that teachers, administrators, counselors, and learning specialists are most knowledgeable about what to study.

The developmental and societal counseling program goals need to be studied in accordance with the current curriculum program offerings. In reviewing the curriculum to meet children's needs, the following questions should be asked:

1. Do the school's curriculum offering support the school counseling program objectives (developmental and societal needs) in the primary and intermediate grades?

2. Are the school counseling program objectives geared to the maturational development of the children?

3. Are the school counseling objectives taught in accordance with sound learning theory?

The desired data can be gathered by reviewing the elementary school's textbooks and related educational aids, subject curriculum outlines, lesson plans, and via classroom observations. The purpose for conducting a curriculum assessment is not to negatively criticize or to find fault, but to review curriculum design, delivery methods, and the degree to which the curriculum addresses children's developmental and societal needs.

Assessing The Learning Environment. Learning takes place in the context of a social system (the school) which mirrors the complexities of the community which it serves. Climates of the school and the community impact significantly on what is learned, when it is learned, and how it is learned. The environmental assessment process is concerned with identifying ways in which both the school and the community can improve upon the teaching/learning climate for the benefit of children.

The physical climate consists of those factors which are directly observable. Some examples of physical factors that can contribute to or inhibit the quality of services delivered to children are classroom lighting, heating, air circulation, available space, noise levels, furniture arrangements, availability of needed resources (budget, teaching supplies, media resources, and equipment), length of school day, and scheduled breaks for teachers and children.

While the physical factors must be considered when studying the environment, the not so obvious and easily observed psychological climate also must be addressed when assessing the learning climate. The psychological climate is affected by such issues as the physical and mental maturation of children, peer relationships, pupil-teacher interactions, self-esteem, attitudes toward learning and education, and a variety of societal issues (economical, sociological, medical, demographics, multi-cultural/ethnic, political, legal, technological, and educational) which can affect any community. Anyone or a combination of these psychological climate issues can and do impact significantly on the needs of children and their readiness to learn.

And while the elementary school counseling program cannot address all of the physical and psychological issues impacting on the teaching/learning process, it must respond to those climatic conditions and issues which are within its sphere of influence. Perhaps by establishing school and community partnerships, cooperative programs and joint ventures can be established which can capitalize on the strengths of both school and community in neutralizing some of the conditions which place children at risk and in providing quality educational experiences for all children.

After the learning environment (school and community) has been assessed and the data have been evaluated, the Counseling Program Committee can offer suggestions and a plan of action in designing a teaching/learning environment that will be physically and psychologically conducive in supporting the successful attainment of the school's targeted academic and elementary school counseling program goals.

ESTABLISHING GOAL PRIORITIES

The most significant aspect of the planning process is selecting goals and strategies upon which the elementary school counseling program will be based. These goals will provide a direct link between the needs of the children and the delivery of program services as determined by the elementary school counselor and members of the Counseling Program Committee.

While a variety of methods exists by which goal priorities can be determined, the proposed method reviews the interactions of the **desired priority program goals list** with the **needs priority program goals list** as determined by the needs assessment. The desired priority goals list represents those goals which best reflect where a strong elementary counseling program should be if it is to meet the needs of children. These goals were first identified during the early stages of the planning process and sequenced in a hierarchial fashion from high priority to low priority in accordance with their worthiness of attainment as perceived by the Counseling Program Committee. The needs priority goals list reflects the degree to which those same goals are actually being met. This goal list is sequenced from high need (goals are not being met) to low need (goals are being met), thus reflecting the varying degrees of success in goal attainment. Arrange as shown in Figure 2.2.

Desired Priority Program Goals (List from highest to lowest)	**Needed Priority Program Goals** (List from highest to lowest)
1.	1.
2.	2.
3.	3.
4.	4.
5.	5.
.	.
.	.

Figure 2.2. Counseling goals priority list.

By comparing the two lists, the Committee can begin to identify four categories of program goals as illustrated in Figure 2.3.

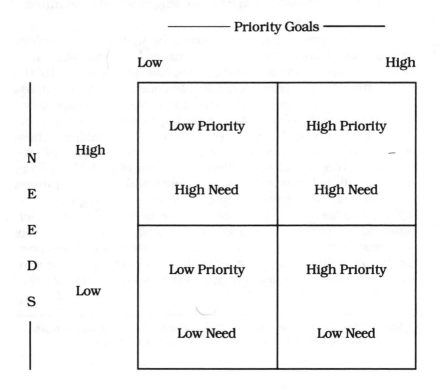

Figure 2.3. Developmental goals priority grid.

High Priority—High Need Goals

These goals are not only thought to be very important by the Counseling Program Committee as ones that need to be addressed (high priority), but are the very same goals which are not being met through the school curriculum (high need). The children's developmental and societal needs for whatever reason are therefore presently going unattended. Consequently, goals falling into this category are of top priority and need to be addressed.

High Priority—Low Need Goals

These goals are not only thought to be very important (high priority) by the Counseling Program Committee, but they also are being adequately met by the school counseling program (low need). The Committee needs to review the expenditure of resources, program activities, and time spent developing these high priority goals to determine what program resource adjustments, if any, can be made in maintaining quality, while redirecting a resource surplus to those goal areas that need further development or refinement.

Low Priority—High Need Goals

While the Counseling Program Committee thinks these goals are important, they are the least important to be addressed of the many goals that have been listed. However, the Counseling Program Committee also needs to be aware that these goals are not being met. If they are important enough to be maintained as program goals, the Counseling Program Committee will need to assess curricular offerings, the behaviors being taught, how they are being taught, and the conditions of the learning environment in order to make recommendations which will lead to goal attainment.

Low Priority—Low Need Goals

As with category three, these goals are thought to be important even though they are near the bottom of the desired program goals list. However, unlike the preceding category, these goals are being met. After reviewing this group of goals, the Counseling Program Committee will have to decide if all of these goals are to be maintained and at what level of commitment (resource expenditure).

Once the Counseling Program Committee has identified the elementary school counseling program goals to be given priority, they should seek consensus in agreeing that these goal statements clearly reflect the needs of the children, that they support the educational and counseling philosophies of the school, and that they address the unique needs and characteristics of the community.

DEVELOPING PROGRAM OFFERINGS

With the needs assessment information collected and analyzed and the priority program goals selected, the Counseling Program Committee is ready to ask and answer the following questions.

1. What new elementary school counseling programs should be offered?

2. What existing elementary school counseling programs should be continued without modification?

3. What existing elementary school counseling programs should be modified in terms of what is being taught, how it is being taught, and when it is being taught?

4. What additional resources or modification in resources will be needed in developing new programs and in modifying existing programs?

5. What existing elementary school counseling programs should be discontinued because they are no longer needed?

6. What positive and negative environmental conditions exist in the school (physical and psychological) that need to be addressed in meeting the priority program goals of the elementary school counseling program?

7. What positive and negative environmental conditions exist in the community (physical and psychological) which need to be addressed in meeting the priority program goals of the elementary school counseling program?

8. What societal issues affecting children's needs must be addressed (economic, sociological, medical, demographic, multi cultural/ethnic, political, legal, technological, educational)?

Goal Clarity

Goal statements are the blueprints of program design in that they operationally define the expected behavioral outcomes to be achieved through the program. Program strategies (objectives) are simply smaller goals which, when properly sequenced, clarify the steps to be achieved in meeting the main goal. When the strategies have been satisfied, the goal will have been automatically attained.

Goal statements and strategies (objectives) should be stated in outcome terminology so that they are

1. behavioral, clear, concrete, specific, operational;

2. measureable, or in some way at least verifiable clear when they have been accomplished;

3. realistic, not set too high, capable of being accomplished with available resources;

4. worthwhile, not set too low, not petty or meaningless; and

5. adequate, that is, goals that are substantial translations of the mission of the system and that de facto satisfy real needs and wants. (Egan & Cowan, 1979, p. 126)

Identifying and Selecting the Goal Strategies

Many different strategies can be employed to satisfy the accomplishment of any given goal. Planning for program effectiveness requires the identification and selection of goal strategies that will be appropriate in purpose, adequate in scope, effective in achieving the desired goal, efficient in resource expeditures, and generate positive outcomes with few negative side effects. The following steps are recommended in developing a comprehensive program plan for each priority goal.

1. Organize the elementary school counseling goal priorities according to the five dimensions of child development and the societal issues which impact significantly on child success.

2. For each goal listed, brainstorm all the possible ways of reaching the goal.

3. Analyze each alternative strategy from varying points of view in order to determine its feasibility.

   a. Study the driving (school and community) and restraining forces (school and community) that will need to be addressed for each strategy.

   b. Review the required resources needed in terms of their availability and/or accessibility in implementing the strategy. Resources like the following need to be considered: Personnel, funds, equipment, facilities, time, knowledge, skills, political influence. etc.

   c. Evaluate each strategy according to such criteria as appropriateness, adequacy, effectiveness, worthwhileness, efficiency, and possible side effects (positive and negative).

4. Select the goal strategies and methods of implementation that best satisfy the selection criteria as presented in the previous step.

5. For each goal strategy identified, determine

   a. the necessary steps to achieve the strategy (objective);

   b. the activities to be utilized in carrying out each step;

   c. a schedule for completing the strategy and activities;

   d. the resources necessary for processing each strategy and related activities;

   e. who is to benefit from goal attainment;

   f. who will need to be responsible for implementing the strategy and directing the activities;

g. what specific tasks must be accomplished when, and by whom (Tasks are the smaller steps associated with the implementation of each activity); and

h. what evaluation methods will be used to monitor the progress of strategy attainment.

6. As a final step to preparing the program plan for implementation,Lewis and Lewis (1983) have suggested that each selected goal strategy and activity be reviewed by asking the following questions.

a. Does the service [strategy] fit program goals and priorities?

b. Are available or potential resources adequate for service provision?

c. Can the service [strategy] be accepted by the community member and consumers?

d. Can the service [strategy] be delivered by available or potentially available service providers?

e. Can the service [strategy] meet the policy constraints within which the agency [school] or program must work?

f. Do the potential benefits of the service [strategy] appear to outweigh the estimated costs?

g. Can we measure service [strategy] effectiveness?

h. Can we develop an implementation plan?

i. Are there serious risks involved in implementing the strategy? (pp. 33-34)

Developing an Implementation Plan

The planning process is now near completion. All that remains is the development of an implementation action plan which is a formal document designed to carry out the plan. Each program goal statement should have a clearly stated list of strategies (objectives). Each strategy in turn should have accompanying activities/procedures and tasks which, when implemented, will result in the strategy being attained. In order for the plan to be complete, basic resources must be identified, a time schedule prepared, the cost determined, service providers selected, and evaluation methods outlined and ready for implementation.

We have included a set of key questions that we believe should be asked in preparing the implementation plan. These questions when answered will provide the necessary data for filling in the *Program Planning Sheet* (Figure 2.4) for each elementary school counseling program priority goal.

1. What are the major activities and tasks necessary to implement the goals and strategies which have been selected?

2. Who are the people that will be responsible for performing the activities and related tasks?

3. What is the time frame and sequence of activities and tasks for each goal and set of strategies?

4. What resources will be needed to perform the activities and tasks for each program strategy?

5. How will the goals, strategies, activities, and tasks be monitored and evaluated?

The *Program Planning Sheets*, when completed, will prove to be very useful in developing a comprehensive counseling program time line, formulating a resource allocations and budgeting plan, and creating a comprehensive evaluation plan which is internally consistent with the elementary school counseling program plan.

As Lewis and Lewis (1983) have suggested:

Effective planning lessens the use of unclear, fuzzy goals, brings commonality of purpose and expectation to various concerned groups, focuses concern on ends rather than solely on means, helps specify desired outputs, and attempts to relate resource allocations to goals. (p. 36)

Primary Grade _____ Intermediate Grade _____

Dimension of Counseling: **Social Development**

Goal: _____

Outcome Strategies	Activities & Tasks	Time Frame	Service Provider(s)	Resources/ Cost	Evaluation Methods

Figure 2.4. Program planning sheets.

BIBLIOGRAPHY

American Association for Counseling and Development and ERIC/Counseling and Personnel Service Clearinghouse. (1985). *Counselors: Agents for educational excellence.* Conference Proceedings: January 13-15, 1985. Orlando, FL. Falls Church, VA: Authors.

American Association for Counseling and Development. (1987). *The future of school counseling: Bibliography of materials.* Alexandria, VA: AACD.

American School Counselors Association. (1984). *Role statement on the elementary counselor.* Alexandria, VA: AACD.

College Entrance Examination Board. (1986). *Keeping the options open recommendations: final report of the commission on precollege guidance and counseling.* New York: College Board Publications.

Dinkmeyer, D., & Caldwell, E. (1970). *Developmental counseling and guidance: A comprehensive school approach.* New York: McGraw-Hill.

Egan, G., & Cowan, M.A. (1979). *People in systems: A model for development in the human service professions and education.* Monterey, CA: Brooks/Cole.

Elkind, D. (1978). *A sympathetic understanding of the child birth to sixteen (2nd ed.).* Boston, MA: Allyn and Bacon.

Elkind, D. (1981). *The hurried child: Growing up too fast too soon.* New York: Addison-Wesley.

Gannon, M.J. (1977). *Management* (2nd ed.). Boston, MA: Little, Brown.

Gesell, A., & Ilg, F.L. (1946). *The child from five to ten.* New York: Harper & Row.

Goodlad, J. (1984). *A place called school: Prospects for the future.* New York: McGraw Hill.

Havighurst, R.J. (1953). *Human development in education.* New York: Longmans, Green.

Lewis, J.A., & Lewis, M.D. (1983). *Management of human service programs.* Monterey, CA: Brooks/Cole.

Maslow, A.H. (1954). *Motivation and personality.* New York: Harper & Row.

McCandless, B.R. (1967). *Children: Behavior and development.* New York: Holt, Rinehart and Winston.

Szilagyi, A.D., Jr. (1984). *Management and performance (2nd ed.).* Glenview, IL: Scott, Foresman.

Terry, G.R., & Franklin, S.G. (1982). *Principles of management* (8th ed.). Homewood, IL: Richard D. Irwin.

Worzbyt, J.C. (1978). *Elementary school guidance: Program planning, organization and implementation.* (Title III ESEA Report). Harrisburg, PA: Pennsylvania Department of Education.

ORGANIZING THE ELEMENTARY SCHOOL COUNSELING PROGRAM

Every elementary school counseling program needs an organizational structure to carry out its philosophy and mission. The organizational function of management is designed to provide the necessary structure to bring people and resources together and to arrange them in an orderly and coordinated pattern to accomplish the planned objectives of the program.

While developing an organizational structure that encompasses a K-12 school counseling program is preferable, many school systems do not have highly centralized district wide counseling programs. With that in mind, the focus of the organizational structure presented in this chapter will apply to single elementary school units.

THE PURPOSE OF ORGANIZING

Many elementary school counseling programs are not viewed as programs but as the activity of one person in the school who has been assigned the role of elementary school counselor. Often times parents, teachers, administrators, and the public are confused about the practice of elementary school counseling as well as when and how to access the counselor's services. When people are uninformed about a particular program, this lack of understanding can create confusion and resentment. Active or passive disorganization leaves much to be desired and often results in a program which functions below its potential and receives the brunt of much negative criticism.

When elementary school counseling programs are organized for success, the organizational structure will promote collaboration and negotiation among individuals and groups (Ivancevich & Matteson, 1987). This activity will improve the effectiveness and efficiency of communications within the elementary school. An effectively organized program will have a positive and visible impact on the school, will clearly delineate and encourage the active participation of all school and community workers, and will specify the nature of the program's services to be provided and how to access those services.

Elementary school counseling programs which are organized for effectiveness will be viewed not as the activity of one person, but as a comprehensive support service designed to enhance the educational process and to help facilitate a meaningful teaching/learning environment for all children (Worzbyt, 1978). A support service of this magnitude will require the collective input and activity of the entire school community.

DESIGNING AN ORGANIZATIONAL STRUCTURE

Schermerhorn (1986) has indicated that organizational design is a decision making process. Once program planning has been completed, an organizational design is needed to carry out the mandated philosophy and mission of the elementary school counseling program. This process can best be achieved by having the Counseling Program Committee respond to the following questions:

- What are the primary goals and objectives that the organization should be designed to meet?

- What continuing activities need to be performed in order to implement the strategies that have been selected as part of the planning process?

- How can the necessary activities be divided so that individuals or groups can be assigned responsibility for performing them?

- Once activities have been grouped into specific jobs, what kind of authority and responsibility should be assigned?

- How and by whom should decisions be made?

- How specialized should roles and jobs be?

- Who should control the work being performed?

- How can communication and coordination among members of the organization be facilitated?

- How can job or role descriptions be developed to take into account both functions and accountabilities?

- How can coordination and communication with the external social environment be facilitated? (Lewis & Lewis, 1983, p. 75)

The answers to these questions will provide the Counseling Program Committee with direction in formulating an organizational design that will bring all the necessary resources together in meeting the planned program goals of the elementary school counseling program. The actual structure that is developed will be unique for each elementary school counseling program in that the goals, needs, size, environment, and available resources of every elementary school will differ. Even more critical than these variables will be the varying orientations and philosophical beliefs of every Counseling Program Committee. Since every committee is unique, elementary school counseling program organizational structures will reflect these differences. *The success of an elementary school counseling program will not be measured in its sameness or differences when compared with other programs, but the degree to which the organizational structure facilitates the attainment of its mission.*

ELEMENTARY SCHOOL COUNSELING: ORGANIZING FOR SUCCESS

Elementary school counseling programs seem to function best when they are organized in such a manner as to involve school and community resources, mirror the educational program structure of the school, and are designed for action in meeting the developmental and societal needs of children. For these purposes to be realized, the chosen organizational structure must be purposeful, relevant, and easily explained to those school and community members who will be providers and recipients of elementary school counseling program services.

We believe that the major components of any successful elementary school counseling program must consist of the following:

1. the tripartite,

2. the dimension of school counseling (developmental & societal),

3. the program functions,

4. the program elements, and

5. the program providers and recipients.

Without all of these components working together in a systematic and organized manner, an elementary school counseling program cannot hope to successfully meet the developmental needs of children.

The Tripartite

The major focus of elementary school counseling programs is to establish broad-based, comprehensive, and developmental programs which function within the curriculum and are designed to facilitate human growth and learning. Elementary school counseling programs can best accomplish this goal by creating physical and psychological environments which support the teaching/learning process. In order to accomplish this end, a strong base is required. Counseling programs are like three legged stools. They derive their support from paying attention to:

1. the child,

2. the behaviors to be learned, and

3. the conditions of the learning environment.

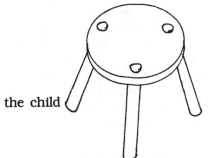

the child

behaviors to be learned

the learning environment

Figure 3.1. The tripartite.

The Child. The child must always be the focal point of the elementary school counseling program. Of utmost importance in understanding children in relationship to the educational process is that they are multidimensional in nature with many developmental and diversified needs to be met. If educational and counseling programs are to capitalize on children's potential through the teaching/learning process, the elementary school counseling program must be geared to meeting children's needs in ways in which they learn best (learning theory applications).

Behaviors to be Learned. An elementary school counseling program must be able to identify the critical behaviors that need to be learned and at what stage in the child's development the learning should take place. Determining what behaviors children need to learn will eminate from the educational philosophy of the school. The school, in developing its educational philosophy and mission, must understand child growth and development and the societal issues (economical, sociological, medical, demographics, multicultural/ethnic, political, legal, technological, & educational) which impact both on children and the community and create needs which must be addressed.

Elementary school counseling programs exist for the purpose of supporting the educational system by assisting teachers, parents, educational specialists, and society in identifying, defining, and teaching (learning style) those behaviors which are most critical for children to learn when they need to learn them. Likewise, the counseling program assists the educational system in critically evaluating what is being taught, when it is being taught, how it is being taught, and whether or not the behaviors even need to be taught in relation to children's needs and the school's philosophy and mission.

The Learning Environment. The teaching/learning process can only be successful to the extent that the conditions of the learning climate support learning. The elementary school counseling program is concerned with developing sound physical and psychological educational learning climates. Knowing what can be done to help children feel comfortable and supported, unique and special, and experience a sense of personal power in shaping their own destinies is an ever increasing challenge for elementary school counseling programs. Children learn best in those environments which support their developmental needs and those created by society.

A three legged stool cannot stand much less support any weight, with a missing or defective leg. The same can be said for an effective elementary school counseling program that is not supported by the tripartite. Elementary school counseling programs serve the educational system best when they assist the school in developing educational programs that address the complex developmental and societal needs of children, teach the behaviors that need to be learned in addressing those needs, and do so in an educational climate which fosters self-confidence, positive self-worth, and a never-ending love for learning and continued self-growth.

Dimensions of Elementary School Counseling

The *program* of elementary school counseling is organized according to a systematic classification of child developmental needs and societal issues which influence the teaching/learning process. The five dimensions of child development are physical, social, self-concept, cognitive, and career. The societal dimension issues which impact on children's lives are economical, sociological, medical, demographic, multicultural/ethnic, political, legal, technological, and educational.

The educational program of the elementary school likewise revolves around the same five dimensions of child development and the mentioned societal dimension issues which impact upon the community and the educational process. From these developmental and societal dimensions emerge the needs of children which stimulate the subsequent educational and counseling program goals designed to meet those needs. While teachers play a significant role in addressing children's academic needs, the elementary school counseling program focuses on developing an educational climate designed to enhance the teaching/learning process in meeting children's developmental and societal needs. Elementary school counselors, with their understanding of child growth and development, learning theory, and the creation of conducive teaching/learning climates, make natural partners with teachers, administrators, and parents in meeting the educational mission of the school.

Physical Dimension. Learning and physical maturation are very much related. Children have physical maturation needs that must be addressed if they are to learn to the best of their ability. Topics like the following are representative of the many facets of physical maturation which are directly related to and have a profound effect on the teaching/learning process.

body imagery	school readiness
laterality	stress management
body in space	relaxation
touch (tactile)	eye-hand
physical care	coordination
diet/exercise	large & small muscle
rest	development
visual perception	growth changes
auditory perception	sex differences
physical coordination	sexual identity
balance	role identification
	hyperactivity

The elementary school counselor and the counseling program can assist parents, teachers, and administrators in developing an educational curriculum which is sensitive to the physical needs of children. When necessary, specially designed programs also can be created to meet the special needs of parents, teachers, and children that cannot be addressed through the curriculum.

Social Dimension. McCandless (1967) defined socialization as ". . .a learning-teaching process that, when successful, results in the human organism's moving from its infant state of helplessness, but total egocentricity, to its ideal adult state of semi-conformity coupled with independent creativity" (p. 421). This definition concerns itself with a process by which human beings become human as they learn the ways of the culture and at the same time become individuals in their understanding, interpretation, and transformation of learnings into personally unique behavioral outcomes.

Social development, as a dimension of the elementary school counseling program, is concerned with what children need to know and what skills they need to develop in order to function successfully in the various social units in which they are members. Children are members of a family, a classroom, small work or play groups, clubs, church affiliations, and the list continues. In order to be contributing member of a group, the following topics are representative of what children will need to know and practice.

sharing	group rules
taking turns	following directions
listening	giving feedback
being assertive	receiving feedback
body language	managing feelings in
verbal	a responsible
communication	manner
skills	human rights
making friends	responsibilities

Classroom climate, peer relationships, and teacher-pupil interactions are all aspects of group dynamics having a direct bearing on the teaching/learning and socialization process. How children feel about and relate with peers and adults in their world cannot help but influence what is or is not learned.

Self-Concept Dimension. The major focus of this dimension is the child as a person. While this is a true statement for the other dimensions as well, the self-concept dimension assists children in self-understanding and in developing a utilization of self for the benefit of self and society. The elementary school counselor, in working with parents and teachers, emphasizes the importance of building a positive self-concept and self-esteem in children. This can only be accomplished if school personnel are taught how to play a purposeful and active role in providing the required information, skills, and self-confidence building environments that will enhance children's self-esteems.

Elementary schools that target the self-concept dimension as a worthwhile goal will want to consider addressing the following child-related topics.

feelings & acceptable	choices
modes of	building self-esteem
expression	climates
fears	values
wishes	recognizing one's
successes	uniqueness
strengths	developing personal
talents	and responsible
failures	power
how to create a new	Feeling connected to
self-image	people, places, and
centering	things
psychocybernetics	
(positive mental	
picturing)	

Children and important adults in children's lives are taught how they can develop more positive feelings toward themselves and others. They will come to understand that the power rests within themselves to create their own unique identities and that they can have as much happiness as they choose to have. The self dimension of an elementary school counseling program helps to create the positive attitudes and self-confidence that will stay with children into their adulthood. Those feelings help to open the doors to learning, controlling fear, and practicing moderate risk taking.

Cognitive Dimension. How children think and learn is the focus of this dimension. The elementary school counselor understands how children learn, the application of learning theory, the importance of matching teaching and learning styles, and how children's varying stages of physical maturation can affect cognitive processes.

The elementary school counselor is prepared to work with parents, teachers, and children in enhancing the cognitive development of children so that they meet their needs and become capable of dealing more adequately with their environment. Some of the cognitive development skills that schools should be addressing are the following:

thinking skills
decision making
skills
goal setting skills
values clarification

processing
information skills
communication skills
problem solving skills
cognitive
restructuring skills

Career Dimension. Children need assistance in identifying fulfilling roles in their environment. They need to understand who they are; what their life purpose is; and their place in the family, school, community, and society at large. Children, like adults, derive meaning from life by participating in life situations that give their lives meaning.

The elementary school counseling program helps children to understand the values of a work oriented society and assists them in identifying themselves as contributing members of society. Parents, teachers, administrators, and community members play a significant role in helping children by exploring a variety of career related issues like the following:

the use of leisure time	economics
hobbies	positive work habits
work responsibilities in the home	school subjects and work relationships
the value of work	career awareness
exploring career clusters	self-awareness

By exploring the world of work, children learn to broaden their own life perspectives. They come to understand the importance of work in society, how what they do at home and school relates to the world of work, the importance of developing useful work habits and skills, and the connection between academics, leisure time, hobbies, and work related training experiences. Exploring career development issues help children derive meaning from life, assume responsibilities, and appreciate their contributions to the family, school, and society.

Societal Dimension. In addition to addressing the developmental needs of children, the elementary school counseling program must be cognizant of societal issues which impact on what children will need to know in order to function in society today and tomorrow.

Some of the major societal issues that impact on children's lives today are the following:

economical	political
sociological	legal
medical	technological
demographics	educational
multicultural/ethnic	

Elementary school children are learning about computers, drug and alcohol education, children's rights, AIDS, careers, death education, wellness, and a variety of other topics which have escalated in importance because of the societal issues at work which demand their understanding and involvement. Elementary school counseling programs therefore must be sensitive to both the developmental needs of children and the societal issues which create varying life situations which children are and will be expected to address in the future. Effective elementary school counseling programs must stimulate academic understandings, teach developmental life enhancing skills (physical, social, self-concept, cognitive, and career) and prepare children how to live responsibly in an ever changing democratic society.

Program Functions

The communication functions (referred to as triple-C functions) of *counseling, consulting,* and *coordinating* form the network through which elementary school counselors perform their work roles. The successful implementation of the elementary school counseling program services hinges on the interpersonal relationships which develop between and among people. The elementary school counselor, using the three communication functions, brings program goals and the necessary resources together to get the job done.

Counseling. An effective way of relating with children is through counseling. Counseling is characterized as a process which fosters a relationship between one or more children and the counselor. The counseling process creates a warm-trusting environment, one which encourages and supports children in self-exploration for the purpose of fostering learning, personal growth, and self-understanding. Children are encouraged to explore their feelings, state their wants, and to learn about themselves. The counselor helps children self-explore by using a variety of skills which assist them in self-disclosure. Role playing, creative play techniques, art, open ended stories, music, and other forms of self-expression may be used to reduce anxiety and help children find their most self-expressive modes. Ultimately, the counseling process helps the counselor and children to successfully communicate with each other. This leads to helping children understand themselves, identify their goals, and develop a responsible plan for goal attainment. Counseling not only helps children address their most immediate concerns, but teaches them skills in self-management.

Most counseling sessions at the elementary school level focus on self–growth and developmental issues. Occasionally, children seek counseling for personal problems or are referred to counseling by parents and school personnel for remediational concerns.

Consulting. Consultation is a collaborative process which takes place between the elementary school counselor and an intermediary (teacher, parent, educational specialist, or administrator) who represents the educational and developmental interests of the children.

The purpose of consultation is to best meet the needs of children by improving the teaching/learning process. Counselors often consult with teachers or groups of professionals to share information, ideas, skills, interpret data, and make mutually agreed upon decisions regarding action plans that will benefit children.

Counselors may consult with parents to learn about children's needs and concerns, to assist them with parenting skills, to discuss child growth and development issues, and to learn from the parents how the school's educational and counseling programs can best serve their needs.

Consultation is a very useful communication function which allows the counselor to tap a variety of school and community resources in order to better understand ways in which the developmental needs of children can be met. These same community resources also have a pulse on what societal dimensions the school and elementary school counseling program need to watch and address in positive ways for the benefit of children.

Coordinating. Coordination is the planned and systematic process of organizing people and the required material resources (funds, equipment, materials) to attain the elementary school counseling program goals. The elementary school counselor is responsible for integrating the counseling program into every facet of the child's school and community life. This infusion model works best when the counselor seeks total participation of school and community participants.

As a program coordinator, the counselor involves the school and community in program development, maintenance, and evaluation activities. In many ways, *the elementary school counselor functions like a conductor of a large symphony orchestra.* The counselor must understand the elementary school counseling program and be able to convey that understanding to the various players so that everyone understands their parts. The counselor must understand how best to utilize the talents of each and to integrate that talent into a coordinated whole. The harmony and effectiveness of an elementary school counseling program rests with the counselor (conductor).

Program Elements

Program elements of an elementary school counseling program are those special programs, activities, techniques, and procedures which are created and implemented for the purpose of operationalizing the program goals. The program elements are organized according to child needs and learning climate conditions which were assessed and then selected as program goals (Chapter 2).

Child Need (Goal) Elements. Those programs and activities which are selected and developed to meet children's needs fall into this category. For example, an elementary school counseling program wishing to develop the self-concept dimension of development would need to determine what behaviors to teach, at what grade level to teach them, and what teaching methods to use in teaching the new behaviors. Following these decisions, the counselor, working with other school personnel (consultation), would develop the program to be implemented and would bring together (coordination) all the necessary resources (people, budget, materials, equipment) needed to provide the service. Occasionally some children will need special services that will require specialized training and attention. In those instances, the counselor may meet the children individually or in small groups and provide a direct counseling service. At times, parent groups may be formed so that the counselor can assist them in working with their children at home.

Deciding what to teach children about the self-concept dimension can be determined by examining the needs assessment results and developing the program according to the tripartite. A knowledge of learning theory and child growth and development are thus needed in addition to the needs assessment results.

While the developmental needs (goals) of children must be met, a second set of needs created by societal issues also must be addressed. Children need to be prepared to act in a responsible and effective manner in all life situations that will or could have a significant impact on their lives. Consequently as a result of societal needs assessment results, some elementary school counseling programs may feel compelled to create special programs designed to meet those needs. Many elementary school counseling programs have created drug and alcohol education programs, school drop out programs, wellness programs, ethnic and cultural programs, school pride programs, and computer programs. These programs and ones like them are created for a purpose. They are added to the curriculum to the extent that they are absolutely necessary in maintaining and/or enhancing the teaching/learning process and in helping children meet societal expectations. While the school may be capable of developing new programs in response to a variety of societal issues, the Counseling Program Committee should ask whose responsibility it is to address these issues? The counselor, using his/her consultation and coordination skills, may need to involve community support services in meeting some of the special needs of children, thus easing the burden of the school which may already be pressed to its limits.

Learning Climate Supporters. Elementary school counseling programs are successful to the extent that they meet the developmental and societal needs of children. However, programs, activities, and procedures are effective to the extent that they are supported by positive climatic conditions. Most elementary school counseling programs are supported by the standard climate supporters such as public relations, staff development, budgeting resources, available counseling program space, office support and resources, and parent/community volunteer support. Each of these programs, individually and collectively, is designed to provide the necessary resources and people support required to build and maintain self-confidence building environments where children can live and learn.

Maximizing humanistically oriented child-centered teaching/learning environments is the third dimension of the tripartite. The first two dimensions were addressed in developing the special programs and activities in meeting children's needs while the third dimension focuses on creating the right environment (physical and psychological) which will support the teaching/learning process.

As the counselor and the Counseling Program Committee develop each of the climate supporters, they need to think about how each can best contribute to a successful learning climate.

1. **Public Relations.** The most effective public relations are conveyed through having an excellent school counseling program. Children, parents, teachers, administrators, and community supporters will seek out the services of an elementary school counseling program that can meet their needs. They will likewise want to contribute their talents in support of a successful elementary school counseling program once they understand how they can help.

2. **Staff Development.** One of the most effective ways to enhance the learning climate of the school is to treat teachers and staff with respect. Provide them with training that when implemented will contribute to a positive and healthy school climate. For example, teach (most often done through consultation) custodians, cafeteria workers, and office personnel how they can contribute to a positive school climate. Work with teachers and administrators on how they can contribute to children's positive self-esteem. Staff development can be a fun and energizing experience for school personnel and can contribute greatly to a positive school climate.

3. **Budgetary Resources.** Financial resources in most school districts are always short of what the school counselor would like to have in order to operate a successful program. Keeping this in mind, the creating

of the actual budget should be based on the estimates of the expected budget and on the needs for the coming year. Expected needs are to be based on the counseling program goals and what resources will be needed to implement those goals. The counselor will need to consider equipment, supplies, travel, telephone, postage, printing, and related costs. When possible, the counselor will want to consider ways in which budgetary limitations can be delimited. This can be accomplished by looking to ways in which program needs can be satisfied without depending totally on a counseling budget that is already strained to the limits.

Networking with other schools, making needed materials, borrowing equipment, and involving the school community in budget stretching activities are just a few ideas to expand a tight counseling budget.

4. **Program Space.** The availability and effective utilization of space is critical to the success of an effective elementary school counseling program. The school counselor and the Counseling Program Committee need to consider space, or the lack of it, and how it will impact upon meeting the counseling program goals. The arrangement of children and furniture in any counseling activity should be considered. How children are positioned, the size and climatic conditions of the room, and the lines of communication that are established can either contribute to or destroy an otherwise well planned counseling activity (Quirk & Worzbyt, 1983).

The counselor's office likewise needs to communicate a positive climate and be designed and located in the school building where children will feel comfortable talking with the counselor. Office size, furnishings, location, color scheme, privacy, and related climatic conditions (physical and psychological) are important considerations for counselors to think about when setting up or rearranging an office. While we recognize that many counselors are limited on what they can do about their office size and location, they can still exercise some control over aspects of the physical and psychological climate of their office space.

5. **Office Support and Resources.** Elementary school counselors who have secretarial assistance and the use of voice recording-transcribable equipment, desk computer, tape recorders, VCR, duplicating and transparency equipment, and private telephone will be able to make more effective and efficient use of their time in meeting the needs of children. Counselors are required to maintain accurate program records, file correspondence, create and duplicate program materials, and maintain an active consulting and inservice training program with school personnel. With office support and resources, school counselors can manage a very effective program by delegating many of the routine, yet important, tasks to a cadre of parent volunteers who have office management and secretarial skills.

6. **Parent/Volunteer Program.** Many elementary school counseling programs rely on parent/volunteer programs. While the number and size of these programs vary from school district to school district, the one important ingredient that is often lacking is proper planning and training programs for volunteers. Most school districts that utilize volunteer groups do so to strengthen and enhance the quality of services to children. However, volunteer programs that are poorly organized and lack a training component tend to create climatic conditions that interrupt the teaching/learning process instead of contributing to it. More will be said about this topic in Chapter 6, *Breathing New Life Into an Existing Program.*

Program Providers and Recipients

Elementary school counseling programs are designed to provide a direct service to children. Children will gain immensely from a well planned and organized program in that their developmental and societal needs will be met in a climate (physical and psychological) that supports effective teaching and learning.

In meeting children's needs, parents, teachers, administrators, and the community also benefit from the activities of the elementary school counseling program. For in order to be a successful provider of services, the various volunteers need to be given information, taught skills, and have their own self confidence enhanced so that they can improve upon their ability to help children learn. The process is thus circular in nature. As teachers, parents, administrators, and community volunteers (service providers) contribute to the growth and development of children (service recipients), they also benefit from the activities of the elementary school counseling program as well.

WHY THE ORGANIZATIONAL STRUCTURE WORKS

The organizational structure works because it takes the guesswork out of planning, actuating, and controlling a successful comprehensive program. A counseling program that is organized around child development and societal needs, has clearly stated goals which reflect the behaviors to be learned, and addresses the creation of positive climatic conditions designed to enhance the teaching/learning process, cannot miss in having a positive impact on children.

A counseling program that is clear in its philosophy and mission is one that has vision, direction, and purpose. Elementary school counseling programs will continue to remain relevant, purposeful, and meaningful as long as they continue to monitor and reflect the needs of children, school personnel, and the community.

Improving elementary school counseling programs begins with the development of an organizational structure which supports programs and activities because they are justifiably needed, not because they are popular. An organized elementary school counseling program that has twenty-twenty vision addresses the special needs of all children not just those in need of specialized attention. A well organized elementary school counseling program requires less administrative and clerical attention from the counselor because the program encourages and supports the helping hands of many who are eager to take their place in making elementary school counseling a success. And perhaps most important of all, a well organized elementary school counseling program welcomes expansion. As more people come to understand how they can support a counseling program and are invited to participate, the school not only increases its support base for the program, but also maximizes the quantity and quality of services it can deliver.

BIBILIOGRAPHY

Ivancevich, J.M., & Matteson,, M.T. (1987). *Organizational behavior and management.* Plano, TX: Business Publications.

Lewis, J.A., & Lewis, M.D. (1983). *Management of human service programs.* Monterey, CA: Brooks/Cole.

McCandless, B.R. (1967). *Children: Behavior and development.* New York: Holt, Rinehart and Winston.

Quirk, J.P., & Worzbyt, J.C. (1983). *The assessment of behavior problem children: A systematic behavioral approach.* Springfield, IL: Charles Thomas.

Schermerhorn, J.R., Jr. (1986). *Management of human service programs.* Monterey, CA: Brooks/Cole.

Worzbyt, J.C. (1978). *Elementary school guidance: Program planning, organization and implementation.* (Title III ESEA Report). Harrisburg, PA: Pennsylvania Department of Education.

ACTUATING THE ELEMENTARY SCHOOL COUNSELING PROGRAM

The third step in operating an elementary school counseling program is actuating, which more simply stated means moving to action. The planning and organizing phases of management have laid the groundwork for mobilizing program plans, people, and the organizational structure toward goal accomplishment.

Actuating centers largely around creating the enthusiasm, drive, and energy in people to want to achieve the desired elementary school counseling program outcomes. The process of actuating, as we shall describe it, is to be accomplished in two phases. **Phase I: Orientation** is designed to aid school personnel, families, and community volunteers in their understanding and utilization of the elementary school counseling program. **Phase II: Training and Development** is designed to prepare school, family, and community participants for their direct involvement as providers of program services.

The elementary school counselor and Counseling Program Committee are faced with some major challenges in actuating an effective elementary school counseling program. Those challenges are related to developing a human resource staff and working environment which enable people to function together effectively and efficiently, to enjoy what they are doing, to develop new skills and abilities, and to ultimately become champion supporters of the elementary school counseling program.

While the primary focus of any elementary school counseling program must be on meeting children's needs so that they can learn to the best of their abilities, counselors must likewise remember that children's needs can never be successfully addressed until they meet the needs of those people who provide the services. Elementary school counseling programs function best when teachers and other service providers

- understand the philosophy, mission, and goals of the program;

- understand how to take advantage of the program;

- are provided with opportunities to access program services;

- see a particular advantage or reason for becoming involved;

- participate in meaningful ways in shaping the program;

- receive recognition for their contributions to the program;

- are informed about what is expected of them when delivering program services, are supported, and are given continuous feedback; and

- experience a personal sense of accomplishment for their participation in the program.

A successful actuating process is one that is designed to meet the needs of service providers so that they will understand and feel comfortable with the idea of both utilizing program services and providing them as well.

PHASE I: ORIENTATION

While orientation is a time consuming process, it is not a waste of time. When carefully planned, orientation can provide a needed forum for mutual interactions between the school counselor and the people seeking to know more about the program. Orientation activities are designed to systematically stimulate hopeful expectations, positive attitudes, and create new and supportive behaviors in response to elementary school counseling. The intent of this socialization experience is to achieve the best possible match between the elementary school counseling program and those who will be using and providing services.

The socialization of teachers, parents, administrators, and community supporters, as stated earlier, begins with orientation activities (Phase I) and later extends to training and development experiences (Phase II). *Orientation activities familiarize school personnel and community supporters with all aspects of the elementary school counseling program and ways in which they can contribute to the success and well being of that program* (job responsibilities).

Done well, orientation enhances peoples' understanding of the elementary school counseling program and shapes their effective utilization of program services. When done well, results speak for themselves in the consistency of program quality and in the increased satisfaction of those who have received services.

As important as orientation activities are, the unfortunate fact is that they are frequently neglected when implementing a new program or modifying an existing one. When this occurs, the uninformed and misinformed are often left to fend for themselves. They learn about the counseling program on their own and from casual contacts with peers. Otherwise well intentioned and capable individuals often end up receiving misinformation and forming inappropriate attitudes and/or behaviors which ultimately detract from a quality program.

Planning the Orientation Program

Prior to beginning the orientation program, the counselor and Counseling Program Committee will need to plan the orientation process. Some things to think about are

- identifying goals to be met,

- outlining the strategies to support each goal,

- developing the specific activities to support those strategies, and

- locating and securing necessary resources to accomplish those goals.

Once an orientation proposal has been developed, it will need to be cleared by appropriate administrators prior to its implemention. These people will want to know of the benefits of such a program, before approval will be given.

Orientation Payoffs

In establishing an orientation program three significant payoffs make it a worthwhile process. Orientation reduces anxiety, reduces start-up time and expense, and builds a support base.

Reduces Anxiety. Program participants come to understand that an elementary school counseling program is a support service designed to help teachers, parents, and administrators provide quality education to children. The information helps to reduce the fear that the counselor is taking over other people's jobs, that the counselor is an evaluator of teachers, and that anyone who uses the services of the counseling program must be ineffective in doing their job.

Reduces Start-up Time and Expense. Getting a successful school counseling program functioning as it should is no easy matter. That process can be eased along more quickly when parents, teachers, children, and administrators possess the necessary information, skills, and self-confidence to access services.

Builds a Support Base. Orientation programs tend to build trust, positive attitudes, and program support more quickly when the mystery is taken out of elementary school counseling. As people's confidence builds in the program as well as in their own ability to contribute to its success, they become more willing supporters and take pride in themselves and the program's accomplishments (Schermerhorn, Jr, 1986).

Orientation as a Process

The orientation process centers around meeting with parents, teachers, administrators, children, and community leaders and telling them about the elementary school counseling program and what it has to offer them. This soft 'tell and sell' process is designed to get these various groups excited about the program's potential and to begin stimulating their thinking about how they can avail themselves of the program's services.

The counselor and Counseling Program Committee will want to think about orientation as a process which will last several months. In so doing, they should plan their short, but exciting strategies accordingly and select a variety of colorful message catching vehicles to communicate what needs to be known. In some ways, the counselor and Program Committee are like computer salespeople selling a very saleable product. While the product cannot sell itself, a number of intriguing features about the product, once understood, is enough to bind the sale. The computer salesperson does not tell the customer about all the features of the product, but interacts with the customer and identifies those computer features that will most interest the customer in buying the product. Over time, through a variety of orientation procedures, the customer learns more about the computer, what it can and cannot do, and learns to make more effective uses of the system. The same customer probably would have been scared off by a computer salesperson who tried to tell too much, too soon.

Some valuable lessons can be learned from the computer salesperson analogy as it applies to selling elementary school counseling programs. They are as follows:

1. let the counseling program features sell themselves by introducing their capabilities in meeting the participants' needs,

2. don't push program participants to buy into the counseling program using a hard sell approach, and

3. think of orientation as a continuous never ending process. The initial steps to be taken should be designed to appeal to the customer's needs, interests, and curiosity.

As with selling any product, not every person will become an automatic advocate. The counselor and Program Committee are encouraged to work with those people who are ready to become involved and give the others time to come around. Many staunch supporters and recipients of counseling services were once non-advocates who chose to become involved because they were influenced, not by the counselor, but by the testimony of their peers. With time and a saleable track record, many new program users and supporters will join the ranks.

When teachers, parents, children, administrators, and community supporters begin to make use of the elementary school counseling program, the orientation process is said to be working. These results however are not obtained by accident. Program participants must first understand and practice the philosophy and mission of elementary school counseling as it is planned and organized if the program is to meet needs of children.

Orientation Activities with Teachers

The counselor and Counseling Program Committee can involve teachers more readily in the counseling program through inservice activities, group meetings, seminars, and classroom demonstrations. The focus of these sessions should be on introducing the nature of elementary school counseling

(Chapter 1) and the organizational structure (Chapter 3) to teachers. More specifically, the counselor can introduce and discuss program goals, review program expectations in meeting children's needs, and share with teachers how they can hope to benefit from participating in the program.

The orientation process can be facilitated by meeting with teachers individually and by grade level to discuss such issues as the five dimensions of development, learning styles, and effectively managing environmental conditions as they impact on the teaching/learning process. The counselor and Program Committee also should explore with teachers a variety of ways in which they would welcome the opportunity to work with them. Providing teachers with a checklist containing a variety of involvement possibilities is one way of assessing their interests in the counseling program.

Orientation Activities with Parents

The counselor, who desires a well rounded and integrated school counseling program with maximum benefits to children, will certainly want to include parental participation in the program. The counselor and Counseling Program Committee can begin introducing the elementary school counseling program through newsletters, informal discussions with parents, speaking at a variety of community organizations frequented by parents, and by being as visible as possible at parent-teacher organizations, school open houses, and other school social events.

As parents become somewhat familiar with the school counseling program, more formal orientation approaches can be utilized. Slide/tape or video presentations depicting the role of the counselor, video tape presentations of the counselor conducting classroom counseling activities with children, and live demonstrations of various counseling methods and techniques help to convey the essence of the elementary school counseling program to parents.

For the most part, parents are eager to learn, especially if they are well taught. They want to know about the normal growth and development of their children, about their social and emotional maturation, about sibling rivalry and how to address it, and about how to develop more effective parenting skills. They are especially concerned about helping their children to learn and develop the skills and understandings necessary to live full, satisfying, and productive lives. Orientation activities should be so designed and implemented that parents see the potential that the elementary school counseling program has to offer.

As interest builds in the program, orientation activities should be developed to help parents identify ways in which they can contribute to strengthening the counseling program. Parents can learn to make major contributions in two ways. First, they can be taught how to contribute to the school's understanding of their children. In doing so, they will gain a better understanding of their children and how the school works with them. Second, parents can make a difference by becoming parent volunteers in the counseling program, a process that is discussed at some length in Chapter 6.

Orientation Activities with Children

Since school counseling programs exist for the benefit of all children, it is especially important that they understand and become involved in the counseling program.

As with parents and teachers, the orientation process begins with the first contact and the first impression. Children need to warm-up to the counselor first before they can be expected to participate in the program. The counselor can begin introducing the program in an informal way by spending time with the children, listening to them talk, enjoying their company, learning their names, and recognizing children with a friendly hello, pat on the back, or an appropriate comment.

As children become more acquainted with the counselor as a person, more formalized activities can be employed in conveying the essence of the counseling program to them. Classroom visitations, the use of filmstrips, participation in small group developmental counseling sessions, bulletin boards, and prepared reading material are all useful vehicles to be used in teaching children about the counseling program and how to make use of the services.

The orientation sessions should convey that the program is for all children and that the counselor is always ready to listen to them discuss their interests and concerns in a caring and confidential setting. The children also will be interested in knowing about the kinds of topics, issues, and developmental skills that the counselor will be addressing in individual, small groups, and classroom settings. The more interesting and live examples the counselor can convey through a variety of mediums, the clearer will be children's understanding of the elementary school counseling program.

With time and additional modeling, the counselor can teach children how they too can contribute not only to their own growth,but to the growth of others as well. In this way, they will learn to become providers of program services and contribute to the strength and success of the elementary school counseling program.

**Orientation Activities
with Administrators**

The management of an effective elementary school counseling program depends on the support that the program receives from school board members and administrators. A big mistake made by many counselors is taking for granted that the school board and administrators understand the philosophy and mission of the counseling program. While others wrongly conclude that the success or failure of the counseling program has little to do with their involvement or lack of it.

Those elementary schools that have the strongest and most highly developed counseling programs are the ones where counselors communicate with and involve their administrators and school board members. Those are the schools where administrators and school board members know and understand the program's philosophy and mission, organizational structure, and goals.

Counselors who hope to build strong administratively supported elementary school counseling programs must plan and execute an orientation program for administrators. That program needs to demonstrate why and how children, teachers, parents, community members, administrators, and school board members are better off because they have this program. Counselors need to meet formally and informally with school board members and administrators to inform them about school counseling practices and successes. More specifically, school board members and administrators need to be shown how they can derive the most benefit from the counseling program and the counselor's expertise. Unless administrators are well oriented, the elementary school counseling program will function much as a computer in the hands of someone who does not know how to use it. The potential is there on both sides, but productivity will remain limited until the mystery regarding its potential is released.

Orientation Activities with Staff

Another group of people who have much to offer children and the school counseling program in general are the school bus drivers, custodians, cafeteria workers, teacher aides, and secretarial staff. These people interact with children on a daily basis and often either make or break the day for children.

School counselors first need to befriend the school staff. They need to listen to and talk with them about their jobs, how they feel about the school and what it is trying to accomplish, their concerns for and about children, and what role they think they play in the teaching/learning process.

Often the school staff sees little or no relationship between their job functions and child development issues. For this reason alone, orientation activities are a must. The focus of the orientation activities initially should be on helping bus drivers, custodians, cafeteria workers, and secretarial staff understand the counseling program and meeting children's needs in relationship to the tripartite as explained in Chapter 3. Once the school staff understands what children's needs are and the significance of meeting those needs in relationship to the teaching/learning process, the counselor and Program Committee can begin to explore how they can make a positive difference in children's lives.

Some topics of particular importance where school staff can have a positive influence on child development are building positive self – esteems, developing child-adult relationships, improving communication skills, learning assertive child management skills, and learning appropriate observation skills. These types of activities can help the staff connect in positive ways with the school and highlight their importance as members of the educational team.

The staff also will personally benefit from the orientation program in that their own self-esteems will be raised and they will have developed some skills that will help them to work more effectively with children.

The school staff can and does play a very important role in contributing to the physical and psychological climate of the school. When taught how to go beyond their current contributions and encouraged to do so, staff can touch children's lives in some very positive ways.

Orientation Activities with the Community

Elementary school counseling programs function best in communities where members mutually understand and support each others' interests and goals. The school looks to the community for financial support, participation in a variety of counseling related program activities, and continued feedback and support regarding the management of an effective elementary school counseling program. Likewise, the community looks to the school to provide a quality education for all children that will ultimately benefit them personally and the community collectively.

The orientation process begins with the school counselor and Program Committee becoming knowledgeable and understanding of the community's needs and support services. This can be accomplished by interacting with businesses, industries, and social service agencies. The counselor should become familiar with community living standards, the economic condition of the community, and related societal issues which impact significantly on the community. In addition, community workers should be asked their views on education and what ideas they have which could make education more purposeful, meaningful, and relevant. This is a necessary first step in fine tuning education (counseling) program offerings in response to community involvement.

Once the counselor is familiar with the community and its needs, a second level of activities can begin. These orientation activities are designed to familiarize the community with the elementary school counseling program. Counselors are encouraged to speak before community groups, make informal contacts by telephone, and make on-site visits (agency, industry, business). Making use of the radio, television, newspaper, flyers, and newsletters are other ways in which the orientation process can be furthered.

The message should be directed toward exploring ways in which the school counseling program and the community can encourage and develop partnerships which will mutually benefit the needs of children and the community. In Chapter 6 is discussed the importance of school and community partnerships and the benefits of engaging in this practice.

PHASE II: TRAINING AND DEVELOPMENT

As has been demonstrated, parents, teachers, administrators, school board members, child service specialists, and staff personnel have important roles to fulfill in contributing to the strength and success of any elementary school counseling program. However, easing these perspective volunteers into the school counseling program is a task not to be taken lightly.

Training and Development is the second phase of actuating a school counseling program. The major goal of this phase is to bring people, program activities, and resources together for the purpose of achieving counseling program goals. This phase is to be accomplished in a self-esteem enhancing environment in which program participants are motivated and supported in their endeavor to serve children.

Developing A Supportive Environment

The four major determinants to be addressed in developing a supportive training and development environment of which we speak are connectiveness, uniqueness, power, and models (Clemes & Bean, 1981).

Connectiveness. Program volunteers need to feel a part of the elementary school counseling team and also experience a sense of confidence in themselves as they direct counseling program activities. The counselor and Program Committee have an important role in creating and maintaining a supportive teaching/learning environment. That support also must spill over into the day to day activities of the volunteer participants.

Uniqueness. Program volunteers need to feel positive about their contributions to the counseling program. They need to feel special and be recognized for their contributions to the school counseling program. Creating a sense of uniqueness helps to build motivation, maintain a high energy level, and instill self-confidence.

Power. Program volunteers need to feel that they have an important role in shaping the counseling program. They should be encouraged to participate fully in the training and development process and be given the responsibility to manage their involvement in those activities which they are directing.

Modeling. Self-esteem training environments call for the dissemination of accurate information, the learning of specific skills, and self confidence building activities when preparing program volunteers for action. The modeling process gives participants an opportunity to observe, experience, and practice what they are being taught under the guidance of an experienced trainer.

Process

Now that parents, teachers, administrators, school board members, school staff, and community volunteers understand the nature of the elementary school counseling program and are deriving benefits from the program, they are ready to become program service providers. To be successful, program volunteers need accurate information, specific skills, and the necessary self-confidence to perform their counseling program roles effectively. In accomplishing this end, a four step training model consisting of observing, experiencing, teaming, and soloing will be presented (Worzbyt, 1978). In Figure 4.1 is depicted the process.

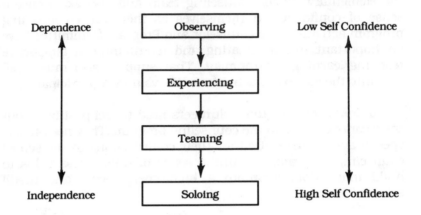

Figure 4.1. Program training model.

As program volunteers advance through the training model, they become more independent regarding their ability to conduct counseling activities on their own. The knowledge, skills, and self-confidence gained from the training experience also tend to enhance the participant's feelings of self-worth. Regardless of the people being trained or the nature of the training experience, the same process is applicable.

Step I: Observing. When teaching any group of volunteers how to conduct a particular activity, one of the best ways is to move from familiar ground to new experiences. Participants are likely to feel more comfortable about the training process.

Observing is the information dissemination and climate setting stage and is designed to provide the volunteer with an understanding of the activity. During this stage, the volunteer has an opportunity to observe the counselor or a member of the Counseling Program Committee discuss and demonstrate the nature of the involvement. Volunteers begin to see how their existing skills can be used, understand the breadth and depth of the activity, and begin to physically and psychologically connect with what may have been previously a somewhat threatening situation.

Before volunteers bring counseling programs into the classroom for the first time, they will need opportunities to observe as the counselor demonstrates ways in which they can become involved. Counselors can accomplish this through workshops, in-class demonstrations, and through individual consultations. Films, video tape presentations, simulations, and role plays are all suitable ways to demonstrate and discuss volunteers' involvement in classroom and other counseling activities.

Following the demonstration (observing), time should be taken to discuss what happened, why it may have happened that way, and respond to volunteers' questions and feelings. A series of observation sessions may be necessary before volunteers feel comfortable enough to move to Step II.

Step II: Experiencing. *Experiencing* is the second phase of the volunteer training program. After having observed a particular activity, technique, or procedure, volunteers are ready to experience what they have observed.

Volunteers who are learning how to conduct a classroom counseling activity will gain much by experiencing the learning activity in the same way that the children will experience it. *Experiencing* may take place in formal training sessions or informally in small group activity sessions. During *experiencing* sessions, volunteers become more familiar with the new activity and develop a better understanding of how to conduct the activity because of having experienced it first hand.

Regardless of the nature of the activity, volunteer training programs should not skip the *experiencing* phase. Only when people have been personally touched by an experience can they process the experience in a meaningful manner. Understanding and experiencing are natural prerequisites to Step III: *Teaming.*

Step III: Teaming. Teaming is the skill and confidence building phase. As volunteers become familiar with activities, procedures, and techniques, their purposes, and how to manage the new situation, they are ready to participate in a teaming experience with the counselor.

Teaming allows the counselor to teach the volunteers in a controlled and non-threatening environment how to handle their new responsibilities. During this step, which may require a number of sessions, the counselor gradually turns more and more of the responsibilities for leadership over to the volunteer.

Each *teaming* experience should be followed by a review of what has taken place. The review is designed to encourage volunteers to talk about the experience, to examine their progress in achieving the intent of the activity, to set new direction for subsequent teaming experiences, and to provide the counselor with an opportunity to continue support and bolster confidence. The review process, in addition to the benefits mentioned, serves to demonstrate the importance of taking time to look back when providing direction and support in moving forward.

Teaming continues until both the counselor and the volunteer feel that he or she is ready to solo. The counselor must pay particular attention in not letting the helping relationship continue beyond the point of establishing the volunteer's independence in directing the experience. *Teaming* is designed to provide volunteers with enough understanding and self-confidence about the activity to eventually assume full responsibility for directing the new experience.

Step IV: Soloing. Most people look forward to the time when they can solo, no matter what the experience. *Soloing* is a time filled with anticipation, excitement, and perhaps some reservation. The counselor works closely with the volunteer even at the point of *soloing.* While the counselor, at this stage, does not directly assume an active role in managing the experience, the counselor does provide support and is available for consultation when desired. The counselor continues to provide support, in whatever way possible, until both parties agree that the assistance is no longer needed.

When volunteers (teachers, parents, children, admini-strators, community leaders, school board members) finally solo, they will understand their new responsibilities and will be capable, with some assistance, to become trainer–facilitators themselves. As the training process unfolds, counseling program services can be expanded and more volunteers can be enlisted in providing a comprehensive developmental counseling program that will touch the lives of all children.

BIBLIOGRAPHY

Clemes, H., & Bean, R. (1981). *Self esteem: The key to your child's well-being.* New York: Kensington Publishing.

Schermerhorn, J.R., Jr. (1986). *Management of human service programs.* Monterey, CA: Brooks/Cole.

Worzbyt, J.C. (1978). *Elementary school guidance: Program planning, organization and implementation.* (Title III ESEA Report). Harrisburg, PA: Pennsylvania Department of Education.

CONTROLLING ELEMENTARY SCHOOL COUNSELING PROGRAM

Planning, organizing, and actuating represent critical management functions in establishing well grounded and effective programs. As important as those functions are, they hold little value if the expected program service results do not justify the expenditure of effort and resources in accomplishing the program goals. Ultimately the success of any program can only be determined by evaluating the program's performance against goal standards. If the results are not within acceptable limits, corrective measures will need to be applied. Evaluation and program adjustments, when necessary, constitute the work of management control (Terry & Franklin, 1982).

CONTROLLING DEFINED

Controlling is a proactive process designed to detect and correct significant deviations in program goal outcomes from program standards as clarified in the planning process. If the planning, organizing, and actuating functions of management could be executed without error, no need would exist for the controlling function. Being realistic however, one cannot hope to expect that functions as complex and detailed as these can be executed perfectly. Effective controlling assists the elementary school counselor in evaluating, monitoring, and regulating the actual performance of program goals in order to insure that they are executed as planned.

The planning and controlling functions in elementary school counseling programming are very closely related. They are actually developed at about the same time. The controlling function cannot exist without carefully detailed plans which identify the intended commitments to action and future accomplishments. The controlling function grows and develops from the planning process. The closer the linkage between these two functions, the greater the potential for a successful elementary school counseling program.

REASONS TO EVALUATE

Elementary school counseling programs serve to identify and solve environmental and educationally related climatic conditions (problems) in the school and community which impact negatively on children and the teaching/learning process. These problems are then corrected in order to improve upon the teaching/learning process and to meet children's needs so that they can learn more effectively. In the process of meeting this end, the Counseling Program Committee conducted a comprehensive needs assessment (Chapter 2) with the tripartite as its focal point. Children's needs were identified, behaviors to be learned were specified, and the school and community environments were studied to determine ways in which they could best support the teaching/learning process. Following the needs assessment, program goals were identified and prioritized to meet the most critical needs. The Counseling Program Committee then developed strategies, selected activities, and committed resources to carry out each of the counseling program goals.

A final step in the management process is needed to inform the Counseling Program Committee how well the counseling program is doing in solving those problems identified during the needs assessment. The elementary school counselor depends on the controlling function to monitor performance, to make the right program decisions, and to provide continuous feedback to those service providers responsible for keeping the elementary school counseling program on target.

Monitor Program Performance

Monitoring program performance is one of the most important functions of management. The Counseling Program Committee will want to know what kind of an impact the counseling program is having on meeting children's needs as identified in the needs assessment. The Program Committee will want to review each program goal in terms of its appropriateness, adequacy, effectiveness, efficiency, and side effects. Some program goals may need to be adjusted or eliminated depending on the results. While other goals may be very appropriate, they may still be falling short of expectation because the necessary mix of resources, activities, and strategies may need to be adjusted in order to reach goal attainment.

Monitoring program performance is only possible to the degree that the Counseling Program Committee has set specific standards during the planning process for each program goal. Knowing whether or not the elementary school counseling program is working as planned requires clearly stated program goals with observable and measurable criteria. Without such standards, evaluation is pointless.

Make Program Decisions

While monitoring program performance is an important step in controlling, it can be a rather meaningless activity unless something is done with the results. Data take on meaning when they are interpreted and used for self-corrective purposes for staying on target. The target in elementary school counseling programs is the goal which is designed to meet a critical need. Keeping the goal and need in mind, the Counseling Program Committee will be continually making decisions that will meet the desired program outcomes. Decisions regarding goal elimination or adjustment, strategy design, activity selection and modification, and resource allocations will have to be made routinely throughout the school year if the controlling function is to produce favorable results.

Feedback to Service Providers

Without feedback to service providers, the elementary school counseling program will function like a missile without a guidance system, rarely if ever hitting the target. Service providers need to know how they are doing during program implementation and what they can do to make constructive improvements in the delivery of services. Feedback not only helps to keep the counseling program on target, but also is an important source of motivation and satisfaction. Service providers will feel better about themselves and the program when they know that they are making a significant contribution.

Program adjustments resulting from planned decision making also are more easily made and supported when the service providers are included in the team effort to provide quality services to children. Planned feedback generates positive results in a supportive climate which fosters purposeful change.

Control Process

The control process comprises three definitive steps which are

1. measuring the program performance as executed;

2. comparing the program performance results with the program standards (criteria); and

3. ascertaining the unacceptable differences, if any, and implementing corrective action.

In essence, the Counseling Program Committee is concerned with what is currently happening in the elementary school counseling program and then comparing the results with what is expected. With that information, the Counseling Program Committee must then decide which program outcomes are acceptable and will continue as they are, or which are not and will require remediation. In Figure 5.1 is graphically depicted the process to be presented.

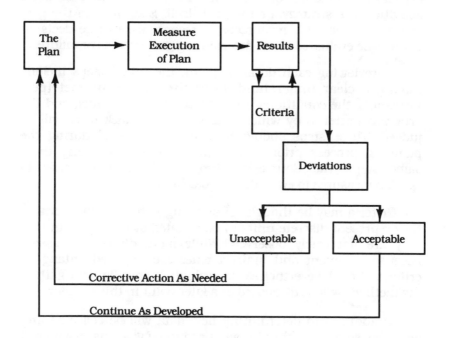

Figure 5.1. The control process.

Measuring Execution of The Plan

The elementary school counseling program consists of many different sets of plans that work together in meeting children's needs including program plans, budgetary plans, organization plans, implementation plans, and evaluation plans. Regardless of the plans to be evaluated, the process works in the same way.

Every plan consists of resources, activities, strategies (objectives), and goals. The resources must be of sufficient quantity and quality to create the desired activities. Selected activities must support the chosen strategy (objective). The selected strategy needs to produce the desired goal outcome. And finally, the selected goal itself must be free of obstacles in meeting the needs to be addressed. Goals may fall short of expectation because of problems associated with resources, activities, the strategy, or the goal itself. Each link in the goal chain, starting with resources, represents a separate decision point to be evaluated when determining goal success or failure.

In reviewing each decision point, the initial steps include having a clear understanding of the goal to be met (performance), the conditions under which it is to be met, and the criterion (criteria) by which goal success, or lack of it, will be judged. These steps should have been completed during the planning process prior to goal implementation. Using these same steps, the Counseling Program Committee needs to develop measures to evaluate the goals to be studied.

Criteria may be thought of as being either tangible in that they represent discrete units to be counted or intangible in that they are not easily observed. While more difficult to assess because judgment and indirect clues are required, intangible criteria should nevertheless be evaluated. Specific data gathering methods will be discussed at a later point in this chapter.

In addition to determining how data will be collected and analyzed, some thought also will need to be given as to who will collect and analyze data and when they should be analyzed. While responding to these questions will require some thought, answers can be found by examining the goal criteria to be met. *What are we hoping to achieve through goal attainment? How will we know when we have succeeded? What data and in what format will best satisfy our need to know how we are doing? Who will collect data and how can the information be collected so as not to cause any undue hardship on those who must provide and analyze the information?*

These are critical questions to be answered, because without a planned method for data collection and analysis, the remaining two steps in the control process cannot take shape in an effective, efficient, and adequate manner. The potential negative side effects from relying on a poorly planned controlling process could result in a devastating blow to an otherwise potentially positive counseling program.

Comparing Results With Standards

Program performance evaluation is determined when the actual program results are compared with the established criteria. The significance of the differences between performance and standards requires the interpretation of the Counseling Program Committee. Since this is an ongoing and continuous process, adjustments in the controlling process often require little loss of time or expenditures of expensive resources.

Program providers are continually consulted for their input and are kept informed about necessary changes in program design. The Counseling Program Committee need not concern itself with minimal deviations or exceptions in performance from the standards. However, significant exceptions or outstanding variations from the criteria will require the most effort in the controlling process. The exceptional cases will require the remedial action.

To illustrate, the counseling program may have as one of its goals for all children at the sixth grade level to verbally demonstrate their ability to use a six step decision making model when processing a given decision making activity. If 90% of the children are able to successfully demonstrate each of the six steps, the Counseling Program Committee, while interested in helping the remaining 10% succeed, may view this goal as being met. The degree of deviation from the standard is not significant and therefore does not require a program change for this goal. The acceptable standard, if possible, needs to be decided prior to implementing the activities, thus avoiding the temptation to adjust expectations (standards) on the bases of results.

While each goal will have specific and unique criteria to be evaluated when comparing performance with standards, there are some general criteria which apply to all goals during the planning and evaluating functions. Goals can be studied in terms of five criteria according to Craig (1978). The criteria are appropriateness, adequacy, effectiveness, efficiency, and side effects. By studying these criteria, specific questions become apparent from which measures can be designed to secure the desired data.

Appropriateness. This is basically a value laden category which questions the suitability or proper fit of the chosen resources, activities, strategies, and the goal itself in meeting the identified program needs. In other words, do most people support the goal and the selected means to attain it? While the answer was yes during the planning process, the Counseling Program Committee will again need to reflect on the appropriateness of each dimension of the plan during implementation and at its conclusion.

Adequacy. Program plans are successful to the extent that resources, activities, and strategies are sufficient in number and development to accomplish the specific need. The Counseling Program Committee will want to evaluate the degree to which specific program needs are being met, and if they are not, whether an adequacy problem exists in the plan (resource, activities, strategy, and goal).

Effectiveness. To what extent are the selected resources, activities, strategy, and the goal capable of accomplishing the desired results? Program plans may be appropriate and adequate, but be incapable of producing the desired effect. When this occurs, program resources, activities, strategies, or the goal may need to be eliminated or altered in order to meet the specific program need. Evaluating program plans for their effectiveness helps to identify and eliminate resources that are not being used, to rewrite some activities and remove others that don't support the strategy, and to alter a program goal that does not have the necessary impact to solve the problem (need) for which it was intended.

Efficiency. The Counseling Program Committee will want to evaluate the cost effectiveness of the program plan. This can be accomplished by comparing the estimated cost (time, money, numbers of people, etc.) with the actual cost and the quality of the obtained results produced by the plan. Could the same results be obtained for less money? Could certain activities be combined in producing the same strategy? Do the achieved results justify the expenditure of resources?

Side Effects. Every program plan will produce or create planned and unplanned conditions, some of which will impact positively and others negatively on the counseling program. To what extent did program resources, activities, strategies, or goals produce the anticipated side effects? Can the side effects be tolerated or will some counseling program plans need to be revised or eliminated?

To evaluate resources, activities, and strategies for every program goal would be very tedious and would receive negative marks on the five evaluative measures. As we have stated earlier, the Counseling Program Committee can streamline the evaluation and controlling process by focusing on the major program goals and looking for significant deviations and exceptions in program expectations versus program outcomes. When these deviations are noted, a closer look at program resources, activities, strategies, and goals are in order.

Implementing Corrective Action

The last step in the control process insures that operations are adjusted and that efforts are made to achieve the planned results. Whenever significant deviations are identified, immediate and intensive action is necessary. Long delays and less than quality responses cannot be tolerated when addressing significant variances in anticipated program results.

If the Counseling Program Committee has done a careful job of program planning and designing the evaluation, the necessary information should be available for making the required changes. However, having the right information will not insure remedial action. The effective use of evaluative information requires that those who collect the data

1. present the information in a way that increases the possibility of acceptance,

2. make sure the right information gets to the right people at the right time, and

3. summarize how evaluative information about the plan will be used in the organization. (Craig, 1978 p. 108)

Information that is presented in a nondescriptive and threatening manner and is shared in an untimely fashion with people who are neither in a position to implement the needed changes nor are motivated to do so will result in the collection of useless information and an aimless and wasteful counseling program.

Information. Evaluative information is only useful to the extent that it is applied in a corrective fashion and keeps the counseling program on target. If the counseling program staff is to accept the notion of remedial action, program changes must be presented in a non-threatening manner. In order to meet this end, presenting evaluative feedback in a way that increases the possibility of its acceptance is the goal. This can be accomplished by

1. providing continuous feedback (formal and informal) through existing channels of communication and decision making;

2. clearly specifying, in a nonjudgmental fashion, the existence of any problem and what makes it a problem;

3. naming the benefits that could result from correcting significant deviations or variances in program plans;

4. providing some alternative courses of action that could be explored in meeting the previously unmet criteria;

5. inviting the participation of key people who will share their ideas in exploring remedial courses of action;

6. identifying persons who need to be involved, what they will need to do, and what initial steps will need to be taken;

7. indicating where the changes will need to take place in the counseling program;

8. stating how the changes will be orchestrated;

9. seeking questions, avoiding surprises, and alleviating fears regarding the corrective actions to be taken; and

10. acknowledging any anticipated rough spots in making program modifications and describing how they will be addressed.

Right Information—The Right People—The Right Time. While preparing and presenting evaluative information in an effective manner is critical to its acceptance, making sure that information gets to the right people in a timely fashion is equally critical if data are to serve a useful purpose. Several key questions need to be asked before any corrective action can be implemented.

1. What is the nature of the corrective action to be taken?

2. What organizational level is most equipped to facilitate the corrective action (operational, administrative, policy, etc.)?

3. Who has the power (formal/informal) and responsibility for making the decision?

4. What information will the decision maker(s) need in order to make the necessary decision?

5. When must the decision maker(s) have the information in order to make a timely and cost effective decision?

If, for example, during the controlling process, the Counseling Program Committee received feedback from the primary grade teachers that they needed more information on self-esteem development before they could adequately meet the child development goals in that area, a number of decisions would need to be processed in order to effect the desired change. The feedback from teachers will help the Counseling Program Committee organize the evaluative data, understand problems, and identify plausible solutions. The information also will reveal the organizational level(s) that will need to become involved in making necessary decisions that will better equip teachers to service children's needs in the area of self-esteem. By next responding to the preceding five questions, a proposal for change can be developed and submitted to the appropriate decision makers for their review and disposition.

Reporting the Actions to be Taken. The final step in implementing the proposed corrective action(s) takes place once final approval has been received from the decision maker(s).

Corrective action is most likely to occur when certain key ingredients are present in evaluative feedback reports. Those ingredients are

1. names of those people who will be held responsible for implementing the corrective action(s);

2. a detailed accounting of the corrective action to be taken, specifying the resources to be made available, a description of the activities to be implemented in meeting the accepted strategy, an outline of the strategy, and clearly stated criteria to be met in meeting the goal;

3. a time table for completion of each phase of the corrective action;

4. a schedule for reporting the progress of the action being taken; and

5. a description of the accepted reporting format (verbal feedback, written report, norms, statistical accounting, etc.) and the names of those individuals who are to receive the information.

This final step helps to insure that the controlling process recommendations will be carried out and that the desired actions will be met. *Accountability and responsibility are key factors in implementing or making remedial adjustments in any action plan.*

Types Of Control

Davis (1951) and Donnelly, Gibson, and Ivancevich (1981) have referred to three types of control and have identified them as **preliminary control, concurrent control,** and **feedback control.** Preliminary control takes place before the elementary school counseling program is placed into action and includes the development of a philosophy, mission statement, policies, procedures, and rules designed to insure that program activities are carried out as planned. Without preliminary control, an elementary school counseling program could easily be tempted to be all things to all people and operate without a clear focus as to its purpose. Preliminary control influencers assist the school counselor, administrators, faculty, and the school community members to make difficult decisions in choosing only those goals, strategies, activities, and resources which reflect the philosophy, mission, and policies of the school and elementary school counseling program.

Concurrent control takes place during the action phase of carrying out the program plan. This type of control is the heart of any operating control system (Terry & Franklin, 1982). This process includes providing direction, monitoring, and fine tuning of all activities as they occur. Concurrent control requires having an in-depth sense of what is to happen, when it is to happen, how it is to happen, and who is responsible for making it happen. Concurrent control helps to insure that the plan will be carried out in accordance with all of the conditions as set forth in the plan.

Feedback control most closely approximates that which has been described in the preceding pages. Feedback control relies on the use of information which has been supplied about previous action in order to correct possible future deviations from acceptable standards. Feedback control is necessary because program goals may not be met even though preliminary and concurrent control procedures have been implemented.

Feedback data will assist the Counseling Program Committee in taking a close look at the goal plan (resources, activities, strategy, and the goal) and determining what corrective actions may be warranted, if any, in meeting counseling program standards.

All three types of control measures are critical to the success of any elementary school counseling program. They provide the elementary school counselor and Program Committee with an opportunity to review the counseling program from a variety of angles and to ask such questions as the following:

1. Was the goal plan really worth the effort?

2. Did the plan have a significant and positive impact on meeting children's needs?

3. Was the need being addressed critically enough to warrant the expenditure of these resources?

4. Was this program goal and plan central to the elementary school counseling program philosophy and mission?

DATA COLLECTION METHODS

Now that the controlling process has been explained, let us return to Step 1, *Measuring Execution of the Plan,* and review a variety of ways in which to obtain the desired data. Data collection begins with identifying the questions to be asked at each discussion point in the goal plan. The decision points represent the various links in the goal plan (Resources—Activities—Strategy(ies)—Goal). Each goal has criteria (standards) to be met in meeting the needs for which the goal was designed. These criteria can be measured through data collection methods. A measure represents a quantity and/or quality factor that can be expressed as data. After data have been collected, analyzed, and interpreted, a decision can be made regarding the degree to which the goal standards (criteria) have been met.

As we indicated earlier, every link in the goal plan chain can be evaluated in terms of its appropriateness, adequacy, effectiveness, efficiency, and side effects. Determining how often, what, and how much to evaluate is critical. Measuring only those things that will yield the most critical information needed is an important guide to consider when controlling the elementary school counseling program. Asking the question, "How will the counselor and Counseling Program Committee know whether this resource, this activity, or this strategy (objective) meets the five evaluative criteria?" is a good place to begin. In order to answer these questions, some form of measurement and data collection method will be required.

Some easy to use and some rather complex data collection methods are available from which to choose when deciding which methods will provide the most useful data for the measure being sought. In Figure 5.2 is a list of very useful and familiar ways to collect data.

---

observation	research design
questionnaire	(experimental,
interviews	surveys,
financial records	case studies)
pupil records	academic
ratings scale	assessment
(peers, faculty,	instruments
administration)	check lists
institutional records	anecdotal
and policy	records
statements	opinionnaires

Figure 5.2. Data collection methods.

Using the grid in Figure 5.3, the Counseling Program Committee can begin to identify various measures it wishes to evaluate regarding each goal plan and how best to secure the data. As an example, the Program Committee may wish to evaluate the success of its fourth grade communication skills development program which can be accomplished by comparing the expected results (standards) with those actually obtained. By asking the right questions and choosing the most effective data collection methods, the Committee will be able to determine how successful the communication skills program has been in addressing the children's needs.

GUIDELINES TO EFFECTIVE CONTROLLING

The controlling function is clearly an important dimension of managing an effective elementary school counseling program. We have made a number of important suggestions throughout the chapter which we would like to reemphasize as practical guidelines when implementing the controlling process.

Goal Statement: To have children behaviorally demonstrate their understanding of 3 out of 5 communication skills as outlined in the social skill development program.

Measure (Questions)	Collection Method	Source	Collector	Report Form
1. How many children can follow 2 step directions correctly?	Obervation Checklists Rating Scale Self Report	Teachers Children	Teachers	Teacher Use Only
2. How many children speak one at a time in planned group discussions?	Observations Checklists Rating Scales Self Report	Teachers Children	Teachers	Teacher Use Only
3. How many children are able to verbally repeat back what others have said before speaking?	Observations Checklists Rating Scales Self Report	Teachers Children	Teachers	Teacher Use Only
4. Does the Communication Skills Program seem to be achieving the desired results?	Opinionnaires Attitude Survey Interviews Experimental Research	Parents Teachers Children	Counselors Teachers	Administrators & School Board members. Prepared by counselor twice a year

Figure 5.3. Sample data collection grid.

1. Recognize controlling not only as it reflects on the past but also as future oriented. The success of this process rests not only on what happened yesterday, but how these new data will shape the tomorrows.

2. Since the control process cannot be all inclusive when monitoring an elementary school counseling program, select those decision points which are most critical to program survival and future growth (resources, activities, strategy, and goals).

3. Before deciding what to measure, first think about what decisions will need to be made and what information will be required to make those decisions. This action will help to eliminate the collection of needless information and the wasteful use of people's time.

4. Select the standard with care because the key to successful controlling is the standard against which an action plan is evaluated both during and after its implementation. Controlling diminishes in its effectiveness when standards become inexact.

5. Utilize multiple controls because they are more beneficial to use when evaluating goal plans than to rely on just one measure. Evaluating the appropriateness, adequacy, effectiveness, efficiency, and side effects of program goals will give a broader and more in depth look at the goal than any one measure can provide on its own. Keep in mind, however, that not every goal needs to be evaluated by all five measures.

6. Subject the controlling process to evaluation methods. As Terry and Franklin (1982) have indicated, to have good controlling at low cost is entirely possible as well as poor controlling at high cost. The controlling process should be subjected to the same five evaluating controls listed in Guideline 5 in order to determine its contribution, or lack of it, to the counseling program.

7. Identify and utilize key personnel in the controlling process. These individuals should not only be motivated

to participate in the process, but have the authority to do so. They should, likewise, be given the authority and responsibility to either manage the corrective action to be taken or to handle it directly themselves. Without immediate and planned remediation, the controlling process serves little or no value.

8. Have the Counseling Program Committee, in addition to engaging in feedback control, pay equal attention to preliminary and concurrent control functions. This will help to insure for a solid elementary school counseling program.

Yes, the controlling function does require the expenditure of time, money, and use of human resource skills to keep an elementary school counseling program on track. Often this must be accomplished utilizing crude social science evaluation measures and the interpretation and utilization of incomplete and fragmentary data. While no perfect measures exist that will tell us exactly what we may want to know, nor no perfect solutions to our problems, these do not represent justifiable reasons for eliminating this valued process. With practice and some risk taking, new skills will emerge as will a significantly stronger more reliable and valid controlling function.

For those school districts and individuals who have neglected this dimension of program management (controlling), the following quote by Wrenn (1962) may encourage some to overlook their own inadequacies and the problems associated with controlling, and take the plunge.

> More mistakes can be made by counselors (school districts) who assume that they know but never attempt to find out than by counselors (school districts) who conduct studies (evaluations), but do so poorly. (p. 146)

BIBLIOGRAPHY

Craig, D.P. (1978). *Hip pocket guide to planning and evaluation.* San Diego, CA: Learning Concepts.

Davis, R.C. (1951). *The fundamentals of top management.* New York: Harper & Row.

Donnelly, J.H., Jr., Gibson, J.L., & Ivancevich, J.M. (1981). *Fundamentals of management.* (4th ed.). Plano, Texas: Business Publications.

Terry, G.R., & Franklin, S.G. (1982). *Principles of management* (8th ed.). Homewood, IL: Richard D. Irwin.

Wrenn, G. (1962). *The counselor in a changing world.* Washington, DC: American Personnel and Guidance Association.

BIBLIOGRAPHY

CHAPTER 6

BREATHING
NEW LIFE INTO
AN EXISTING PROGRAM

For those school districts that have had an elementary school counseling program in place for some time, keeping that program exciting, viable, and purposeful can be a challenge. Like people, programs can lose their vitality if they continue to function in the same way year after year. That is why breathing new life into an existing program can be an uplifting and rewarding experience for all who are involved in the energizing process.

While many ways exist to energize an existing counseling program, we would like to share ideas that have been passed to us by our colleagues in the field. Any time new ideas are added or old ideas are modified, program energizers have been created. This chapter will elaborate on a number of ways to spark new vitality into an existing program, stimulate school and community participation, and revitalize a commitment to the elementary school counseling program.

This chapter will address six (6) vital areas of commitment and will suggest some ways in which counseling programs can be strengthened through

1. parent volunteer support,

2. networking: a spiderweb of support,

3. environmental connectiveness,

4. pupil service interfacing,

5. school and community partnerships, and

6. public relations.

PARENT VOLUNTEER SUPPORT

Parents have been, and always will be, a vital source of volunteer support in our schools. But as with any resource, parent volunteer activities need to be meaningful, carefully planned, guided by school personnel, supported by adequate resources, and monitored in terms of their effectiveness. Likewise, parent volunteers must clearly understand the nature of the commitment prior to volunteering their services. They should be interviewed (screened) prior to their acceptance into a volunteer program, receive appropriate training, be given constant feedback on how they are doing, and receive proper recognition for their services. Keeping these points in mind, volunteer programs can be very successful and rewarding to parents, teachers, and children alike.

As with any successful volunteer program, much needed planning goes on behind the scene before the program is set in motion. To assist counselors with the process of identifying, planning, implementing, and managing parent volunteer programs, we offer the following.

Things to Think About

1. How can parent volunteers best serve the school counseling program?

2. What program goals (dimensions of counseling) are amenable to parent participation?

3. In what new ways might parent volunteer groups be of benefit to the counseling program?

4. When should volunteer activities begin and how long (days, weeks, etc.) should they continue?

5. Who should be involved in developing, implementing, and managing the volunteer program?

6. How will parents, teachers, children, and the school benefit from the program?

7. What initial steps should be taken?

8. What other questions need to be addressed before the planning process begins?

People with Whom to Talk

Many people in the school community are not only willing to volunteer their service, but have good suggestions as to ways in which volunteers can provide a valuable service to the school counseling program. By talking to parents, counselors can find out what their talents and interests are. Parents frequently will have talents such as writing, secretarial skills, artistic talents, photography, and carpentry skills. Some unique ways of making use of these talents and others like them are mentioned later in this section. In the meantime, the counselor can talk with a number of groups and individuals to help them understand ways in which they can contribute to the quality of education in the school. The following groups and individuals are but a few of the many resources that can be contacted.

1. Social service clubs and agencies (Groups in this category look for special projects and ways to help the community.)

2. Administrators and school board members

3. Teachers

4. Parent leaders

5. Parent volunteer organizations, parent-teacher groups, Boy Scouts, Girl Scouts, YMCA, YWCA, and similar organizations

6. Neighboring school districts that have parent volunteer groups

7. State, regional, and national professional association personnel and office holders. These people travel widely and are exposed to a number of interesting ideas and programs. This is a valuable resource to tap.

8. Senior citizens

Things to Do

1. Brainstorm ways in which individual parents as well as parent groups could best serve children (directly and indirectly) in a school district.

2. Identify the program goals (dimensions of counseling) most amenable to parent participation.

3. Develop a rationale in support of parent volunteer programs. In that rationale

   a. explain the reason(s) for supporting such programs;

   b. review the potential risks and state why they are worth taking and how they can be minimized;

   c. identify the benefits that could result from volunteer programs both to the volunteers and those served by the programs;

   d. address questions that the school/community may have regarding plans to implement particular volunteer programs;

   e. support an open invitation for participation in developing the process necessary to implement volunteer programs; and

f. provide a plan of action outline for implementing parent volunteer programs to include program goals, description of activities, initiation and completion dates, potential problems and solutions, needed resources, and means of evaluation.

4. Contact formal and informal leaders in the school and the community and assess their interest in the program.

5. Survey the parents for the purpose of identifying a volunteer pool.

6. Introduce the program to the parent volunteer pool.

7. Identify those who wish to volunteer their time, meet the qualifications, and subscribe to the program standards.

8. Provide the volunteers with a copy of the district's training manual for parent volunteers.

9. Run the training program. Be sure to support the parent volunteers in every way. Treat them with kindness and promote a positive self-esteem enhancing environment for them while they work.

10. Set the volunteer program in motion. Depending on the nature of the parent volunteer program, a network of a number of community resources (state, regional, national) may be necessary in support of the district's parent volunteer effort.

Suggested Activities

While the list is endless regarding ways in which parents can assist the counseling program both directly and indirectly in providing support to children, here are but a few.

1. **Counseling Newsletters and Brochure Assistance**

   Many parents have writing skills, clerical skills, and artistic ability. They could form a volunteer team, guided by the school counselor, to write a monthly newsletter, and develop brochures and audio tapes on counseling program topics of interest that could be loaned to children and parents.

2. Classroom Counseling Aids

Counselors are always in need of props to use in small and large group counseling sessions with children. Parents who like to sew can make puppets, stuffed animals, and masks. Other parents can assist the counselor in developing a picture file. Pictures can be drawn or clipped out of magazines, and photographs can be taken to illustrate and support various teachings in the five dimensions of counseling. Likewise, parents with carpentry and related skills in the trades can contribute their talents in similar ways to benefit the school counseling and educational programs.

3. Clerical Aids

Since most school districts are not able to provide sufficient clerical help for school counselors, a parent volunteer clerical aid pool would help to free up valuable counselor time to work directly with children. As with every volunteer program, specific guidelines would need to be developed specifying the nature of the work to be done by the volunteers and at the same time maintain necessary confidentiality standards.

4. Library Assistants

Parents can catalogue books, review reading material for bibliography topics and listings for teacher use, read stories to small groups of children, and plan library displays.

5. Cafeteria Aids

Rather than have parents police children's behavior, have them function as spotters identifying children who are displaying appropriate (desired) behavior. Spotters can hand out coupons or tokens which can be turned back to the classroom teacher for special privileges such as going to the library and participating in a variety of activities during free time.

6. **Playground Monitors**

Parents can be very helpful to teachers in monitoring playground activity. While parents should not replace the teacher on the playground, another set of eyes can help to improve playground safety.

7. **Parent Resource Networking**

While networking is a topic to be discussed in greater detail in this chapter, counseling programs have a number of resource needs. Parent volunteers can establish a number of useful networks that will improve counseling programs (information networks, career awareness networks, and various interest networks).

8. **Strength Sharing**

Many parents have skills which can be shared with children. Sharing one's strengths is not only a rewarding experience for parents and children alike, but it is also a form of modeling worthy of emulation. Children should be given an opportunity to share their strengths with parents.

9. **Special Interest Programs**

Parents can coordinate a variety of worthwhile skill-building programs for children. Babysitting certification programs, latchkey safety training, fire safety, making a safe home, children's rights, and caring for a younger sibling are but a few of the many types of programs staffed by parents that can benefit children.

10. **Activity Period Programs**

Some elementary schools coordinate an afternoon activity period one day a week. Selected parent volunteers run a series of interest groups, hobbies, and sporting events from which children may choose. The activity sessions change every five weeks, giving children an opportunity to participate in up to two new experiences each 10 week quarter. This volunteer program, while a lot of fun for parents and children alike, requires much advanced planning prior to its implementation.

11. **Room Parents**

Most schools have a room parent program in the primary grades. These parents assist teachers in planning and conducting parties and related activities.

12. **Tutoring**

Parents who have teaching skills (elementary school) may be interested in serving as parent tutors for children.

13. **Parents as Partners**

Some school districts have a club or organization called *Parents as Partners*. This is a group for parents that has both a professional and social purpose. Parents have an opportunity to socialize with each other and perform a useful purpose in working closely with the elementary counselor in providing a variety of direct services to the program. These parents meet with the counselor throughout the school year and provide support services as needed.

NETWORKING: A SPIDERWEB OF SUPPORT

A network is as the title implies, a series of interconnecting lines like the fabric of a net which link people, places, and information centers. Networks exist because they serve to bring people, places, ideas, and resources together for the benefit of those who use them. Our transportation networks (road, rail systems, air routes, and nautical navigation routes) are designed to move people, needed goods, medical supplies, and produce rapidly, efficiently, and safely to their destinations. Our tele and audio communication links (telephone, radio, television, satellites, and computers) exist for the purpose of collecting, organizing, maintaining, and releasing needed information in the most expedient, systematic, and efficient manner possible to sources whose very survival may depend on that information.

People networks, also being very popular, exist among individuals who share common interests, who wish to promote specific causes, and who may be collectively contributing to the growth of a common body of knowledge. Networking has made a significant difference in the quality of life which we all enjoy. We are able to access a variety of services quickly, manage our time more effectively, and have been able to expand our resources significantly. And while networking is not a particularly new concept, we have not fully explored or made use of the creative potential which it holds for us in improving the quality of education and human services for children.

If elementary school counseling programs are to provide a wealth of services to parents, teachers, and children; are to strengthen collaboration among schools, community agencies, colleges and businesses; are to address special needs and interests of a diverse school population; and are to do it in a cost effective manner, then networking is neither a luxury nor a frill, it is a necessity.

Things to Think About

Questions should revolve around ways in which networking can facilitate and enrich the quality of counseling services to children. Not only is considering a variety of networks important, but also is the diversity of delivery systems as well.

1. In what ways can an elementary school counseling program make use of networking?

2. What program goals (dimensions of counseling) can be best served through networking?

3. What kinds of networks already exist that a counseling program could access (information networks, crisis intervention networks, special educational needs networks, etc.)?

4. How are networks established and when should they be dropped?

5. Who should be involved in networking?

People with Whom to Talk

1. Authors who have written articles on networking and networking strategies.

2. Community leaders who have helped establish various types of networks (hospital administrators, directors of resource centers and libraries, politicians, and lobbyists).

3. National network coordinators for political campaigns, fund raisers, and professional association public relations coordinators.

4. At the local level, state department of education personnel, school administrators, and counselors who have made use of networking strategies.

Things to Do

Networking can be viewed in terms of the people to be served and the nature of the services to be provided. The delivery system (fabric) to be utilized can be determined by exploring the cost, speed, accessibility, and purpose of the network.

Organizing and expanding cooperative networks of learning systems are primary goals of elementary school counseling programs. The purpose of this type of network is to link community members and learners with educational opportunities. At various times, we are all learners and can benefit from networking opportunities. At other times we function as providers of mutual support services and can assist others.

Networks are established for the purpose of getting things done through people in a more effective and efficient manner than could be done without the support.

Networks tend to be rather fluid and free of the structure associated with organizations. Their boundaries are not well defined nor should they be. Networks may be short lived and many form rapidly as the need dictates. As needs of people and programs vary and tasks to be accomplished shift, so do the shared values, interests, goals, and objectives. The strength of the network lies in the deep commitment of its members to a shared position or common cause. Seldom are any two (2) networks alike.

In forming a network, here are a few ideas to get the counselor started:

1. Refer to the dimensions of elementary school counseling. Identify the goals that the program wishes to support as determined by the needs assessment.

2. Take a separate sheet of paper for each program goal to be attained. Write the goal in the center of the paper. Draw concentric circles around the goal and label each circle moving out from the center in the following manner; school, community, state, and nation.

3. Brainstorm a list of all the people, organizations, departments, and community resources that might be able to support the various goals in any way. Include familiar people and groups as well as other potential sources of help. Identify businesses, social service agencies, industry, churches, educational institutions, and other learning systems that could be networked in meeting the counseling program goals.

4. Select the desired resources from the list for each goal. Place the information on the appropriate concentric circles—(school, community, state, and nation).

5. Study the networks for each goal and determine how these groups, organizations, and people can best serve

the counseling program. This can be done by examining needs for each goal area. Remember that networks differ in types: people networks, information networks, fund raising networks, brainstorming networks.

6. Once the types of networks that would be most useful are determined, develop a questionnaire on rolldex cards for the purpose of collecting the needed information to access the network.

7. Mail out the cards with a letter explaining the purpose of the network and how the group/organization/person being contacted can be of service to the counseling program.

8. As the cards are returned, organize them by goal area (dimensions of counseling) for easy access.

9. Make use of the network. Provide positive reinforcement to the network participants. Networks function best when network participants not only provide services, but are the recipients of services as well. Therefore explain to those who offer their help that the counseling program will share information and ideas with other network participants, if desired.

10. When the network has outlived its usefulness, do not be afraid to discontinue using it.

Networking is an exciting way to breathe new life into an existing program. Fresh ideas, new faces, the availability of multimedia resources, and an opportunity to interact with experts in the field, serve to stimulate a renewed interest in the elementary school counseling program. Like the intricate interlocking root system of a stand of giant sequoia trees, networking provides the means through which an elementary counseling program can be nurtured, grow strong, and maintain its strength because of the depth, breadth, and diversity of its support systems.

Types of Networks

Elementary school counseling programs can make effective use of different types of networks.

1. **Speakers Bureau.** Inservice programming can be expensive. However, many groups and organizations would be willing to come for little or no cost to the district because of the free advertising for the organization. Social service agencies perform a community function and would be willing to do training in school districts because it is a part of their agency's mission. Other groups might be willing to trade services. School counselors and related support personnel need to interact with the community and let various support groups learn about their workers. When given the opportunity, various school and community specialists can conduct training sessions for each other at no or very limited cost, thereby contributing to each other's knowledge and upgrading the availability of high quality professional services.

2. **Topic Networks.** Topic networks consist of people who have an interest in a specific area and want to exchange ideas, materials, and expertise on a particular subject area (self-esteem, stress management in children, parenting, children of alcoholics, divorce, etc.).

3. **A Child Advocacy Network.** School districts are dependent upon a number of social service agencies in meeting the special needs of children. Often times to access these services as quickly as the need arises is difficult because the school and the various social service agencies have not developed a close working relationship. A child advocacy network would open the lines of communication more quickly and speed up the delivery of services.

4. **Information Networks.** National and state computerized information networks on practically every topic imaginable can be accessed by school districts for free, or in some cases, a membership fee is required.

Suggested Activities

Since networking is an important topic, children can benefit from understanding the concept and make use of what it has to offer. Children need to understand that networks evolve from specific goals. They represent informal linkages and are designed to facilitate action toward the desired goal.

1. Have children discuss the meaning of the term network and brainstorm as many different examples as possible (roads, telephone lines, electric lines, bus system, railroads, television networks).

2. Ask children to identify networks that they have used and for what purpose.

3. Have children name some networks in their community that their family, friends, or neighbors have used. (Meals on Wheels, Red Cross blood donation networks, telephone network, emergency health care network, phone network, car pooling, U.S. Mail).

4. Have children discuss some of the following networks and learn as much about them as possible.

   a. Childfind

   b. Block parents

   c. Poison control

   d. FBI Most Wanted List

   e. Organ donation and procurement networks

   f. Health networks

   g. Business networks—McDonalds, Amway, Shaklee, oil companies

   h. Home extension and homemaker networks

   i. Buying cooperatives

5. As children become more interested in networking and how it touches their lives, have them explore possible networking projects in which they could become involved.

   a. Developing a resource directory on community wellness.

   b. Accessing information networks for the purpose of collecting data on a class project.

   c. Selecting a special area of interest, network with others who share the same hobbies, sports, interest in computers, etc.

   d. Developing a computer network among class members.

   e. Developing a foreign student pen pal network.

ENVIRONMENTAL CONNECTIVENESS

While creating positive, growth–producing physical and psychological environments should be everyone's responsibility, it is often left to the elementary school counseling program to facilitate such surroundings. Most schools recognize the importance of orientation programs during periods of academic transition, but they pay much less attention to developing and maintaining a healthy climate for children throughout their entire school careers. They seem to do even less for teachers, parent volunteers, and community resource people who provide direct services to children. The lasting impression that we sometimes create is that knowing and knowledge takes precedence over feelings, emotions, thoughts, and reason. And yet we continually hear from parents, teachers, and alumni, that their lasting impressions revolve around the degree to which they were able to successfully connect with the physical and psychological environment of the school. Rarely are academic issues ever discussed.

Elementary school counseling programs can play a significant role in helping children, teachers, parents, and community helpers to create and maintain supportive, warm and academically stimulating climates. Building such climates can be fun experiences and can draw people together. The school building can undergo a transformation, a face lift, both in terms of its physical as well as its psychological characteristics. Building environmental connectiveness is just one more way the counseling program can take on a new look and energize itself and the school.

Things to Think About

1. What factors constitute the physical and psychological climate of the school?

2. How can the school (parents, teachers, children, administrators, and school board members) best influence these factors (physical and psychological) in a positive direction?

3. What blocking agents (physical and psychological) exist within and outside the school that impede progress in enhancing the school climate?

4. How might these blocking agents be neutralized or eliminated?

5. What are the physical and psychological needs of children, parents, teachers, and administrator?

6. How can the school best address the needs of all people within the system?

7. When should the process of enhancing environmental connectiveness begin?

8. Who should be involved in the process?

9. Where should environmental connectiveness begin?

10. What first steps should be taken to develop and maintain the desired school climate?

People with Whom to Talk

All school personnel (providers and recipients of services) should participate in the process of building a new school climate. Talk with children, parents, teachers, school board members, and educational specialists. Find out what suggestions they have for strengthening physical and psychological comfort in the school.

Things to Do

1. Learn as much as possible about environmental connectiveness. Read, talk to people, and observe what goes on in the environment.

2. Identify the warm fuzzies (the positives) and the cold pricklies (negatives) in the environment (physical and psychological).

3. Brainstorm ways in which all people in the school environment can contribute to the physical and psychological positives thereby enhancing the school climate. (Activities for teachers, parents, children, administrators, etc.)

4. Explore ways in which physical and psychological negatives can be reduced or eliminated. Develop a plan to do so.

5. Become familiar with a variety of circumstances in which children become disconnected and how the school can help re-establish connectiveness. Children can become disconnected when they experience a loss through divorce, death of a loved one, relocation, illness, rejection by peers, or when experiencing any period of transition in their lives.

6. Teach children and adults the necessary skills which will help them connect more readily with their environment. (Communication skills, interpersonal skills, decision making skills, values clarification and self-

understanding skills, stress management skills, assertiveness training skills, relaxation skills, goal setting skills, and conflict management skills). Above all, teach children how to develop a positive self-esteem.

7. Brainstorm ways in which the school can connect more readily and positively with the community and with visitors who enter the school for the first time.

8. Improve the physical climate of the building so that everybody feels relaxed.

Suggested Activities
(Physical Connectiveness)

The school environment has both a physical and psychological dimension. Physically, the building consists of space, heat, light, air currents, doors, walls, rooms, pictures, equipment, materials, furniture, and people. The arrangement and interaction of these factors create a climate which we experience and relate to in some fashion. Our perception of the physical environment drives our thoughts, feelings, wants, and behaviors. These conditions represent the psychological climate of the school as we alone experience it. Therefore, both the physical and psychological climate of the school are important as separate and as interactive determinants in creating a desirable learning climate. What follows are some practical activities and suggestions that can be implemented in creating a positive, warm, and accepting physical school climate.

1. The classroom and school building can be decorated with familiar objects and pictures that are meaningful to children.

2. The school should be made physically comfortable. (Climate controlled, free of drafts, and properly lighted.)

3. The classroom furniture should be movable and arranged as needed to facilitate learning.

4. Children should be helped to feel comfortable in the building and familiar with offices, rest rooms, multi-purpose rooms, etc.

5. Children should be encouraged to make their own physical space comfortable in whatever acceptable ways possible.

6. Teachers should inform children of the classroom and school rules in a positive manner.

7. A daily routine of classroom activity should be established. This gives some stability and predictability to school life. A word of caution, stability and predictability are not synonomous with rigidity. Fostering an organized environment that is flexible, exciting, and interesting is important.

8. Take some time to talk with children about their environment and physical changes that could be made to help create or enhance a stronger bond between themselves and the school. What can the school librarian, cafeteria workers, bus drivers, administrators, teachers, and parent volunteers do to make a difference? Greeting children as they get off the bus, a warm smile, a pat on the back, and a word of encouragement are all physical positives that can make a difference in the lives of all children.

9. In addition to attending to the physical needs of children, what can children, parents, teachers, and administrators do for each other? Just coming up with unique ways of saying "I appreciate you" is a fun challenge. Here are a few ideas that administrators and school boards can implement on behalf of teachers.

   a. Sending positive notes for a job well done.

   b. Sending doughnuts and coffee to the teachers lounge once a month before school begins.

   c. Having feature articles written on classroom teachers for publication in the local newspaper.

   d. Standing in for a teacher once a week for a thirty minute free break.

10. The Counseling Program Committee can assist school personnel in making a list of ways in which they can connect more readily with the community in a positive manner. Select a few ideas from the list and implement them.

Suggested Activities
(Psychological Connectiveness)

While creating a positive warm physical plant is important, what goes on between and among people (children, teachers, parents, administrators, and educational specialists) is especially critical in developing a psychological climate of connectiveness. We all need to feel satisfied in our relationships with people, places, and things in those environments which are important to us.

To experience a feeling of being disconnected with an important aspect of the environment causes pain (physical and psychological), stress, a sense of loss, and a feared inability to cope with the present and an unknown future. Since all of us are in a continuous state of connecting, disconnecting, and re-establishing new lines of connectiveness within our environment, an important aspect is to know something about the process, ways in which we affect it, and how the school and community can enhance the process. Indeed, one of the most effective ways of breathing new life into any program is to feel connected to it in a positive way.

1. Develop support systems for children and adults who are trying to cope with change in their lives. (Loss through death, divorce, separation, illness, relocation, surgery, or other dimensions of adjustment).

2. Recognize people's uniquenesses and share with them their positive attributes.

3. Teach children, teachers, and administrators how to give helpful, and yet nonjudgmental, feedback.

4. Develop programs which give people personal power through skill development which enhances psychological

connectiveness. (Goal setting skills, decision making skills, values clarification skills, stress management skills, assertiveness skills, thinking skills, interpersonal communication skills, etc.)

5. Teach parents, teachers, administrators, and children how to interact with each other in nonthreatening, nonjudgmental ways.

6. Let the major focus of psychological connectiveness revolve around activities and interpersonal exchanges which promote positive self-esteem in all people.

7. Teach effective modeling techniques to build connect-iveness. Determine what positive models are to be created and think of the best delivery systems available to teach them. Make use of television, art work, music, literature, posters, the school intercom, class plays, poetry, billboards, video cassettes, advertisements, and any other available means to model the desired beha-viors. When models are taught effectively, children, parents, teachers, administrators, and community leaders will begin to emulate the desired actions. The results will stimulate a positive,warm,growth-enhancing environment.

8. Other topics to consider when developing positive psychological environments are the following:

listening	interpersonal
self-disclosure	barriers
self-awareness	negotiation
confrontation	conflict management
communication skills	developing trust
interpersonal skill	understanding
development	feelings

PUPIL SERVICES INTERFACING

The purpose of Pupil Services Interfacing is to suggest ways in which members of the pupil service team,in cooperation with one another, can "help to breathe new life" into an elementary school counseling program. Our intent is not to discuss pupil services management issues or to go into an indepth description of the role and function of each of the key players on the team. While we recognize the importance of this topic, space simply does not allow us the opportunity to do so. Pupil service personnel would consist of psychologists, social workers, health professionals, counselors, and speech and hearing specialists.

The basic purpose for pupil services is to provide children with an equal opportunity to be educated. Pupil services are designed to provide children with the necessary information, understandings, life skills, and self-confidence to develop the requisite action plans necessary to modify their environments and to develop themselves in positive and socially acceptable ways. In order to accomplish this end, the on-going process of meeting children's needs, identifying and teaching behaviors to be learned, and creating physically and psychologically growth producing learning environments requires working with the whole child, not just the parts (intellect, emotional, social, personal). According to Holt (1975), each specialist who provides a special service for children must (1) recognize the child as a whole, (2) be cognizant of the services of others, and (3) understand the working relationships which exist among the various service units that can only be effective when the team functions through a coordinated effort.

In striving to provide each child with an equal opportunity to be educated, the pupil services team must support the educational goals of the school system. Pupil service interfacing requires all members of the pupil services team to work together in providing both direct and indirect services to all children, not just to those who are experiencing developmental deficits or to those who significantly deviate from the norm. "Effective interaction between the pupil services team and the instructional personnel in the elementary school is a necessary prerequisite for making pupil services an integral part of the education of children" (Holt, 1975, p. 78). Pupil services team members must view themselves as expediters of learning for all pupils and not merely as interventionists in crises or remedial situations for some children. Indeed, the primary focus for all pupil service personnel must be to enhance the maximal development of all children thereby reducing the need for remediation.

Perhaps two of the biggest problems or roadblocks standing in the way of pupil service team building is time and a reticence on the part of some specialists to view themselves as environmental engineers in developing and maintaining growth-producing learning climates within the school community. The first roadblock can be resolved by establishing team building as a high priority item and setting aside time each month to meet. The second roadblock may require a bit more effort to resolve since it will involve a redefinition of team members roles and some attitude adjustments regarding new thoughts about pupil service interfacing activities in the school community.

A high priority to keep in mind, as the pupil services team explores new ways of working together for the purpose of enhancing services to children and their families, is that of "breathing new life into an existing program." Pupil services personnel should thus view the process as a way of building more fun, excitement, and enthusiasm into their own work life and gaining as much from *interfacing* as they give back to the school system.

We have found that when pupil service specialists work in isolation and get caught up in the same routine day in and day out they begin to lose some enthusiasm for their work and find themselves getting stale. They begin to lack the drive and dedication they once had. Pupil service interfacing can help them to break out of the old routines and stimulate new thoughts and ideas.

In order to assist the elementary school pupil services team get started in developing interfacing activities, we have provided some ideas that have been used by school specialists.

Things to Think About

    1. How can the pupil services team most effectively meet the needs of children?

2. What role can the pupil services team play in curriculum design?

3. What role can the pupil services team play in public relations programming?

4. What role can the pupil services team play in teacher inservice programming, parent workshops, and in networking with community resources?

5. What role can the pupil services team play in developing and enhancing the learning/living climate of the school?

Note: Brainstorm as many ways as possible to involve the pupil service team in providing direct and indirect service to all children. Select a few specific ideas and think about how they might become a reality.

People with Whom to Talk

Meet with all of the pupil service team members in the district and discuss the questions listed under *Things to Think About.* Many pupil service specialists will enjoy the opportunity to engage in activities other than assessment and report writing. Getting together with colleagues supporting differing professional points of view can be a stimulating experience for the participants and can lead to some very innovative pupil service activity in the school district. Talk to the following people about ways in which they would like to work together in providing services to children and their families.

1. Psychologist

2. Social worker

3. Health professionals

4. Counselors

5. Speech and Hearing specialists

6. Other school district pupil service teams

7. Local, state, and national associations of pupil service supervisors

Things to Do

1. Call a meeting of the pupil services team for the purpose of exploring pupil service interfacing activities that could benefit the development of all children in the district.

2. Present reasons which support pupil service interfacing activities. How might pupil service team members, children, the teaching staff, and the administrators benefit from this approach?

   Possible responses might include the following:

   a. Team members will have an opportunity to support one another and learn more about the potential of pupil services by working together on a few common projects.

   b. The school community will come to understand pupil services as an integrated team which supports the interests of all children.

   c. A team effort in pupil service programming will send a stronger message to the school and the community of the importance of child development and learning life skills in addition to academic learning.

   d. Pupil service specialists, working together as a team, can be a powerful resource in teacher inservice training and providing consultation services in the school district.

   e. A functioning pupil service team can become an effective resource for the school administration to rely on when responding to human service problems and needs of children.

f. A pupil service team also can function as a "think tank" in coming up with innovative ideas to create the most conducive learning environments for all children.

g. An effective pupil service team also has the necessary resources to conduct limited institutional research for the school district.

Note: While there are many positive benefits to any school district in creating an active pupil service team, we also recognize that the team must be selective in supporting a limited number of activities.

3. Create a pupil services council. In large school districts with multiple pupil service workers, a representative from each of the specialty areas (psychologist, social workers, health workers, counselors, speech and hearing) could serve on the council. Workers then could be rotated on and off the council thus giving all personnel a chance to participate on the council and to provide direct service to children.

The function of the council would be to serve as an advisory body to the administration. The council could suggest and coordinate teacher inservice training, make suggestions regarding the development and enhancement of living/learning environments for children, help to develop positive school-community relationships which enhance the operation of the school, help to coordinate school–wide evaluation efforts, and take an active role in public relations programming in the school system. The council might also function on a regular basis as a "think tank" to improve such pupil service activities as making referrals, delivery of human services, developing a more effective pupil tracking system, and brainstorming innovative ways to improve the self–esteem of children and the working climate of the system.

Suggested Activities

The effective utilization of the pupil services team requires a plan for the delivery of services to pupils, teachers, and the school. Breathing new life into an elementary school counseling program takes place when pupil service personnel take a new interest in their jobs, work more smoothly together, are supported by the school district administrators and the teaching staff, and have some fun in using their creative potential to develop exciting, stimulating, and enthusiastic learning environments.

1. Create counseling activities in the counseling program dimension areas to be used by classroom teachers.

2. Develop teacher inservice programs designed to aid teachers in such activities as classroom management strategies, effective parent-teacher conferencing, developing a positive self-esteem climate, and working with special need populations.

3. Develop and implement a comprehensive program for expectant parents and parents of preschool children that will improve family capabilities to provide in-home learning environments that will develop readiness for learning. Such a program would need to address health, nutritional, social, and psychological needs of children and related non-academic influences which affect children's motivation and attitudes toward learning.

4. Meet with school administrators, teachers, parents, and other pupil service workers to study the needs of children.

5. Generate as many solutions as possible in meeting the needs of children. Have fun with this activity and don't be concerned with evaluating the responses as they are given.

6. When the pupil service team runs out of ideas, have them select a couple of possibilities and develop them.

Remember the main purpose of pupil service interfacing is to create in practice what so often is expressed on paper, an organized, coordinated, and well developed pupil services team which functions as a system, as well as by units, in providing services to all children in the school district.

SCHOOL AND COMMUNITY PARTNERSHIPS

School and community partnerships are designed to provide opportunities for the school and community to work together for the betterment of each other. Children learn about their communities and how they can participate in making them a better place to live. Likewise community members are encouraged to become involved with their schools to learn about ways in which they can contribute to helping develop caring and productive citizens.

The concept of school and community partnerships is not new, but it has only been sporadically applied. The rationale for developing partnerships is simple. Neither entity can afford to function independent of the other. The schools, once considered a central force of activity in many communities, have found themselves under fire because of the loss of public confidence. The schools have been both criticized and supported for trying to, almost single-handedly, address all of society's ills and still provide a comprehensive education for all children.

School and community partnerships involve the full participation of the school and community in identifying and addressing each others' needs. This process must utilize the children as well. Our children represent a vast untapped resource as problem solvers, service providers, and humanitarian advocates. What better way is there for children to become fully involved citizens than to contribute, in meaningful ways, to the growth and development of their communities? After all, children are not merely preparing for citizenship, they are citizens and need opportunities to be recognized as community supporters.

Community and school partnerships can serve as the mechanism for encouraging necessary dialogue between the elementary school counseling program and the public. The process can become a key strategy for mobilizing resources in search of excellence in education and in breathing new life into the school's counseling program.

Things to Think About

1. In what ways can children benefit from community involvement?

2. In what ways can the community benefit from their participation in school related activities?

3. What community needs exist that the school can help address?

4. What needs does the school have that the community can help meet?

5. What significant role can the community play in developing child citizens through community involvement and service?

6. In what ways can children contribute to the health and well-being of people in the community?

7. How can school and community linkages contribute to such ideals as human rights, caring, respect, trust, cooperation, sharing, and responsibility?

8. What kinds of community service projects exist, or are needed, in which the school and community can develop working partnerships?

9. How can the school counseling program and the community begin to develop the bridges necessary to cultivate the desired partnerships?

10. Who should be contacted?

People with Whom To Talk

Most communities are ready and want to get involved. Parents, the private sector, and community agencies eagerly await the opportunity to become partners in education. In order to begin the process, a team of interested school and community people need to convene in order to discuss the concept of partnerships and potential benefits to school and community.

In *Pedagogy of the Oppressed*, Freire (1970) has stated that the most ready learners are the ones who understand their communities and understand that the importance between their communities and themselves lies in their own capacities to influence events or be influenced by them. When this realization takes place, learners adapt quickly to the learning environment and learning takes place for a very specific and real purpose. In addressing the issue of partnerships, school and community planners need to be convinced of the importance of joint projects involving children as the vehicle for stimulating acquired learning and improved skills and capabilities. Community service itself can become a natural bridge toward acquiring advanced learning. While various groups, community agencies, businesses and industries, and individuals could be contacted in exploring the questions under *Things To think About*, we have included a few sources from which to draw.

1. Representatives from established school and community partnerships

2. American Red Cross (ARC)—local chapter of Youth Services, American Red Cross, National Headquarters, 17 & D Streets N.W., Washington, DC 20001 (The purpose of ARC is to know about community needs and to mobilize and train people to meet those needs. The ARC cooperates well with schools and communities in addressing community needs.)

3. Interested social service agencies that meet community needs

4. Local hospital representatives

5. School district representatives (teachers, administrators, counselors)

6. Business and industry representatives

7. Parents

Things To Do

Before beginning a collaboration program, the step with which to begin is to identify those specific needs that can be best served through school and community linkages. The most significant reason for school/community programs is for their collaborative benefits and to provide opportunities for children and community volunteers to benefit from what each has to offer. The following sequence of steps is offered to initiate collaborative school/community partnerships.

1. Get organized. Rather than initiate a system wide plan, start with one school. Invite teachers, parents, counselors, and administrators to serve on a steering committee to explore children's needs as determined by the needs assessment results.

2. Assess the community's needs as well. Provide the children with an opportunity to learn about their community and its needs by having them talk with various representatives from community agencies, voluntary action centers, and various businesses and industries whose job it is to know about community needs and projects.

3. Match school counseling program needs and goals with community needs and goals. Make a list of those community project opportunities that will satisfy the school counseling and academic program objectives.

4. Call for Community Project Proposals. After the community needs assessment has been completed, invite various community groups, businesses, industries, and agencies to submit project proposals to the school which will involve the participation of children. Provide proposal guidelines to all interested parties. The guidelines should specify the nature of the project, level of child involvement (numbers of children and age levels),

location of activity (school, home, business), the number of hours required to complete the project, volunteer assistance provided, resources provided to complete the project (money, materials, and people), and the school's investment (time, money, people, and other resources).

5. Identify and select community projects. The Steering Committee needs to decide among the various projects, which ones to pursue. Decisions can be made on the basis of need (school and community), student capabilities, time required, and resource (financial, human, and material) commitment.

6. Meet with community project partners. During these meetings, proposals need to be discussed in detail and a final determination made by both the school and community as to their feasibility and ease of implementation.

7. Select, develop, and plan projects for implementation. The Steering Committee, in concert with the various community volunteers, plan and develop each project to be implemented.

8. Implement the projects. When the planning process has been completed, the children, with school and community support, are ready to become involved in contributing to and learning more about their community. The number of community needs projects in which a school participates is up to the school and will be determined by a number of factors, many of which are outlined in the project proposals.

9. Provide feedback and evaluation. Community projects take on a significant meaning when feedback and evaluation are a part of the process from start to finish. Children and community volunteers should be given an opportunity to talk or write about their experiences. Questions, like the following, help participants to focus on themselves in relationship to the activity. What

feelings are expressed by the children and the volunteers? What was it like to help people in the community? How did those helped feel? What was it like for community volunteers to work alongside children? In addition to discussing feelings, the *Keystone Learning Model* (Part II Introduction) also has participants examine what they have learned from the experience in relation to themselves and others and how those new learnings can be transferred and applied in new or different settings.

The community service projects are designed to foster learnings about self and others, the community, citizenship, service, and the school and its role in a modern society.

10. Continue the learning in a continuous, cycle format. As school and community collaborations grow and develop, the community will become more aware of school system needs and will want to support the school much in the same way that the school supports the community through community service projects.

Note: As with the planning and implementation of any new program, be sure to obtain clearance from the school board and have school personnel support before starting. Other points not discussed here, but which need to be addressed, are the development of clear job descriptions (volunteers), a recruitment plan to obtain community volunteer assistance, a training program to orient community volunteers and teachers to the community service project concept, and a continuous feedback and monitoring plan to recognize and support all program participants. The giving of awards, certificates, and luncheons are but a few ways to stimulate and maintain interest in this worthwhile program.

Suggested Activities

Breathing new life into a school counseling program takes place every time a well planned and supported change in programming occurs. Involving children in community service projects is not a new idea. Community needs and child activities have long co-existed, but seldom have they interfaced or mutually benefited from their interdependence. Now is the time to form partnerships with the community in working with the aged, the young, the handicapped, the hospitalized, the terminally ill, health organizations, community action and safety agencies (e.g., firemen, policeman, medics, the blind association, the American Red Cross, the Boy and Girl Scouts, the YMCA & YWCA). The humanitarian, ethical, social, and community values that help young people develop today will have a critical impact on the future of our country.

When selecting community service projects, look for activities that will develop life skills, decision-making skills, and personal management skills. Look for activities that will help children mature, grow, and develop individually and socially; learn group processes and experience group involvement; and develop healthy attitudes and wholesome values. Community service projects can accomplish these attributes by helping children to utilize and extend their interests, talents, networks, and feelings of self-worth and personal power in the interest of helping others and their community.

The number of opportunities is endless for developing partnerships with the community. Here are a few ideas. As activities are selected, contact community groups for needed resources to complete the various projects.

1. Collect, repair, and make toys for children. Ask parents and business and industry for their support in supplying needed materials, equipment, and people resources to assist with the project. Groups like the Salvation Army, Big Brother Big Sister, and the Lions Clubs sponsor projects of this type for needy children. Many different grade levels or work teams in a school can work together on this project with job responsibilities varying with the skill levels, abilities, and interests of the children.

2. Have the Steering Committee contact various health groups in the community and identify their needs. Children can work beside community volunteers in

making bandages, assembling first aid kits, or preparing mailings for a coming health event.

3. Have the children and members of the Steering Committee work with various community agencies and citizens in identifying needs regarding the environment, the elderly, the handicapped, opportunities for community leisure activities, and more effective use of public buildings. Children can learn much about their community by reading about these topics and seeing what they can do to make their community a better place in which to live.

4. Have the children survey their own needs and contact various community groups to assist teachers and school personnel in sponsoring such activities as a school health fair, a drug and alcohol prevention program, and participating in special topics/causes such as fingerprinting and missing children, environmental protection, and children's safety (toys, traffic, bicycle, home, fire) programs.

PUBLIC RELATIONS

Public relations (PR) is not a topic which is new to elementary school counseling. Over the past several years, it has received a great deal of attention from the American Association for Counseling and Development (AACD) and more specifically from the American School Counselor Association (ASCA). Each year for the past several years ASCA also has published a public relations kit for school counselors which has provided the profession with much technical assistance and many effective ideas for promoting school counseling.

Public relations programs, if handled effectively, can do much to breathe new life into an existing program. Children, teachers, administrators, school board members, parents, and members of the school community can, and often do, contribute to the public relations efforts of the school counseling program. As an energizer and a forum for cooperative planning and interaction, PR activities are second to none.

Public relations is a process which conveys responsible activity on the part of the school counseling program to make the public aware of and understand its planned educational efforts. As a process, it is not only designed to let people know about the elementary school counseling program, but to engender community participation and support whenever and wherever possible. That participation can come in the form of a kind word, financial support, and volunteer efforts in the school.

The key to effective public relations starts with effective communication–two-way communication. Message sending and receiving between the school and community is a daily activity and often has a more far reaching effect on public attitude than some of the more formalized activities that we call public relations.

Because we believe that effective public relations is central to successful counseling programming, we have included it as a way of breathing new life into an existing counseling program. While space does not allow us to develop the topic fully, nor is this necessary with the wealth of ready and available materials, we will highlight a few major points regarding the implementation of PR programming.

Things To Think About

1. Does the school counseling program consider PR a high priority activity or do they merely give lip service to the idea?

2. Does the PR program operate from a comprehensive long-range program?

3. Has the school counseling program considered the different publics that are vitally concerned with counseling programs in the schools and made plans for involving them in the PR program?

4. Has the school counseling program planned a comprehensive coordinated two-way communications program? Have all publics a viable means for sending messages to

the school? Does the school know if the various publics are satisfied with the school counseling program?

5. Does the school have an effective school counseling public relations inservice training program for all employees? Are efforts being made to make them aware and help them with their PR skills?

6. Has the school counseling program identified public relations talent on their staff and have they assigned them PR responsibilities?

7. Does the school counseling program have adequate support to back the PR program in terms of needed resources (financial, materials, equipment, time, people)?

8. Has the school counseling program identified a variety of communication channels in order to reach a variety of audiences in the community?

9. Does the school's PR program operate on the basis of honesty, openness, and cooperation with the media?

10. Has the school counseling program considered the importance of the school climate toward counseling? The attitudes held by the staff and children are vitally important to the success of any program.

11. Does the school counseling program give appropriate recognition to staff, children, parents, and community supporters for their contributions to school counseling?

12. Is there a plan for the assessment and evaluation of the school counseling PR program?

People with Whom To Talk

Consult with people, professional organizations, and community groups like the Chamber of Commerce who have experience with PR programming. Some specific examples of people and groups to contact are as follows:

1. The American School Counselor Association

2. ERIC/CAPS

3. The American Association for Counseling and Development (AACD)

4. The National School Public Relations Association

5. Local organizations of the YMCA-YWCA, The American Red Cross, The Chamber of Commerce, and radio and TV stations

6. Public Relation specialists in the community (business, industry, agencies, and school districts)

7. School counseling programs at the national, state and local levels that have been recognized for their public relations efforts

Things To Do

1. Public relations programs must be planned. They should espouse a statement of purpose, have clearly stated objectives, and an identified support system. Each school counseling program must decide for itself the meaning of a well planned PR program. Public relations programs should, however, be internally consistent with the counseling program. "Effective external communication systems obtain their strength and credibility from effective internal communication systems" (Ellison, 1985, p.4).

2. Select the key publics to be reached. Public relations is a two-way communications process and must touch those publics who will be most influential in determining the success of the school counseling program. Some key people who can either help or hinder the school counseling program are

   a. opinion and power leaders in the community,

   b. senior citizen leaders and families who no longer have children in school,

c. teachers and staff,

d. parents and families of enrolled children,

e. elected and appointed officials,

f. children in school,

g. business and industry,

h. local media, and

i. service clubs and organizations.

3. Evaluate the current status of the school counseling program. The school counseling program needs to assess its current communication effectiveness. By assessing the public's perceptions of school counseling, program strengths and liabilities can be targeted. Assessing perceptions is critical, for school counseling will be judged like any other program, not as it is, but as it is perceived to be by those who will be doing the judging. Opinion surveys and attitude assessment devices are very effective tools for obtaining a quick pulse on the publics' assessment of the school counseling program.

4. Plan for school and community involvement. One of the most effective ways to build a successful PR program is to encourage active participation by staff and community members. A PR network can be established to link key people in the school and the community as a means of encouraging two-way communication, publicizing the counseling program, and responding to questions and misunderstandings about the counseling program before rumors have a chance to evolve. As the network expands, so will community and school support for elementary school counseling.

5. Select a variety of communication channels. Successful PR programs not only know their various publics, but how best to influence or inform them about counseling

program issues. The frequency with which specific channels are used also will be determined by such variables as time, cost, availability of talent, and the nature of the message to be communicated.

Regardless of the communication channels utilized (TV, radio, newspaper, newsletters, meetings, etc.), the purpose of PR is to build a large reservoir of good will rather than to patch the dikes in a crisis (Cooper, 1986). Keeping this in mind good PR begins with an effective school counseling program, one that establishes a reputation for truthfulness, openness, and reliability.

6. Develop an active and planned PR program. A public relations program which evolves from the school counseling program will be in tune with the school's needs assessment results and the counseling program objectives. Following this format, PR exists for the benefit of supporting the counseling program and is not viewed as a separate entity unto itself.

   Public relations is everybody's business and needs to be broad-based and continuous in terms of its involvement. Parents, teachers, children, school board members, administrators, and community supporters need to understand their PR responsibilities and how they can support a calendar of weekly or monthly PR activities.

7. Evaluate PR effectiveness. Every PR program should compare effectiveness against cost. Program effectiveness is measured in terms of goal outcomes achieved. Goal outcomes can be measured by the number of people reached, positive attitude changes achieved, the receipt and understanding of accurate information, and attendance and/or participation of people in various programs sponsored by the school counseling program.

   Program cost can be determined by estimating the dollar value needed to convey the PR message per contact. Cost factors include a calculation of the number of employee hours spent on the project, materials and equipment rented or purchased, consultation fees, and loss of productivity in the completion of other assignments because of additional PR responsibilities given to employees.

Public relations ideas need to be tested in order to determine whether or not they are too costly for the return accrued. Perhaps other and more cost effective ways can be utilized to accomplish the same derived outcomes. In other instances, the desired outcomes may not be measurable. If that is the case, the PR idea is probably not working and should be discarded or modified and reevaluated.

Suggested Activities

Any activities that help to create good PR practices are PR activities. Deciding what those activities should be and how to implement them are determined by following the suggested courses of action stated under *Things To Do.* Therefore rather than provide a list of PR activities that may or may not be useful to every school counseling program, we would like to share a few unique PR ideas that colleagues have shared with us.

1. Provide new children, parents, and visitors with a welcome letter and information packet about the school counseling program.

2. Offer mini-courses, lectures, and discussion nights on various topics of interest to anyone who would like to attend. Topical suggestions are decision making, assertiveness training, stress management, and self-esteem development. What makes this approach unique is that the programs are not just geared to parents, but to all members of the community.

3. Create multiple channels for establishing a positive self-esteem building climate in the school. Involve the entire school community in offering and implementing a variety of suggestions for developing a physical and psychological sense of connectiveness.

4. Have children write a personal letter to their parent(s), senior citizen, or community member telling them about the school's counseling program and how their personal participation will help to enhance the learning environment. These same people also can be invited to participate in school/family events.

5. Identify as many different behaviors, activities, and communications that tend to block effective public relations and figure out how to neutralize or eliminate them. The focus of this activity must be on "fixing the problem" and not "fixing the blame."

6. Establish a "good idea box" to gather parent and teacher suggestions and opinions regarding ways to improve the school counseling program. Parents will need to be given varying opportunities to share their suggestions (phone, newsletter, tear offs, conferences, etc.) with the counselor. As ideas and opinions are shared, the senders should be supported and when suggestions are implemented, the person making the suggestion should be duly recognized.

In response to the "good idea box", a school superintendent pledged the following and attached these statements to the box. These comments are well worth taking note of by counselors in establishing positive PR with all publics.

a. I will respond to every suggestion signed by the sender,

b. I will read suggestions each week,

c. Each suggestion implemented will be done so with appropriate credit to the sender,

d. I will implement as many suggestions as possible.

e. In cases where reality completely precluded implementation, I will explain why,

f. Suggestions which can't be implemented "as is" will be used to produce more suggestions until we come up with new, useable solutions,

g. I may ask senders for more information before I respond to them or implement them.

h. I may ask senders to help implement the suggestion.

i. I believe the only way we can be a better institution and create a better work place is by gathering suggestions.

j. You talk, I will listen. As long as you agree to listen equally when I talk. (Ellison, 1985, p. 6)

Remember that the primary focus of any effective counseling program is to initiate ideas and actions rather than respond defensively to criticism. We also must be realistic and recognize that people evaluate counseling programs based on their perceptions of them and not on a rational, organized accounting of the facts, or the program's success or relevance. Such perceptions are formed primarily on the tone of quality of relationships built by the school with its publics (Jackson, 1985).

While school counselors and volunteers in counseling programs must first be concerned with how well they do their jobs, they also must establish ongoing PR practices which extend to the daily discussions between and among friends and neighbors. These low keyed and less sophisticated PR practices can often be more influential or damaging than those which require much time and costly resources to implement.

BIBLIOGRAPHY

Cooper, L. (1986). Take the guesswork out of school public relations. *Education Digest, 56,* 13-15.

Ellison, B. (1985). Involve your total school staff in public relations. *Journal of Educational Public Relations. 8,* (1), 4-7.

Freire, P. (1970). *Pedagogy of the oppressed.* New York: Seabury Press.

Holt, F.D. (1975). The pupil personnel team in the elementary school. In S.C. Stone & B. Shertzer (Eds.), *Guidance monograph series x: Elementary school guidance.* New York: Houghton Mifflin.

Jackson, P. (1985). How to be a manager of change: Positioning the schools to earn real lasting public support. *The School Administrator, 42* (11), 10-12.

PART II

COUNSELING
AND THE
CURRICULUM:
A TEAM APPROACH

PART II

COUNSELING AND THE CURRICULUM: A TEAM APPROACH

A factor which is of critical importance in the development of a successful elementary counseling program is the integration of the counseling services into the curriculum to the greatest extent possible. This requires that a team approach be developed to include the school, home, and community. In Part II, we will focus specifically on integrating the elementary school counseling program into the total educational system via the teaching/learning process as a means of accomodating children's needs.

As we view the needs of the child, we readily see that these needs do not exist in isolation; therefore, to deal with them in the isolation of a counselor's office is not possible. This does not mean that individual counseling is never warranted, but it does suggest that most of the changes will take place within the classroom setting. For this reason, we feel that close cooperation between teacher and counselor is essential to a succesful program.

In attempting to provide a vehicle through which this cooperative effort can be fostered, we will look specifically at five dimensions of developmental needs which we feel must be addressed through the curriculum. These five dimensions are:

1. physical development,

2. social development,

3. self-concept development,

4. cognitive development, and

5. career development.

Although the five areas are all interrelated, specific activities have been developed to address each area separately in the following five chapters. The intent is that the "Keystone Learning Model," as presented in the following section, will enable the reader to provide students with valuable learning experiences.

KEYSTONE LEARNING MODEL

Everything that occurs in the environment represents a learning experience. We are exposed to many such experiences daily, yet many go unrecognized because they are not in our field of awareness. Consequently, many valuable learning experiences never register with us and the loss is ours.

Activities in the five chapters in Part II are designed to enhance the teaching/learning process in meeting children's needs and are presented through a learning model for helping children glean meaning from those life situations which address the five dimensions of development.

Before presenting these activities, we should first describe our learning model which consists of five major dimensions in a keystone configuration. Our belief is that the appropriate use of the model represents the "keystone" of a successful lesson.

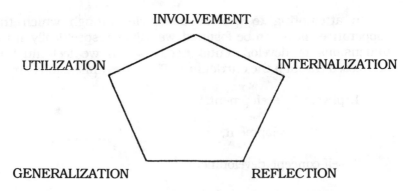

Figure II.1. Keystone Learning Model: Five major dimensions.

In using the learning model, three important premises are utilized:

1. experience consists of everything that happens to us,

2. learning can take place in every experience, and

3. the process of learning involves combining experience with meaning. This enables children to understand and clarify the meaning of their life experiences and apply these new learnings to subsequent life experiences.

The five phases of The Keystone Learning Model are described in detail as they relate to the five developmental dimensions of the elementary school.

Phase 1 Involvement

The involvement phase of the learning model represents the experiencing domain of the model from which all learning is derived. Because everything that happens to us is an experience, all experiences provide us with an opportunity for learning. These experiences influence our lives and our environment and affect what we learn. Since this is the case, we can enhance children's sense of awareness and therefore increase meaningful learning for them by taking advantage of existing learning experiences. As children enter into any experience, they begin to generate data which will be processed in the other phases of the learning experience model.

Phase 2 Internalization

In this phase, the children increase their involvement in the experience. This requires that children begin to internalize the content of the experience and reflect on the process. This is the point in the model when children describe and discuss observations and begin to reflect on what has taken place.

Internalizing is a natural activity and is the outgrowth of those experiences of which we are aware. Most of us are compelled to talk or write about what we have experienced with others. As we internalize, we describe our experiences, our feelings, what we observed, our field of awareness, and our expressions of the experience. We usually do not have to be primed for this to take place as we are anxious to validate our experience with others and to establish a sense of connectiveness with those who shared the experience.

While internalizing is a natural experience, it can be enhanced so as to increase the child's involvement, help the child internalize the experience, and begin the reflection process while still experiencing the event. This can be accomplished in a variety of ways, the easiest of which is to pose questions regarding the life situation which stimulate and heighten awareness. A second method is to create a script which takes the child through the experience much in the same manner as a travelogue is designed to guide and highlight points of interest that might otherwise go unnoticed.

Phase 3 Reflection

The reflection phase challenges children to find meaning in the activity in relation to the learning experience.

Unfortunately, in most life experiences, learning stops with the involvement or internalization phase and the remainder of the learning process remains undeveloped. The reflection phase is designed to stimulate thinking about the implications of what has been internalized. Children are helped to focus on what they have learned from the experience. The purpose of reflection is to derive meaning from the experience. Children can respond by saying "I learned _____ about myself," or "I now understand _____ ."

Phase 4 Generalization

Generalization is possibly the most important phase in the learning model because it involves the child in relating the learnings of the activity to other experiences. A crucial point during this step is that the child is able to make the connection between the current activity and how learning from the activity can be applied to other life situations.

Generalization also encourages children to think about the implications of what has been learned. This stage is designed to broaden the context of learning in that children are taught to transport the concepts learned in the activity to other environments and experiences, thereby broadening their learnings and understandings in meeting new life experiences.

Phase 5 Utilization

As children begin to broaden and heighten their field of awareness and clarity by being able to generalize meaning and understandings, they are ready to apply what they have learned to other situations. In Phase 4 they learned the connection, but in Phase 5 they utilize and apply the learning by setting new goals and becoming involved in new life situations. This is the phase when children gain a value of learning for the future. The utilization phase stimulates the creation of new experiences which allow for the development of new insights which have grown out of previous experiences.

And so, the learning process continues in a never ending cycle of Involvement, Internalization, Reflection, Generalization, and Utilization. Each time the cycle is completed, the breadth and depth of learning is expanded.

In the succeeding chapters in Part II, we will follow a format which provides a brief review of the research for each developmental area, identify some basic needs and skills to be developed, and provide a series of activities which can be integrated into the curriculum to aid in meeting these needs.

The activity component of each chapter has been designed to form the bridge between the curriculum content and the dimension of development being addressed.

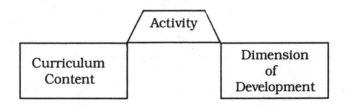

Figure II.2. Keystone Learning Model: Activity bridge.

DIMENSION
OF PHYSICAL
DEVELOPMENT

The physical development of the child is of utmost importance in the educational process as it is central to successful learning. This is especially apparent in the elementary school because those children who are slower in physical development often experience social difficulties as well as learning problems because of their physical development. In this chapter, we have addressed several areas of physical coordination activities which we hope will provide opportunities for enjoyable learning as well as increase physical coordination and dexterity in children.

RESEARCH ON PHYSICAL DEVELOPMENT

Various factors of a physical maturational nature affect the teaching/learning process. Such aspects as eye-hand coordination, large and small motor development, visual and auditory perception, growth changes and sexual identity, all have an impact on student success or lack of it. Such needs must be identified, understood, and addressed in order to enhance learning.

In addition, activities designed to enhance the physical development of children tend to promote more socialization within the classroom because children usually perceive them as being fun. Such activities also allow children to set both realistic and individualized goals.

Carlson (1982) saw the importance of physical activity in developing and maintaining interpersonal relationships. Children, through physical activities, are provided with opportunities to work together toward team objectives and goals; thus promoting friendships within the classroom group.

Hillman and Runion (1978) suggested that people learn best through active participation and enjoy learning more through active involvement in the learning process.

The use of physical activities also is a very effective technique when working with children who are identified as hyperkenetic. According to Koester and Farely (1981), children with special needs respond especially well to physical activities because through such activities they are able to meet their stimulation needs in a condoned environment.

Since additional pressure is being placed on children for academic excellence, an imperative is that children have periods of physical activity to provide variation in their daily schedule. Kaczkowski (1979) suggested that counselors should combine a mixture of verbalization and physical activities that are most helpful to children.

Nelson (1976) stated that "Counselors and teachers alike can provide and use play media with children in order to produce comfort and encourage expression and communication" (p. 206).

Nelson (1976) stressed the importance of the counselor's need to incorporate both physical and psychological activities into the development of the whole child.

NEEDS TO BE ADDRESSED

1. The need to experience variety in school day activities.

Although this is not specifically a need which addresses a particular area of physical development, it is crucial for elementary grade children to experience a variety of learning activities. Those activities which promote active learning in a physical sense not only provide a welcome change in daily routine, but also promote the development of specific physical coordination skills.

2. The need to be able to utilize physical skills in working cooperatively with fellow classmates.

Since much of a school child's day is spent in academic tasks on an individual basis, opportunities for group cooperation activities are needed to promote development of the whole child. Many of these activities will be those which require physical coordination skills.

3. The need to develop specific physical coordination skills.

The development of any skill requires practice. This is especially true of physical coordination activities; thus the need for daily physical exercises and activities.

4. The need to be actively involved in the learning process.

Much research supports the fact that children learn best through active involvement in learning. Physical activities provide an excellent vehicle for active learning to take place.

**5. The need to learn the value
of working together to
complete a task.**

All children need to be aware of the value of working with others. This can be promoted very successfully through physical activities.

SKILLS TO BE DEVELOPED

1. Fine and Gross Motor Skills

Many of the activities in the primary grades are developed specifically to provide for the development of fine and gross motor skills.

2. Eye-hand Coordination Skills

Physical activities which include balancing and catching or throwing objects provide excellent means for promoting the development of eye-hand coordination.

3. Visual Perception Skills

Although most academic tasks promote the development of visual perception skills, this can also be done through activity-oriented tasks. An excellent activity for developing these skills is contained in the activities section of the chapter.

4. Auditory Perception Skills

Children often hear without actually listening. Those parents who call their children several times before being responded to are well aware of this trait. Activities to promote the growth of auditory perception skills will be most helpful in assisting children to be more successful in school.

5. Cooperation Skills

One may debate the concept of cooperation as a physical skill; however, it is most often in the area of physical development where the importance of cooperation is most crucial. An example of this concept is the "Make a Machine" activity which follows in the activity section.

APPLICATION OF
THE KEYSTONE LEARNING MODEL

To provide an example of how the Keystone Learning Model may be applied in activities, let us look at the "Make A Machine" activity which is the first of the Physical Development activities. We will look at each of the five phases of the model and describe what should take place in each phase.

Involvement

During the involvement phase, the children become immersed in the experience. This is the time when the directions are given, the stage is set, and the environment is prepared so that children experience feelings, thoughts, behaviors, and stimulation of the senses. In this particular phase of the "Make A Machine" activity, the children will be motivated to think about the action they will use when it becomes their turn to be a part of the machine. They may also begin to imagine what their machine will look like.

Internalization

In the internalization phase, children will begin to talk about the feelings which have been generated. All of the children will be able to answer such questions as "How did it feel?" and "What was it like?"

Reflection

As children begin to observe the machine in action, they will hopefully begin to notice strengths of particular children i.e. Mark keeps his part of the machine going at a consistent pace and encourages other children to keep the machine operating even though they may be getting tired. Individual children may also begin to recognize their own personal strengths in promoting classroom cooperation.

Generalization

At this point, the transfer of learning begins to take place. Children begin to make statements such as "Gee, since Mark is so dependable and encouraging, he can be the chairperson of our candy sale next month. Mark, too, will begin to generalize in his mind with thoughts of how he can better make use of this identified strength.

Utilization

Children will utilize the information by asking Mark to chair the committee for the candy sale. Mark will utilize his information by working to develop this strength which has been identified.

This, then, completes the circle for the Keystone Learning Model. As children become accustomed to the use of the model, they will find it easy to relate each learning to subsequent life situations.

INTEGRATION OF
PHYSICAL DEVELOPMENT ACTIVITIES

The physical activities on the following pages have been designed to stimulate group cooperation as well as provide children with an opportunity for physical exercise in an enjoyable atmosphere. In addition, some of the activities promote the development of coordination and motor skills. All activities should be presented using the Keystone Learning Model which was presented at the beginning of this section and should be integrated into the existing curriculum. For example, the "Make a Machine" activity described on page 167 would fit beautifully into a social studies lesson on cooperation.

MAKE A MACHINE
(Physical Development Activity No. 1)

Objective: To enable children to use repeated physical movements while participating in a group cooperation activity.

Level: Primary

Materials Needed: None

Procedure:

1. Talk with the children about how a machine works. Discuss what happens when one part of the machine comes loose, breaks off, or just stops working. (The machine breaks down).

2. Explain that they are going to make a human machine by continually repeating a certain movement.

3. Choose 5 persons to come to the front of the class and assign a specific movement to each such as

   a. move your hands in a circular motion,

   b. tap your right foot,

   c. bend down/stand up,

   d. open and close your mouth, or

   e. move your head from side to side.

4. Have the first person begin his/her movement, then the second, the third, the fourth, and the fifth. (Remind children that they must be touching the other members of their machine in some way).

5. Allow the children about one minute to demonstrate their smooth working machine.

6. Choose 5 new children and repeat the activity with different movements.

Evaluation: Each child should have had an opportunity to be a part of a machine. Following the activity, a discussion of ways that working together as a class can be compared to a smooth running machine would be appropriate. It may also be helpful to make a list of all of the daily activities which require cooperation and post it on the bulletin board.

Variations: After the activity has been done one time, allow children to form their own small groups and make a wacky machine of their own. Stress the idea of cooperation by having each person do his/her part to make the "machine" work.

† † †

BALLOON BOUNCE
(Physical Development Activity No. 2)

Objective: To have children work together to successfully complete an activity.

Level: Primary

Materials: Balloons and stopwatch

Procedure:

1. Divide the children into teams of 4 to 6 players each. Instruct each team to form a small circle.

2. Explain to them that the object of the game is to see which team can keep their balloon in the air for the longest time. (The balloon may be hit with the hands only).

3. Provide each group with a balloon.

4. Give a signal when each group is to throw the balloon into the air and try to keep it there the longest time.

5. Recognize the winning team by having those members be the group leaders for a subsequent activity of their choice.

Evaluation: Children will become aware of the qualities which helped the winning team be more successful than some of the other teams. This can be accomplished by having children discuss things which they observed as being helpful, hindering, etc.

Variation: Use a feather and have the groups keep it in the air by blowing on it. See which group can keep it in the air for the longest time.

✝ ✝ ✝

MIRROR IMAGE
(Physical Development Activity No. 3)

Objective: To have the children be able to "mirror" the actions of a partner.

Level: *Primary and Intermediate*

Materials: *None*

Procedure:

1. Ask each child to select a partner for the activity.

2. Discuss what is seen when one looks in a mirror. Explain to the children that they are going to be doing an activity in which one of each pair is going to act as a mirror.

3. Demonstrate to the children how the mirror activity works by choosing a child to do some actions and following the child yourself.

4. Instruct the children to stand and face the chosen partner.

5. Remind the children to complete the movements slowly so that their "mirror" can follow them.

6. After 1 minute, have the children change roles, the mirror now becomes the leader and the leader is now the mirror.

Evaluation: The children will need to discuss the activity in terms of feelings generated while completing the activity. "What made it easier to follow the movements of the other person?" "What made it more difficult?"

Variation: Have just half of the children participating in the activity at a time. The others should act as observers. When the activity is completed, discuss the following questions:

1. Did you see anyone who seemed to be frustrated by the activity? What caused this?

2. What made the activity difficult?

3. Did some things seem to be easier? What made them easy?

† † †

WHO'S MY PARTNER
(Physical Development Activity No. 4)

Objective: To have the children to be able to move through groups and identify their respective partners.

Level: Primary

Materials Needed: One 15 foot to 20 foot piece of yarn for every two children.

Procedure:

1. Have the children number off in twos.

2. Ask all of the number ones to come to the front of the class.

3. Give an end of yarn to each of the number ones.

4. Stretch the yarn pieces out and tangle them slightly.

5. Give an end of yarn to each of the number twos.

6. On a given signal, instruct the children to try to find out who's at the other end of their piece of yarn.

7. Have the "String Partners" to be their partners for a subsequent activity.

Evaluation: Each child will be able to move successfully through the maze and find his/her partner. Following the activity, it may be helpful to allow time for the children to discuss their "strategies" for finding their string partner and to think about additional things they may want to try if they did the activity again.

Variation: Complete the activity with just four pairs at a time but blindfold the team members. They must identify their string partner by the sound of their voice.

† † †

BLOCK RACE
(Physical Development Activity No. 5)

Objective: To have the children learn the value of working together as a team to reach an objective.

Level: Primary or Intermediate

Materials Needed: Old floor tiles or square pieces of cloth or newspaper

Procedure:

1. Instruct each child to choose a partner.

2. Have the children decide which one of them will be the "racer" and which one will be the "placer."

3. Explain that the "racer" can only move forward if he/she has something to step on. The "placer" has the job of moving the tiles forward so the "racer" can keep going.

4. Designate a starting and ending line. When the pairs reach the line, they must reverse roles and come back to the starting line.

Evaluation: Children will gain a sense of the value of working together by discussing the following:

1. What was needed to be successful?

2. Was one job harder than the other? Which one?

3. Were you better at one job than the other? Which one?

Variation: Complete the activity by having the students work in groups of four, three "placers" and one "racer." Discuss why this was easier than just working in pairs.

✝ ✝ ✝

THE MIRROR ME
(Physical Development Activity No. 6)

Objective: To enable the children to gain a better understanding of the physical properties of their bodies.

Level: Primary and Intermediate

Materials Needed: Full length mirror with three pieces of masking tape placed horizontally across mirror and spaced at equal distances on the mirror, construction paper, and crayons.

Procedure:

1. Talk with the children about what they see when they look in a mirror. Discuss briefly that the mirror shows things exactly as they look.

2. Place the mirror in the front of the classroom and explain the reason for the three pieces of tape (To divide the image into three equally spaced portions).

3. Ask each child to stand in front of the mirror and observe only the image that he/she sees above the top part of tape.

4. Instruct the child to go back to his/her seat and draw what he/she saw at the top of his/her paper.

5. When this step has been completed, follow the same procedure with the space between the 1st and 2nd piece of tape, between the 2nd and 3rd, and below the 3rd.

Evaluation: The children should be more aware of the basic makeup of their bodies by viewing them in terms of proportioned areas. Discussion of the following may assist in the understanding process:

1. Was it easier to draw a figure when you looked only at a small portion of it? Why?

2. Were the proportions easier to see? What other ways could you do this activity?

Variation: Use just one child (or the teacher/counselor) as a model and have all the children draw the same figure. Make the drawings life size by using large sheets of butcher paper.

† † †

PARACHUTE ACTIVITY
(Physical Development Activity No. 7)

Objective: To help the children learn the value of cooperation in physical activities.

Level: Primary

Materials Needed: A sheet, blanket or parachute, and several soft articles (nerf ball, balloon, pillow)

Procedure:

1. Place the sheet or blanket on the ground and space the children at equal distances around the outside.

2. Ask children to bend down and grasp the end of the sheet and pick it up.

3. Show the value of teamwork in the following activities:

   a. Making a dome—All children raise the sheet overhead and pull it down very rapidly.

   b. Catching Objects—Place an object in the center of the sheet. Have the children jerk the sheet up and see how high they can throw the object and still catch it in the sheet.

   c. Put additional items (one at a time) on the sheet. See how many objects the children can throw in the air and catch without dropping them.

Evaluation: The children should be aware that working as a team made the activity successful. Talking about teamwork would be very appropriate at this point. Suggested questions to use are What helps it? What hinders it?

Variation: Divide the group into two teams with each team on one-half of the sheet. Place a ball in the center of the sheet. Each team tries to toss the ball off the sheet on the opponent's side.

† † †

BUILDING A TREE HOUSE
(Physical Development Activity No. 8)

Objective: To have the children use their imaginations by taking an imaginary trip to gather materials to build a tree house.

Level: *Primary*

Materials Needed: *None*

Procedure:

1. Explain to the children that they are going to go into the forest to gather materials and then build a tree house.

2. Begin by discussing things they'll need to take— Pantomime gathering up materials (hammers, nails, saw, etc.)

3. Pantomime the following:

   a. Marching into the woods

   b. Gathering materials, sawing board, etc.

   c. Finding a suitable tree

   d. Climbing the tree

   e. Putting up the tree house

   f. Building a chair for the tree house

   g. Sitting down on the chair to talk about the house you built

4. When the children sit down in their chairs to talk about their house, bring the discussion around to individual differences.

   a. Could a very tall person come to your tree house? Someone very short?

   b. Could someone who was wearing glasses?

5. Discuss the need to consider differences in others as we plan activities, and doing certain things to accommodate these differences.

Evaluation: The children should be observed as they complete their imaginary trip and build their tree house. At the conclusion of the activity, a brainstorming session on how individual differences are considered in school each day should really bring the point home. If the children have difficulty getting started on the brainstorming, provide suggestions such as different size desks and chairs for different size children, positioning of people in the room with vision and hearing problems, etc.

Variation: Take a variety of imaginary trips. The children enjoy these and can be very creative. Some examples:

1. a trip to the moon

2. a trip to Africa

3. a trip to the beach

4. a trip to the North Pole

5. a trip through a desert

† † †

TRUST WALK
(Physical Development Activity No. 9)

Objective: To help the children learn better the value of trust.

Level: Intermediate

Materials Needed: Blindfolds for one-half of the class.

Procedure:

1. Discuss the word trust.

    a. Can you think of a time when you trusted someone?

    b. Can you think of a time someone trusted you?

2. Provide time for discussion and examples of trust.

3. Have the children choose partners for the trust walk.

4. Allow the children to participate in the trust walk using the following guidelines:

    a. One of the pair is blindfolded.

    b. The second member will lead his/her partner around a designated area, making sure that no danger comes to him/her. Leading is done by placing a hand under the partner's elbow.

    c. After a few minutes, partners reverse roles.

Evaluation: The children will experience the feelings of trust through participation in the activity. Follow up discussion should include the following:

1. feelings of the leader,

2. feelings of the one being led, and

3. the development of trust

Variations:

1. Complete the activity using only verbal directions for the blindfolded partner.

2. Set up an obstacle course on the playground as the setting for the trust walk.

✝ ✝ ✝

LOOK WHAT I CAN DO
(Physical Development Activity No. 10)

Objective: To have the children demonstrate the ability to do several things at one time.

Level: *Primary and Intermediate*

Materials Needed: *None*

Procedure:

1. *Divide the class into groups of four or five.*

2. *Name a leader for each group.*

3. *Designate a given signal when the leader says "Look What I can Do" and performs an action, i.e., snapping fingers. All persons in the group imitate the action.*

4. *Have the person on the child's right then to become the leader and say "Yes I can do that and I can also do this" i.e., snapping fingers, tapping foot. All repeat the two actions.*

5. *Have the next person on the right say, "I can do both of those and also this" and shows 3 simultaneous actions, i.e., snapping fingers, tapping foot, patting head. All repeat the three simultaneous actions.*

6. *Continue to play until all persons in the group have added an action (The idea is to see how many different actions can be done simultaneously).*

Evaluation: *The children will be able to identify something they learned about their ability to do several things at once. To facilitate discussion, questions such as the following should be posed:*

1. *Did anyone do more than they thought they could?*

2. *What provided the extra incentive? and*

3. *Was anyone fearful of trying the activity? What caused this feeling?*

Variation: *Have two groups compete against each other to see which group can do the greatest number of actions simultaneously.*

✝ ✝ ✝

THE GREAT STONE FACE
(Physical Development Activity No. 11)

Objective: To provide the children with practice controlling facial expressions.

Level: Primary

Materials Needed: None

Procedure:

1. Explain to the children that you are going to be doing an activity which requires that they try to keep from laughing as long as possible.

2. Choose a child to be the "great stone face". This child sits on a chair in front of the room.

3. Each of the other children has an opportunity to come up and try to make the "great stone face" laugh.

4. The child who succeeds in making him/her laugh then becomes the next "great stone face."

5. If you want to add variety to the activity, you may use a stopwatch to see who was able to keep the "great stone face" the longest time.

Evaluation: The children will discover that maintaining a specific pose requires that they exhibit a great deal of control over their body and that the actions of others can greatly affect the amount of control they have.

Variation: Have the children pretend to be a manikin or a statue. Others will attempt to get them to change their position in some way.

✝   ✝   ✝

MY FINGERPRINTS/HANDPRINTS
(Physical Development Activity No. 12)

Objective: To help the children be aware that there is no one exactly like them.

Level: Primary

Materials Needed: Tempera paint, paper.

Procedure:

1. Have each child carefully observe his/her hands.

    a. What are some things you notice about your hands?

    b. Are all hands the same size?

    c. What about fingernails, freckles, moles, scars?

2. Ask the children if the look of their hands will change. Point out that age, weathering, growth, etc. will change the appearance of the hands.

3. Discuss the fact that fingerprints will never change. That is why the police department uses fingerprints as a means of identification.

4. Have each child make fingerprints and handprints on a piece of construction paper.

5. Prepare a class poem or short story about the individuality of each person's hands.

Evaluation: The children will discover that each person has specific characteristics to his/her handprint. Such discussion questions as those posed below may assist the process:

1. What particular thing(s) do you see on your hands that you don't see on someone elses?

2. What other kinds of things affect the way our hands look? i.e., better fingernails, band aids, cuts, scratches, etc.

Variation: Have a blindfolded child try to identify other classmates by shaking hands with them.

✝ ✝ ✝

WHO'S MISSING
(Physical Development Activity No. 13)

Objective: To assist the children in developing a more acute observation skill.

Level: Primary

Materials Needed: None

Procedure:

1. Instruct the children to look around the room and observe all of their classmates.

2. Then have everyone close their eyes while the teacher leads a child from the classroom.

3. When the teacher/leader says "Who's Missing" the children have 5 seconds to look around the room and name the missing person.

4. The person who correctly identifies the missing person gets to be the leader for the next round.

5. At the end of the activity, talk about things the children looked for when trying to identify the missing person.

Evaluation: The children will be able to identify the "missing" classmate. Discussion should focus on such things as:

1. What did you look for in trying to identify the missing person?

2. Was it easier to identify some "missing persons"? Why?

Variations:

1. Have just one person be "it." That person is the only one who can guess "Who's Missing."

2. When the children become pretty good at identifying the missing person, suggest that students sit in a different place each time the leader says "Who's Missing."

† † †

PASS THE DONUT, PLEASE
(Physical Development Activity No. 14)

Objective: To provide the children with an opportunity to practice cooperation skills in a physical activity.

Level: Intermediate

Materials Needed: Plastic straw for each child and construction paper donuts.

Procedure:

1. Explain to the children that they are going to participate in a donut passing relay.

2. Choose one person to help you demonstrate the best passing technique.

   a. Both players put straws between their teeth.

   b. One places the paper donut on his/her straw.

c. The second player must get the donut onto his/her straw using only teeth and the straw.

d. If the donut falls to the floor, the team must begin again.

3. Have the children count off to form teams of four.

4. Announce that at the signal to begin, each team tries to be the first to pass the donut from the front to the back of his relay team. (After several dropped donuts, the children will learn to balance the straw carefully and make slow rather than quick, jerky movements).

5. Provide team winners with the opportunity to choose a fun time activity for a subsequent game period.

Evaluation: The children will be able to show the physical dexterity necessary to participate in the activity.

Variation: Have the children use plastic spoons placed between their teeth (handle between teeth) and pass a marble, button, paper clip, etc.

BIBLIOGRAPHY

Borba, M., & Borba, C. (1978). *Self esteem: A classroom affair.* Minneapolis: Winston Press.

Borba, M., & Borba, C. (1982). *Self esteem: A classroom affair, Vol. II.* Minneapolis: Winston Press.

Carlson, J. (1982) The multimodal effect of physical exercise. *Elementary School Guidance and Counseling, Vol. 16,* No.4.

Dinkmeyer, D. (1973). *Developing an understanding of self and others.* Circle Pines, MN: American Guidance Service.

Farnette, C., Forte, I, & Harris, B. (1979). *People need each other.* Nashville, TN: Incentive Publications.

Farnette, C., Forte, I., & Loss, B. (1977). *I've got me and I'm glad.* Nashville, TN: Incentive Publications.

Farnette, C., Forte, I., & Loss, B. (1977). *At least 1000 things to do.* Nashville, TN: Incentive Publications.

Grimm, G., & Mitchell, D. (1977). *Mostly me.* Carthage, IL: Good Apple.

Hillman, B.W., & Runion, K.B. (1978). Activity group guidance: Process and results. *Elementary School Guidance and Counseling,* Vol. 13, No.2.

Kaczkowski, H. (1979). Group work with children. *Elementary School Guidance and Counseling,* Vol. 14, No.1.

Knight, M., Graham, T., Juliana, R., Miksza, S., and Tonnies, P. (1982). *Teaching children to love themselves.* Englewood Cliffs: Prentice Hall.

Koester, S., & Farley, F.H. (1981). Hyperkenises: Are there classroom alternatives to drug treatment? *Elementary School Guidance and Counseling,* Vol. 16, No.2.

Nelson, R.C. (1976). Relating to children through enjoying choices. *Elementary School Guidance and Counseling,* Vol. 10, No.3.

Nivens, M.K. (1976). The role of physical health in school counseling. *Elementary School Guidance and Counseling,* Vol. 11, No.2.

Reasoner, R.W. (1982). *Building self esteem.* Palo Alto: Consulting Psychologists Press.

Smith, A., Cooper, J., & Leverte, M. (1977). *Giving kids a piece of the action.* Doylestown, PA: TACT.

Thompson, C.L., & Poppen, W.L. (1975). *Guidance for the elementary school.* Springfield, TN: Robertson County Board of Education.

CHAPTER **8**

DIMENSION
OF SOCIAL
DEVELOPMENT

In reflecting on the dimension of social development, counselors must be aware that children have social needs which frequently take precedence over their academic needs. Children must be taught and given the opportunity to practice socially acceptable human interaction skills if they are ever to learn how to build positive and healthy relationships with others. Learning how to function socially must be addressed in the same manner as any academic subject. Children need information skills and the self-confidence in order to function successfully and responsibly in a social climate.

RESEARCH ON SOCIAL DEVELOPMENT

Socialization is a difficult process in which children learn to interact effectively with other children and with adults in their environment. Because school is a social setting, educators must be concerned with how children interact with their peers.

Social development, a critical factor in the educational process, frequently influences, to a great degree, just what and how well each child learns. The dynamics of classroom climate, peer relationships, and teacher-pupil interactions, strongly affect the learning climate of the classroom. Because of the important role of social development in the educational process, Morgan and Jackson (1980) reported that planners of school curriculum programs need to consider a broader range of learning content than has been true in the past. This broader range must include social development activities.

Dlugokinski (1984) stressed that "If children are encouraged to work cooperatively with each other and other community members in their schools, the stage is set for experiencing and appreciating the benefits of connectedness and cooperative activity" (p. 210).

D'Andrea (1983) also pointed to the importance of social development activities for all children. He stated that "Elementary school counselors can more effectively work toward promoting the personal growth of all primary age school children by becoming more involved in consultation with other school personnel during curriculum planning and implementation" (p. 218).

One of the most valuable curriculum additions to promote social development is that of group interaction activities. Piaget (1965) reported that a child's consciousness is altered as a result of group interaction in terms of specific interpersonal skills. Such group activities provide opportunities for children to learn sharing, cooperating and group problem solving, and decision making. The activities provided in this chapter specifically address these particular topics.

NEEDS TO BE ADDRESSED

Needs in the area of social development which we feel are most appropriate within the educational system include the following.

1. To get along with others.

All children have a need to make friends and to get along with their peers. This is, in part, what makes school fun.

2. To have a sense of belonging.

The sense of belonging to a group is a very comforting one. This is why children frequently talk about "my class," "my reading group," or "my team."

3. To work cooperatively.

A strong feeling of accomplishment can be gained from working together to complete a project.

4. To share responsibility.

The idea of "doing one's part" is very important to an elementary school child. It tends to fit in well with the child's sense of fair play.

5. To experience a sense of importance as a member of the classroom.

Each child needs to gain a sense of the feeling that occurs when recognized for his/her special characteristics.

SKILLS TO BE DEVELOPED

In addition to the needs which must be addressed in the dimension of social development, several skills must be developed if the child is to be socially adjusted within the classroom setting. We feel that the five most basic of these skills are as follows.

1. Communication Skills.

For efficient development, the child must learn effective listening skills, conversational skills, and skills in providing feedback to peers and others. The child also must gain experience in presenting clear and direct messages to others.

2. Sharing Skills.

Children who are willing to share are usually well accepted in the classroom social setting. This skill must be regularly encouraged and reinforced, especially in the primary grades.

3. Taking Turns.

If the concept of taking turns is regularly practiced in the classroom, students will naturally develop this habit. Regular positive reinforcement to those children who practice the skill will tend to generate more interest in cultivating this habit.

4. Cooperation Skills.

Opportunities must be provided for children to work together in small groups so that they can learn skills for cooperation.

5. Goal Setting and Decision Making Skills.

Frequently adults feel that they must make decisions and set goals for children who are "too young" to do it for themselves. In reality, though, even very young children are capable of developing these skills if appropriate opportunities are provided for them.

INTEGRATION OF
SOCIAL DEVELOPMENT ACTIVITIES

The elementary school counselor is in a very advantageous position to observe the child in day-to-day socialization activities and to be aware of the school atmosphere and learning conditions which directly affect socialization. Since no two children react in the same way to these influences, the counselor's role is to aid school staff in interpreting these influences and their effect on children. Often a helpful procedure is for the counselor to develop some classroom activities which will promote socialization within the classroom and to work with the teacher in presenting such activities.

The following pages of classroom activities have been developed in such a way that their use will foster social interaction within the elementary school classroom. They are written for use by teachers or counselors; in small groups, or in classroom size groups, as an integral part of the curriculum.

For example, the "Student of the Week" activity could be integrated into Language Arts by having each child write a strength of the chosen student. It also could be integrated into an art curriculum by having each child prepare his/her own poster to be used when that child becomes the "Student of the Week." This process of curriculum infusion will become more and more natural as it is practiced.

After participation in these activities, children will feel more positive about themselves and their classmates, connect more meaningfully with the school curriculum, and will experience many opportunities to practice working together in a variety of school and academically related experiences. In addition, evidence of more positive social interactions among the children on a day-to-day basis should become more apparent.

STUDENT OF THE WEEK
(Social Development Activity No. 1)

Objective: To provide children with an opportunity to receive positive reinforcement from classmates and be recognized for individual strengths.

Level: Primary and Intermediate

Materials Needed: Slips of paper with student's names on them, box or bowl, oaktag or construction paper, polaroid camera

Procedure:

1. Names of all children are placed in a box to identify the "Student of the Week." Each week one name is chosen from the box. That child then becomes the special person for the week. Things will need to be done to help the child feel special, e.g.,

   a. Provide the child with a bulletin board to decorate as he/she chooses.

   b. Make a chart from oaktag or large construction paper which states "_____" is special because:. Each day, one special trait should be identified by the class members and written on the chart. At the end of the week the chart is given to the student to take home. (If possible, the chart should be laminated before the child takes it home.)

   c. Take a polaroid picture of the child to be placed on the bulletin board or on the chart.

   d. Provide special privileges during the week for the child. These can include such things as passing papers, being messenger, etc.

2. Every child in the class should have an opportunity to be the "Student of the Week."

Evaluation: *Each child should be able to describe at least three positive qualities or strengths which were identified by classmates during his/her special week.*

Variations:

1. For those children who have birthdays during the school year, try to arrange their special week during the week of their birthday.

2. Choose a "VIP (Very Important Person)" rather than a "Student of the Week."

3. Allow the child to choose at least one special learning activity during the week.

† † †

DRAW A CARD
(Social Development Activity No. 2)

Objective: *To have the children improve communication/ cooperation and listening skills*

Level: *Primary and Intermediate*

Materials Needed: *Small index cards with statements, questions, or unfinished sentences printed on them*

Procedure:

1. Have the children arrange chairs or sit on the floor in two circles, an inside circle and an outside circle.

2. Give the pack of cards to the first student in the inside circle. That child will draw one card and respond. Questions or statements on the card should be of a positive nature and should include such things as

   a. Tell three things you like about school.

   b. Say something nice about the person across from you.

c. What was the best thing you did during summer vacation?

  d. Tell about your pet.

  e. Tell about your favorite family activity.

  f. Ask someone in the group what he/she likes about you.

3. After completing his/her response, have the child pass the pack of cards on to the next person. The cards continue around the inside circle until everyone has had a turn.

4. Designate children in the outside circle as listeners who may be asked to join the activity through such leader directed questions as "What did Johnny say he liked about Mary?"

5. After everyone in the inside circle has had a turn, have the two groups exchange places so that the outside circle now becomes the inside circle.

6. Pass the cards around the new inside circle until everyone has had a turn.

Evaluation: Children should determine the effect of the activity on their listening/cooperating skills through discussion of questions such as the following:

1. How did you feel when you were on the inside/outside?

2. Can you provide any clues that might help everyone be better listeners?

Variations:

1. Use one large circle for the activity.

2. Have the children prepare the statements and questions that are written on the cards.

3. Divide the class into smaller groups so that each group has just four to five children in it.

✝ ✝ ✝

PENNANTS
(Social Development Activity No. 3)

Objective: To have each child express his/her individuality through an art related activity.

Level: Intermediate

Materials Needed: Felt or construction paper pennants, scrap material, letter patterns, old magazines.

Procedures:

1. Begin by showing samples of pennants for colleges. Discuss the fact that the pennant often identifies a specific school or team.

2. Ask the children to design a pennant for themselves. It can contain either their name or initials and can be decorated any way they wish.

3. Place completed pennants on a classroom bulletin board or hang on walls in the classroom

Evaluation: The children should be able to identify at least two characteristics which show their individuality. This could be accomplished by having each student show his/her pennant and describe it to the class.

Variations:

1. Utilize classroom groups for an activity and have each group develop a pennant to identify their group. This also provides an excellent time to introduce and reinforce the value of teamwork.

2. Have children develop a classroom slogan and put it on a series of pennants.

✝ ✝ ✝

CLASS QUILT
(Social Development Activity No. 4)

Objective: To help children become more aware of how each member of the class makes an important contribution to the group.

Level: Intermediate

Materials Needed: One 12" x 12" piece of cloth for every member of the class, permanent markers.

Procedure:

1. Explain how quilts are made—that each piece of material in the quilt has been sewn on in a special way to provide a pattern. In the past, quilts were made from scraps of old material—each piece often had a personal meaning to a family member.

2. Tell children that each of them is going to be asked to prepare a block of the class quilt. They can draw anything they want on the block but must put their name or initials somewhere on their square.

3. When the squares are all completed, have them sewn together to make the class quilt. (Be sure to emphasize the importance of each person's contribution.)

4. As teacher or counselor, make a block for illustration.

5. Place the quilt on display so that parents, visitors, and others in the school may see it.

Evaluation: The children need to make the connection that each person was an important contributor to the completion of the "class quilt." To assist the children in making connections pose a question such as "What would happen if Johnny didn't make a block?"

Variations:

1. Use the quilt idea to illustrate a favorite class story with each child drawing a scene from the story on his/her block.

2. In addition to the individual blocks, have children work in groups of three or four to make some "team" blocks to form the quilt border.

† † †

HOBBIES GRAPH/CLASS GRAPH
(Social Development Activity No. 5)

Objective: To assist children in becoming more aware of similarities and differences among class members.

Level: Intermediate

Materials Needed: Paper, pencils or crayons, ruler

Procedure:

1. Discuss some similarities of class members as well as some differences.

2. Suggest that it may be fun to actually count the number of each of these similarities and differences and then to make a graph of these.

3. Complete one graph with the children to show them how a graph is constructed.

4. Ask one-half of the children to complete a hobbies graph to show some of the different interests of class members. Suggest that they may want to graph such hobbies as watching TV, reading, sports, building things, collecting things, traveling, etc.

5. Have the remaining children complete a class graph to show certain physical characteristics, i.e., blond hair, glasses, curly hair, blue eyes, freckles, etc.

Evaluation: Children can identify similarities and differences through discussion of questions such as

1. How are we different?

2. How are we alike?

Another appropriate activity at this time would be to identify other areas to be graphed which could show additional areas of similarity or difference. This could include such things as

1. number of persons in my family, and/or

2. classmates' addresses by street on which they live.

Variations: This activity has many possibilities for variations—among them are

1. Feelings graph (how are people feeling right now),

2. Height or weight graph,

3. Favorite TV program graph,

4. Favorite food graph, or

5. Birthday graph.

FAMILY TREE
(Social Development Activity No. 6)

Objective: To help each child feel more of a sense of belonging to the group.

Level: Primary or Intermediate

Materials Needed: Outline of tree on bulletin board or tree branch placed in bucket of sand, leaf patterns, construction paper, paper punch, yarn.

Procedure:

1. Explain that the group will be making a class family tree and that each member of the "family" needs to think of their own special interest so it can be added to the tree.

2. Have each child prepare a colored leaf for the tree. A helpful procedure is to provide patterns or even have leaf shapes already cut out for younger children.

3. Ask each child to print his/her name on the front of the leaf and write one short sentence to describe an interest. "I am Mary Stewart, I like to collect pictures of movie stars."

4. Punch a hole in each leaf, tie the yarn through, and hang it on the tree.

5. Provide time for children to share their interests with the class members.

Evaluation: The children will be able to identify themselves as members of the classroom family. This can be determined through having intermediate grades complete a brief essay entitled "My Role in the Classroom Family" while primary children could be videotaped as they discuss their "family" role.

Variations:

1. Use a large bunch of grapes on a bulletin board with the caption "this is our bunch"—children will write their interests on the grapes.

2. Prepare a class "family" album. Provide a page for each student to write his/her name and interests.

3. Have each child complete a self portrait using colored yarn for hair. Punch a hole at the top, thread yarn through and hang them on the family tree.

✝ ✝ ✝

THE LABEL GAME
(Social Development Activity No. 7)

Objective: To help children explore, within a group setting, feelings generated by the reactions of others to them.

Level: Intermediate

Materials Needed: Strips of paper for headbands for all participants

Procedure:

1. Explain to children that they will be "labeled" in such a way that others will be told how to react to them. They will not know what their label says but others in the class will.

2. Ask for volunteers to participate in the activity.

3. Put a headband with a message on it on each volunteer. (Make sure the student doesn't see what is on the headband). Headbands should have the following messages printed on them. (It may be wise to assign negative messages to the most well adjusted children.)

   a. Listen to me.

   b. Interrupt me.

   c. Smile at me.

   d. Argue with what I say.

   e. Praise my ideas.

   f. Agree with what I say.

   g. Make fun of what I say.

   h. Ignore me

4. Have volunteers sit in a circle and introduce a topic for discussion. Be sure to remind volunteers to react to the person according to what the headband says.

5. After about 5-8 minutes, stop the discussion and ask for reactions from the volunteers. Allow them to guess what they think their headband says.

Evaluation: The children should be able to identify the feelings which were experienced as a result of the activity. To help children do this, an advantageous procedure is to ask such question as

1. How did it feel to be laughed at, interrupted, ignored, praised, etc.?

2. How can we apply this learning to our every day communications with our classmates?

Variation: Do this activity as a whole group activity with several children having the same sign. After a period of time, write the labels on the chalkboard and have the children go stand under the one that they think they are wearing.

† † †

WHAT'S IN YOUR BAG
(Social Development Activity No. 8)

Objective: To have the children share their hobbies and interests with their classmates.

Level: Upper primary and Intermediate

Materials Needed: Paper bags for each child, crayons or markers

Procedure:

1. Direct children to decorate their bag in such a way that it tells something about their hobbies and interests.

2. After this phase has been completed, ask each child to bring in one or two items to put in the bag that will tell others about their hobbies.

3. When each bag is completed, provide a period of time (2-4 minutes) for each child to share the contents of his/her bag with the class. (This is an especially good activity to help children get to know each other at the beginning of the year.)

4. Ask the teacher/counselor to prepare a bag to share with the class.

5. Encourage the children to share as much or as little of themselves as they wish.

Evaluation: The children will be able to identify at least one thing they learned about a classmate. To determine if this occurred, have each child respond to the sentence stem "I learned . . . (If they have difficulty getting started, the teacher/counselor should provide some examples such as "I learned that Suzy and I both like to read mystery books," "I learned that Jason likes to ride a roller coaster," etc.)

Variation: Rather than having the children make a presentation of their bags to the class, have bags displayed so the children may look at them and try to guess whose bag it is. (This is a good way to use this activity after the children know each other pretty well.)

✝ ✝ ✝

FRIENDSHIP CHAIN
(Social Development Activity No. 9)

Objective: To enable children to become more aware of the value of friendship.

Level: Primary and Intermediate

Materials Needed: Strips of colored construction paper ¾" by 6", paste or staples

Procedure:

1. Discuss friendship. What does it mean to have a friend? What kinds of things do friends like to do together?

2. Have each child put his/her name on a piece of ¾" by 6" construction paper.

3. Attach all of the slips of paper in chain like fashion to develop a class "friendship chain" that contains the names of everyone in the class.

4. Ask the children if they would like children from other classes to add their names to the friendship chain. If possible, extend the chain to include all members of the school.

5. Display the chain in a place where it can be seen by all, possibly the lunchroom or the library.

6. Remind the children that the chain should provide a reminder for them of the value of friendship.

Evaluation: The children will observe the value of friendship through a discussion of the chain in terms of how it can be applied to every day classroom living. This process will occur through discussion of the following:

1. How can we be friendlier here in the classroom?

2. What are some ways to be a good friend?

3. How can we promote friendship throughout the school?

Variation: Provide several strips of paper for each child. Have children develop their own personal friendship chains by writing the names of all their friends on the paper. Suggest that they take it home and put it where it can easily be seen to remind them of all the friends they have.

✝ ✝ ✝

PEOPLE POSTER
(Social Development Activity No. 10)

Objective: To enable children to gain a better sense of connectiveness.

Level: *Primary and Intermediate*

Materials Needed: *Chalkboard and chalk or posterboard and markers*

Procedure:

1. *Talk with the children about belonging—ask about groups to which the children may belong such as scouts, church groups, athletic teams, etc.*

2. *Give the children an opportunity to reflect on the positive feelings associated with belonging.*

3. *Explain that the classroom group is another example of belonging and that each person is an important member of that group.*

4. *Tell the children that they will be provided with a pictorial representation to show how everyone in the class connects with the rest of the class.*

5. *On the chalkboard, write the teacher's name in block letters across the board.*

6. *Have each child come up to the board and fit his/her name in so that it connects with the others in a crossword fashion.*

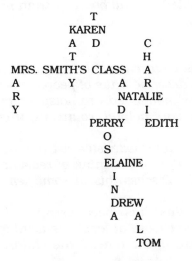

```
              T
           KAREN
           A   D           C
           T                H
 MRS.  SMITH'S CLASS        A
 A         Y        A       R
 R                  NATALIE
 Y                  D       I
                 PERRY   EDITH
                 O
                 S
                 ELAINE
                 I
                 N
                 DREW
                 A   A
                     L
                 TOM
```

7. Display the people puzzle for several days to aid the children in gaining a sense of belonging.

Evaluation: The children will, hopefully, experience a sense of connectedness through a discussion of how the puzzle shows our connection to others. Also a helpful procedure is to talk with the class about other connections they have such as family, Boy or Girl Scouts, church groups, etc.

Variation: Provide small groups with a list of all the children's first names and have them complete their own people puzzles. When they are completed, compare the different puzzles to show the children that many different ways exist for the class to connect.

† † †

LEARNING ABOUT BEHAVIOR
(Social Development Activity No. 11)

Objective: To help the children become aware of their behaviors and understand how these behaviors affect others.

Level: Primary and Intermediate

Materials Needed: Chalkboard or chart paper.

Procedure:

1. Ask the children to think of all the different ways they can to describe traits of people. Some of the things that may be mentioned are noisy, quiet, leaders, followers, happy, sad, helpful, courteous, friendly, rude, etc.

2. After a rather extensive list has been developed, have the children try to think of reasons why people act as they do. Discuss this at some length.

3. When this has been completed, request that the children choose at least one word to describe how they are most of the time. If the children say that none of

the words describe them, ask that they try to think of a word that does describe them.

4. *Ask each child to choose a word from the list to describe the teacher or counselor.*

Evaluation: *The children will be able to identify at least 2 personal behaviors and describe how these behaviors may affect the classroom climate either positively or negatively.*

Variation: *Use a series of pictures exhibiting different behavior traits. Ask each child to choose one and make up a little story or skit to explain why they think that person is acting in that way. (This is a fun activity for the children because they tend to make up some very interesting stories to explain the behaviors.)*

† † †

WORKING IN GROUPS
(Social Development Activity No. 12)

Objective: *To provide the children with an opportunity to practice the skills necessary for successful group work.*

Level: *Intermediate*

Materials Needed: *Construction paper or oaktag, scissors, ruler, old magazines, crayons, scraps of paper, and paste.*

Procedure:

1. *Discuss group cooperation. Stress that when the children work in groups, each of the following should be evident.*

    a. *Everyone in the group should participate.*

    b. *Ideas should be shared.*

    c. *No one should be the "boss." All should work to-gether.*

2. Divide the class into groups of 5 or 6. Provide each group with a piece of oaktag, scrap materials, scissors, etc., and ask them to design a flag for their group. The flag should represent their group in some way.

3. Have the group members work together for about 15 to 20 minutes then bring the groups together to discuss group cooperation. Is everyone sharing ideas, participating, and working together?

4. Then have the groups work together for about 10 to 15 more minutes to complete their flag.

5. Provide time for the children to place their projects with the other groups.

Evaluation: Each group of children will be able to successfully complete a project in the allotted time and will be able to identify specific actions or behaviors which helped to enhance cooperation within their group.

Variation: Provide many opportunities for group work with various tasks. Continue to remind the children of the importance of working cooperatively during group work and of getting everyone involved in the project.

✝ ✝ ✝

INSIDERS VS. OUTSIDERS
(Social Development Activity No. 13)

Objective: To allow the children to experience the feeling of being on the inside of the group as well as the feeling of being "left out".

Level: Intermediate

Material Needed: None

Procedure:

1. Divide the class into two groups with 8 persons forming an inside circle and the remainder of the class on the outside circle.

2. Present the discussion rules as follows:

   a. Only the children on the inside circle may enter into the discussion.

   b. A child on the outside circle may only speak if invited into the inside circle—but he/she must go back to the outside circle after having finished speaking.

3. Introduce a topic of interest to the group. Allow the inner circle children to discuss the topic for about 10 to 15 minutes.

4. Stop and discuss feelings and reactions of both groups.

   a. How does it feel to be a member of the inner circle?

   b. How does it feel when you want to speak but can't because no one will invite you into the inner circle?

   c. How did it feel to be a member of the outside circle?

5. If time permits, choose 8 new persons to be members of the inner circle and have the groups exchange places.

Evaluation: The children will be able to identify various feelings which arise as a result of being an insider versus being an outsider. As a result of this discussion, they should be able to describe at least two things that they as a class can do to help everyone feel like an "insider".

† † †

THE GOOD DEED BOX
(Social Development Activity No. 14)

Objective: To help the children be aware of courteous acts of their classmates.

Level: Primary and Intermediate

Materials Needed: A "good deed" box, slips of paper, and pencils.

Procedures:

1. Prior to the introduction of this activity, prepare a "good deed" box using a shoe box. The box should be covered with Con-Tact or other decorative paper and should have a 1" x 5" slit in the top. (The lid should be covered separately from the box so it is removable).

2. When the box is completed, introduce it to the children as the "good deed" box which should contain descriptions of courteous or friendly acts which the children observe in the classroom.

3. Encourage the children to be alert for these positive acts, to write them on a slip of paper, and to put them in the "good deed" box. (Suggest that they name the student in their description, i.e., "John shared his crayons with Mandy" or "Susie told Mary she would help her learn her spelling words.")

4. At the end of the week, open the "good deed" box and share the information with the class.

5. Positively reinforce the children for showing courteous friendly behavior.

Evaluation: The children will be able to identify and describe at least 10 good deeds which were performed by various class members during the week.

Variations:

1. If "tattling" is a concern in the classroom, use a "Positive Tattles" box where the children are to "tattle" on someone only for doing positive things.

2. Develop a committee of children to be on the lookout for "good deeds" among their classmates. Have them report to the class at the end of the week. Change the committee members each week so that everyone has a turn.

✝ ✝ ✝

MY SHOPPING LIST
(Social Development Activity No. 15)

Objective: To allow the children to make a decision regarding choices they would make for others.

Level: Primary and Intermediate

Materials Needed: Mail order catalogs, paper, scissors, and paste

Procedures:

1. Ask the children to think of a gift they received that really meant a lot to them. Who bought it? Was it for a special occasion? Why is it so special?

2. Request that the children think of four persons who are very special to them.

3. Provide each child with a piece of 8 ½ x 11 paper. Have the child fold it in half and then in half again. When unfolded, it will be divided into 4 sections.

4. Have the children write the names of one of the four special persons at the top of the four sections.

5. *Suggest that they look through the catalogs to find the perfect gift for that person. (Price is no object in this activity.)*

6. *Encourage the children to cut out the picture of the item and paste it on the paper under the person's name.*

7. *If the children wish to do so, allow them to share their gift choices and reason for them with the rest of the class.*

Evaluation: *Each child will be able to identify the perfect gift which they would give to four special persons in their life.*

Variation: *Allow the children to work in groups on this activity and choose gifts for their classmates. Each child in the group will select the name of a classmate from a box with all class members' names in it. The group members will then work together to choose gifts for the persons whose names they have drawn.. This is a fun activity because the children then can tell how they would feel about receiving gifts that were chosen for them.*

† † †

OUR HELPING FRIENDS
(Social Development Activity No. 16)

Objective: *To assist the children to recognize friends who help them in their daily lives.*

Level: *Primary*

Materials Needed: *Bulletin board for placing the names of our helping friends.*

Procedures:

1. *Talk with the children about all the people who help us in our day to day life. Provide time for discussion.*

2. Label these three areas on the bulletin board with the following:

   a. In our home

   b. In our school

   c. In our community

3. Help children to list as many helpers as they can think of under each category.

4. Assign each child the name of one helper and have him/her write a "thank you for your help" note to that person.

5. Allow time for personal delivery to the "school helper."

6. Talk with the children about their feelings toward these school helpers.

Evaluation: Each child will be able to identify at least one helper in each of the three areas.

Variation: Have a helper appreciation day when representatives from school, home, and community helpers are invited to the class. Have the children develop a special program for the helpers (or serve punch and cookies).

† † †

MY FRIEND MOBILE
(Social Development Activity No. 17)

Objective: To encourage the children to think about activities they like to do with all their friends.

Level: Intermediate

Materials Needed: Coat hangers, construction paper scraps, string, scissors, hole puncher, crayons or markers.

Procedure:

1. Use a poem or short story about friendship to promote discussion of the kinds of things friends do together.

2. Ask the children to think of 4 or 5 things they like to do with their friends.

3. Have them cut out circles or other geometric shapes from construction paper and write or draw a picture of what they like to do with their friends on each shape.

4. Punch holes near the top of the shapes and tie string through the holes. Suspend the strings from various parts of the clothes hangers to form a mobile.

5. Suspend the mobiles around the room for the children to view.

6. Allow the children to discuss in small groups some of the things they like to do with their friends.

Evaluation: Each child will make a mobile which describes at least 4 activities which he/she enjoys doing with the friend.

Variation: Have the children work in groups to create their friend mobile. Provide time for groups to share their mobiles with the whole class.

✝ ✝ ✝

FRIENDSHIP RECIPE
(Social Development Activity No. 18)

Objective: To encourage the children to identify the things that make a friendship special to them.

Level: Intermediate

Materials Needed: 3" x 5" "recipe" cards, pencils or pens.

Procedure:

1. Ask the children what they like about chocolate chip cookies. Discuss what are some of the things that go into making a chocolate chip cookie.

2. Talk about recipes, e.g., we use recipes to make things, recipes have special ingredients.

3. Ask the children to think of some of the special ingredients that they think would be important in a recipe for a friend. Work with each child to develop a sample with such ingredients as:

    1 cup of kindness,
    1 dash of humor, and
    1 cup of loyalty.

4. Provide time for each child to create his/her own recipe for a friend.

5. Allow the children to share their recipes with the class or use them to create an interesting bulletin board.

Evaluation: The children will each develop their own personal friendship recipe which contains at least 3 traits which they feel are important to a successful friendship.

Variations:

1. Allow each child to choose a partner and then work in pairs to create their friendship recipe.

2. Divide the class into groups and have them develop recipes for some of the teachers they have had over the years. These recipes will contain ingredients such as humor, kindness, firmness, fairness, patience, etc. (Students really enjoy this activity.)

✝ ✝ ✝

GETTING ACQUAINTED CHECKLIST
(Social Development Activity No. 19)

Objective: To help the children to learn more about their classmates through completing the getting acquainted checklist.

Level: Intermediate

Materials Needed: A getting acquainted checklist, pencil.

Procedure: This is an excellent activity for the beginning of a school year.

1. Explain to the children that they are going to have an opportunity to get to know each other better.

2. Provide each child with a copy of the getting acquainted checklist which contains items such as the following:

   Find someone in the class who

   a. has the same hair color as yours. _____

   b. likes to read mysteries. _____

   c. likes the same T.V. show as yours. _____

   d. has a birthday in the same month as yours. _____

   e. wears glasses. _____

   f. has the same favorite color as yours. _____

   g. is about the same size as you. _____

   h. has sneakers on. _____

   i. has earrings on. _____

   j. has curly hair. _____

3. Explain to the children that they will have 10 minutes to circulate around the room, talk with their class-mates, and find answers to each of the questions.

4. When the activity is completed, discuss it with the children.

Evaluation: The children will be able to answer at least 8 of the 10 questions on their "getting acquainted" worksheet.

Variation: Allow the children to make up their own list of questions that they would like to know about their class-mates. One question for each child. Suggest that they work in small groups and have each person in the group answer the questions from their group members.

† † †

PLAN A PARTY
(Social Development Activity No. 20)

Objective: To assist children in cooperatively working and planning a fun activity.

Level: Primary and Intermediate

Materials Needed: Various types of material and paper scraps, cardboard tubes, foil, styrofoam, crepe paper, paper cups and plates, yarn, ribbon.

Procedure:

1. Choose a theme for the party. It could be a birthday party, a special holiday party, an end of school party, etc.

2. Decide on the number and type of committees you will need, i.e., decorations, favors, games, food.

3. Ask the children to choose the committee on which they would like to serve and divide the class into committee groups.

4. Provide freedom for cooperative planning and working on the specific committees.

5. Set aside time for the actual party that is planned.

6. Following the party, evaluate class efforts by having each group describe the strengths and weaknesses of their particular committee.

Evaluation: Students will demonstrate effective cooperation skills by successfully completing and implementing plans for a classroom party.

Variation: Allow the children to work in small groups to plan several different parties around a variety of themes. Provide time for each group to present their ideas to the class. Have the class vote on the type of party that they would most like to have and follow up by actually having one of the parties.

† † †

MAKE YOUR OWN T.V. SHOW
(Social Development Activity No. 21)

Objective: To provide for children an opportunity to work together to create their own T.V. show.

Level: Intermediate

Materials Needed: Video Taping Equipment—Butcher Paper, Crayons or Markers

Procedure:

1. Talk with the children about their favorite T.V. show. What do you like about it?

2. Divide the children into groups of 4 or 5 and explain to them that they are going to have the opportunity to create their own T.V. show. It can be a comedy, a drama, a game show, a news program, or a documentary.

3. *Provide ample time for the students to write a script, prepare backgrounds if necessary, and practice their programs.*

4. *Video tape each of the groups as they put on their T.V. show.*

5. *Replay each group's T.V. show.*

Evaluation: Children's groups will each present their completed T.V. show to the class demonstrating their organization and cooperation skills.

Variation: Use this same activity in a social studies or career education class. Have the children learn about the different job responsibilities in "putting on" a television program. Explain job networking and cooperation in delivering a successful television production. Perhaps the children could visit a local or regional television studio and view many different responsibilities firsthand.

BIBLIOGRAPHY

Borba, M., & Borba, C. (1978) *Self esteem: A classroom affair.* Minneapolis: Winston Press.

Borba, M., & Borba, C. (1982). *Self esteem: A classroom affair Vol. II.* Minneapolis: Winston Press.

D'Andrea, M. (1983). Social development during middle childhood: Clarifying some misconceptions. *Elementary School Guidance and Counseling, Vol. 17,* No.3.

Dinkmeyer, D. (1973). *Developing an understanding of self and others.* Circle Pines, MN: American Guidance Service.

Dlugokinski, E. (1984). Developing cooperative school environment for children. *Elementary School Guidance and Counseling,* Vol. 18, No.3.

Farnette, C., Forte, I., & Harris, B. (1979). *People need each other.* Nashville, TN: Incentive Publications.

Farnette, C., & Forte, I., & Loss, B. (1977). *I've got me and I'm glad.* Nashville, TN: Incentive Publications.

Farnette, C., & Forte, I., & Loss, B. (1977). *At least 1000 things to do.* Nashville, TN: Incentive Publications.

Gibbs, J., & Allen, A. (1978). *Tribes: A process for peer involvement.* Oakland, CA: Center Source Publications.

Grim, G., & Mitchell, D. (1977). *Mostly me.* Carthage, IL: Good Apple.

Knight, M., Graham, T., Juliano, R., Miksza, S., & Tonnies, S. (1982). *Teaching children to love themselves.* Englewood Cliffs, NJ: Prentice Hall.

Morgan, C., & Jackson W., (1980). Guidance as a curriculum. *Elementary School Guidance and Counseling,* Vol. 15, No.2.

Piaget, J. (1965). *Insights and illusions of philosophy.* New York: Meridean Books.

Reasoner, R.W. (1982). *Building self esteem.* Palo Alto, CA: Consulting Psychologists Press.

Simon, B. (1974). *Meeting yourself halfway.* Niles, IL: Argus Communications.

Smith, A., Cooper, J., & Leverte, M. (1977). *Giving kids a piece of the action.* Doylestown, PA: TACT.

Thompson, C.L., & Poppen, W.L. (1975). *Guidance for the elementary school.* Springfield, TN: Robertson County Board of Education.

Wilt, J., & Watson, B. (1978). *Relationship builders.* Waco, TX: Educational Products Division.

DIMENSION OF SELF-CONCEPT DEVELOPMENT

The self-concept dimension of development is one which is frequently ignored in the educational system because "there is not enough time to complete all of the academic content." While we are aware that the recent educational reform reports are promoting more rigorous academic standards, we contend that a program which promotes the development of a positive self-concept also will show strong academic gains.

RESEARCH ON SELF-CONCEPT DEVELOPMENT

When children enter the educational system, they have images of themselves which have been based on personal experiences during their early years of life. The school must aid children in a continuous development of their self-image through activities aimed at self-awareness and self-understanding.

Understanding of self is an important early step in maturation. If children have an understanding of their likes and dislikes, strengths and weaknesses, and physical characteristics, they are able to make sound decisions. Children, however, do not develop such understandings without assistance. Such assistance must be shown through an affective curriculum aimed at providing experiences for children to gain increased self-understanding/self-concept.

According to Morgan and Jackson (1980), such self-concept education contributes directly to children (1) developing goals and planning for the future, (2) trusting themselves and others, (3) understanding freedom within necessary constraints, (4) achieving a more stable image, and (5) building confidence and security through feelings of confidence and self-esteem.

The effective component of the educational program must not be considered the responsibility of the counselor alone. A team effort, which involves the classroom teacher, who is a prime influence on the elementary school age child, should be utilized. The teacher is a major factor in an elementary school developmental counseling program which, according to Dinkmeyer and Caldwell (1970), should assist children in the following manner:

1. To know and understand self in terms of assets and liabilities; through this self understanding to develop a better understanding of the relationships among personal abilities, interests, achievements, and opportunities. To develop self awareness.

2. To develop self acceptance, a sense of personal worth, a belief in one's own competence, a trust in self and self-confidence; to develop an accompanying trust and acceptance of others.

3. To develop methods of solving the developmental tasks of life as met in the areas of work and interpersonal relationships.

4. To develop increased self direction, problem solving, and decision making abilities.

5. To develop responsibility for choices and actions, to be aware that behavior is goal oriented, and to consider the consequences when making a decision.

6. To clarify feelings so as to become more sensitive to self and to personal behavior.

7. To modify faulty concepts and convictions so that one may develop wholesome attitudes and concepts of self and others; to be able to perceive reality as defined by others. (p. 98)

As counselors and teachers work together to aid children in optimum development of self-concept awareness, they look toward developing children who will be able to assume responsibilities for their actions and decisions. This necessitates that the counseling activities which are provided become an ongoing and integral part of the educational program.

As children grow in self-understanding and self-awareness, a tendency is toward a strong impact on child self-concept as well. In viewing the self-concept, Beane, Lipka, and Ludewig (1980) suggested that educators need to be aware of several factors regarding self-perception. Among these are the following:

1. The children may not see themselves the way others see them because their values may be different.

2. General perceptions of self are quite stable, so continuing, consistent, positive feedback will have more effect than a few random compliments.

3. Adults may influence self-perceptions of younger and preadolescent children easier than adolescents because children are more apt to consider adults as significant others in their lives, while adolescents are more concerned with the opinions of their peers.

Schools have a vital role to play in helping the children develop more positive self-concepts. Wrenn (1980) perceived three major elements in this development:

1. recognizing and stressing personal assets,

2. developing a core of positive beliefs about others and about life, and

3. demonstrating a sense of caring about others.

Educators, in their attempt to develop programs to enhance self-concept development, have approached the problem from a variety of methods. Regular classroom counseling programs directed by teachers and/or counselor have received much attention as one method for providing affective education for all the children. Classroom counseling programs appear to support the suggestion of Beane et al. (1980) that "one way of enhancing self-concept and esteem in the school is to provide a curriculum specifically designed for that purpose" (p.13).

Although considerable support has been provided for the effectiveness of specific guidance packages [i.e., DUSO (Dinkmeyer, 1970), and *My Friends and Me* (Davis, 1977)] in promoting self-concept development, Eldridge, Wittmer, Barakowski, and Bauer (1977) found that the teacher was also an important variable in self-concept enhancement. In a study with EMR students, Eldridge and her colleagues found no significant difference between the experimental groups who were exposed to the DUSO programs and the control groups where teachers were free to develop their own activities for enhancing self-concept. One conclusion that could be deducted is that a good affective curriculum can be "developed" rather than "purchased."

In reviewing the role of the school, Beane et al. (1980) suggested that schools can contribute to the child's self-esteem by

1. creating a climate characterized by democratic procedures, student participation in decision making, personalness, respect, fairness, self-discipline, interaction, and flexibility;

2. minimizing failure and emphasizing success experiences through such practices as team learning;

3. using a variety of grouping patterns rather than always grouping the students by ability;

4. providing for interaction with younger and older people by arranging for cross age tutoring and involving elderly people in school activities;

5. assisting parents to enhance their children's self-perception by conducting workshops for them, holding parent/student/teacher conferences, and encouraging parents to take an active role in their children's learning;

6. permitting students some control over their lives by having them participate in formulating school rules and having them participate in teacher-student planning;

7. including curriculum that gives direct attention to personal and social development; and

8. teaching the students to evaluate their own progress. (p. 27)

One of the school's major objectives must always be to help children feel good about themselves. According to Clemes and Bean (1981), children's self-esteem is most affected by four major determinants. They state that positive self-esteem occurs when children have an opportunity to experience positive feelings about themselves and their environment which result from a sense of connectiveness, uniqueness, power, and models.

A sense of connectiveness is in evidence when children have positive relationships with others and when others approve and respect them. (An activity which promotes a sense of connectiveness is "Who Are These People" which is found in this chapter. Many other activities to promote connectiveness are included in Chapter 8.)

Children feel unique when their own particular strengths or characteristics are noticed by others. All children need to have this special feeling. (The "Things I'm Good At" activity is a good example of an activity to promote uniqueness. Several other activities to promote uniqueness also are found in this chapter.)

Power is felt by children when they are able to use their personal skills and talents in order to maintain direction in their life. (An example of an activity that promotes a sense of power is the "Harvest of Skills." Other activities involving a sense of power are included in Chapter 10).

A sense of models occurs when children are aware that they can make sense out of things, that they can make use of consistent and workable sets of values, and that they have ideas and goals that produce a feeling of purpose and direction. (An activity to promote a sense of models is the "Crystal Ball." Many others can be found throughout Chapters 7 through 11.)

NEEDS TO BE ADDRESSED

**1. The need to be aware of
one's own strengths and weaknesses;
likes and dislikes**

Children need to be able to identify self characteristics and to have the ability to differentiate between personal strengths and weaknesses. They also need to know that all persons have their own set of strengths and that no one is good at "everything."

2. The need to be aware of life experiences which have contributed to one's development

As each of us ponders our own life experiences, we can readily identify personal landmarks and turning points in our own lives. Children, too, need to review their own life experiences.

3. The need to be able to identify and express one's feelings

Feelings play a major role in self-concept development. Children need to be aware of the wide array and variety of feelings they experience each day. They also need opportunities to identify and express those feelings.

4. The need to be aware of one's hopes, dreams and aspirations

No matter how old we are, always looking to the future is helpful. As children progress through the elementary grades, they, too, need to reflect upon what the future may hold for them. Regular activities aimed at helping children do this should promote more realistic perceptions of future pursuits.

5. The need to be able to identify personal values and priorities

While children develop most of their values from their parents, they still need opportunities to evaluate and identify their own values. In this way, children are learning to develop their own framework for living.

SKILLS TO BE DEVELOPED

1. Self-Description Skills

When children first enter school, most of them would describe themselves as being the best, fastest, nicest, etc. However, they soon begin to compare themselves with others and find they do not meet these standards in all areas. They need help in developing self-realization skills in learning to realistically describe themselves in terms of their strengths, weaknesses, skills, likes, and dislikes. Children who can identify and accept their strengths and shortcomings are well on their way to developing positive self-esteems.

2. Valuing Skills

Children need opportunities in deciding what is important to them. Although most basic values will evolve from the child's family life, each also will need to learn the process of valuing in sorting out those things which are important to him/her.

3. Decision-Making Skills

Decision making skills must be developed in all children at an early age and practiced throughout their school experience. Children, who have opportunities to make some decisions on their own, will have an enhanced self-concept having had the experience of deciding something for themselves. This experience also builds self-confidence in children.

4. Feeling Identification Skills

While most children are aware that everyone has feelings, they often describe these feelings in four basic ways: happy, sad, mad, or scared. Children need assistance in developing an extensive vocabulary which suggests both the level and the degree of the feeling being expressed.

5. Prediction Skills

While we do not advocate the development of young "fortune tellers," we do feel that youngsters need opportunities to look at their own future in terms of hopes, dreams, and aspirations. This is part of the process of developing self-understanding.

INTEGRATION OF
SELF-CONCEPT ACTIVITIES

Self-concept activities are the ones which most often do not seem to fit into the regular curriculum and often are added on as a special activity. Our belief, however, is that these kinds of activities can be successfully integrated into the curriculum on a regular basis using the Keystone Learning Model. The "Portrait of a Star" activity can easily be integrated into an art class or a language arts class on creative writing. The other activities listed in this chapter also can be integrated just as easily.

† † †

PORTRAIT OF A STAR
(Self-Concept Development Activity No. 1)

Objective: To have children be able to identify five self characteristics which make them a "star."

Level: Primary and Intermediate

Materials Needed: Picture of each student, large construction paper, markers or crayons, paste or glue

Procedure:

 1. Arrange for each child to bring in a recent photo of self or take a photo of each child prior to the day of the activity.

 2. Have each child cut a large five pointed star out of construction paper. (A helpful procedure is to have a pattern available for those who need one.)

3. Instruct each child to paste his/her photo in the center of the star; then, write a special characteristic in each of the five points of the star.

4. Provide time for the children to share their stars with the class.

5. Display the stars on a bulletin board with a catchy title such as "The Stars in the 4th Grade Galaxy," "A Visit to Our Milky Way," or "See the Stars of Gollywood."

Evaluation: Each child will complete a star and be able to tell the class members about at least 2 of the 5 characteristics which make him/her a star.

Variations:

1. If photos are not readily available, have each child draw a self photo in the center of the star.

2. Have the children make several stars to indicate strengths in various areas such as a sports star, a reading star, etc.

† † †

PERSONAL TIME LINES
(Self-Concept Development Activity No. 2)

Objective: To help children become more aware of significant events in their lives.

Level: Intermediate

Materials Needed: 6 inch x 36 inch strips of oaktag, ruler, markers, crayons

Procedure:

1. Draw a line on the chalkboard and indicate that it represents a period of one month's time.

2. Ask the children to think of important events which have happened in the last month. This could include such things as a holiday, special field trip, big test, class visitor, etc.

3. Indicate the timing of the events along the time line in chronological order, and draw a picture at the point on the time line when the event occurred.

4. Provide each child with a sheet of 6 inch x 36 inch oaktag to make his/her own personal time line beginning with birth date and continuing to the present. Suggest that they include a maximum of 5 to 6 significant events along the time line.

5. If the children need further direction regarding the types of events to include, suggest such things as a special gift, moving to a new home, birth of a sibling, a memorable vacation, etc.

6. Allow the children enough time to share their time lines with the class if they wish.

Evaluation: Children will be able to chronicle significant events of their life based on their personal "time line." To help children clarify their information, pose questions such as:

1. What are some things that help you remember that special event?

2. Would people in your family also categorize that as a special event?

3. Is any event on your list special only to you?

Variations:

1. Reduce the time period of the time line to one year in the child's life.

2. Make a picture time line and ask each child to place photos along appropriate places on their time line.

3. Have children extend their time line for a period of 5 or 10 years and ask them to speculate on significant events in the future.

✝ ✝ ✝

FEELING BOX
(Self-Concept Development Activity No. 3)

Objective: To provide children with an opportunity to talk about their feelings.

Level: Primary and Intermediate

Materials Needed: Several small boxes decorated with Con-Tact paper, pieces of paper with feeling words written on them

Procedure:

1. Prepare the boxes with a variety of feelings words inside. Be sure to include more than just happy, sad, and angry.

2. Divide the class into several groups and provide a feeling box for each group.

3. Have each child close his/her eyes and draw a feeling card from the box. Have each child tell the group about something that made him/her feel that way or make a face to show the feeling and have the group guess what his/her feeling card says.

4. Continue the activities in small groups until each child has had at least two opportunities to share feelings.

Evaluation: All children will have had at least two opportunities to discuss special feelings. The discussion following the activity could focus on:

1. What kinds of feelings are easiest for you to express?

2. Are some feelings more difficult to talk about?

3. Do you experience certain kinds of feelings more often than others? Which ones?

Variations:

1. Have a "Feeling of the Day" activity in which one specific feeling is discussed and each child has an opportunity to give a personal description of the feeling.

2. Use circles for the feelings box and have children draw faces on the circles and put them in the box. When a child chooses a face from the box, he/she must name the feeling, then tell what makes him/her feel that way.

✝ ✝ ✝

NAME GAME
(Self-Concept Development Activity No. 4)

Objective: To provide children with an opportunity to express individual characteristics and personality traits.

Level: Intermediate

Materials Needed: Construction paper, markers, and crayons

Procedure:

1. Instruct the children to make a large seasonal object from construction paper. (Pumpkin, tree, flower, heart, shamrock, Easter egg, etc.)

2. Have each child spell his/her name vertically down the left side of the paper.

3. Have each child write a word or short phrase beginning with that letter to describe himself/herself. Examples:

L   istens carefully
E   asy to get along with
S   ays nice things to people
L   ikeable
I   ntelligent
E   ager to get good grades

C   heerful and friendly
A   rtistic
R   eady to work
O   ften shares pencils
L   ikes to play kickball

4. Provide time for the children to share their name characteristics with the class.

5. Utilize the project to make an attractive bulletin board.

Evaluation: All children will complete a name game shape and share at least two self characteristics with the class. To promote discussion, the following questions could be posed:

1. Would you have liked to add some other characteristics but couldn't because they didn't match the letters in your name?

2. Did you have trouble with any specific letters in terms of your characteristics?

3. Were you sometimes able to think of many characteristics for certain letters?

Variations:

1. Have the children draw names and write a description of another child in the group rather than doing their own name.

2. Allow the children to work in small groups of 3 or 4 and help one another prepare the name characteristics.

✝ ✝ ✝

CRYSTAL BALL
(Self-Concept Development Activity No. 5)

Objective: To provide an opportunity for the children to express their dreams, goals, and aspirations for the future.

Level: Intermediate

Materials Needed: Construction paper circles 12 inches in diameter, markers, and crayons

Procedure:

1. Discuss crystal balls and their use; that fortune tellers use them to predict the future.

2. Ask the children to think about their future. What will they be doing 5 years from now?, 10 years?, 20 years?

3. Provide a large paper circle for each child and instruct them to divide with lines the circle into three parts. Label one section 5 years, one section 10 years, and one section 20 years.

4. Have each child draw a picture or write a brief paragraph in each section to tell what he/she expects to be doing during each time period in his/her life.

5. Allow the children to make a construction paper base for their crystal ball and place it on the bulletin board under a caption such as "What's in Your Crystal Ball?"

Evaluation: Children will be able to choose one of the three sections of their crystal ball and talk with the class about it. A helpful procedure is to remind them to think of current interests and strengths and how they influence what they predict for their future.

Variations:

1. Provide three different smaller colored circles for each child and request that they have a crystal ball for each time period rather than dividing the one large circle.

2. Have the children to take blank crystal balls home and ask their parent(s) to tell what they think their child will be doing in those same time periods. Have the children compare parents' perceptions with their own. Discuss.

† † †

WHAT BUGS YOU
(Self-Concepts Development Activity No. 6)

Objective: To assist children in identifying things that bother them.

Level: Intermediate

Materials: Box of construction paper scraps, pipe cleaners, hole puncher, paste,and scissors

Procedure:

1. Discuss with the children things that "bug" people. To assist them,give some examples such as "When people don't keep their promises" or "When my little sister loses pieces to my game."

2. Provide the children with scrap materials and suggest that they make a weird bug. Remind them that it doesn't need to look like a real bug. They may just use their imagination.

3. Allow for extra creativity by providing pipe cleaners for legs or antenna, a hole puncher for making polka dots, etc.

4. Give each child a piece of white paper (about 1 inch x 5 inches) to write a sentence to tell what bugs him/her.

5. Use the bugs to decorate the bulletin board (with the slip of paper placed directly beneath the child's bug.)

6. Provide time for class discussion about the things that bug them.

Evaluation: Children will be able to describe to the class one thing that bugs them and tell what it is about that thing that is so bothersome.

Variations:

1. Use a large centipede for the bulletin board and make it a "class bug." Have each child write on the centipede's body about something that bugs him/her.

2. Have the children work in small groups to make a group bug. Let each child write what bugs him/her on a sheet of paper which hangs beneath the group bug on the bulletin board.

✝ ✝ ✝

SILHOUETTE ACTIVITY
(Self-Concept Development Activity No. 7)

Objective: To facilitate children identifying at least five personal interests or hobbies.

Level: Primary and Intermediate

Materials Needed: White and colored construction paper, filmstrip projector or other light source, scissors, paste, crayons, markers, and pictures

Procedure:

1. Prepare a silhouette of each child by shining a light on him/her, thus forming a profile and tracing around it.

2. Instruct the children to cut out the silhouette and paste it on a sheet of colored construction paper.

3. When silhouettes have been prepared, have each child either cut pictures from magazines and paste onto the silhouette to show five things in which he/she is interested, or draw pictures of five things he/she likes to do.

4. Assist each child so that when completed, his/her silhouette provides a picture of his/her interests.

5. Display silhouettes on the bulletin board or provide time for children to share their silhouettes with the class.

Evaluation: Children will identify at least 4 or 5 interests or hobbies as part of the silhouette activity. In the discussion portion of the activity, each child will be able to discuss in some detail, one of his/her special interests or hobbies.

Variation: If children do not wish to put anything directly onto the silhouette, permit them to write a brief paragraph or draw pictures on a separate sheet and attach it to the bottom of the silhouette.

† † †

VALUES AUCTION
(Self-Concept Development Activity No. 8)

Objective: To have the children to examine their personal goals and priorities.

Level: Intermediate

Materials Needed: A values auction sale sheet for each child

Procedure:

1. Explain what an auction is and tell the children that each of them will have the sum of $5,000 to bid on items of importance to them. Remind them that items are sold to the highest bidder.

2. Present the list of items for auction. Some of the items which could be included in the auction bill of sale include the following:

   a. to always be happy,

   b. to make the best grades in the class,

   c. to own all the books you ever want,

   d. to be the top athlete in school,

   e. to be the most popular child in class,

   f. to be able to help other people,

   g. to grow up to be a movie star,

   h. to be the class leader,

   i. to live in a beautiful house,

   j. to be able to tell other people what to do,

   k. to always be healthy, and

   l. to have a happy family.

3. Instruct the children to review the list and decide which items are most important to them. Then they should write down the amount they would be willing to bid to attain that item.

4. Conduct the auction and "sell" each of the values to the highest bidder.

5. Evaluate the sale. Are the children happy with their purchases? Would others change their bids in the future to obtain an item they really want?

Evaluation: Children will, at the completion of the activity, have determined which of the values from the list were most important to them. To further facilitate understanding, as part of the discussion, the counselor/teacher may want to pose some of the following questions:

1. Was anyone willing to spend their entire amount on just one item?

2. How did you feel when you didn't have enough money to purchase a value you wanted?

3. Are some other items which are not on the list ones which you really value?

Variations:

1. Use the auction as a group consensus activity by dividing the children into groups and having the children decide as a group what items they wish to bid on for the auction.

2. Have children write lists of 3 things which are important to them. Use these items to prepare the auction bill of sale.

† † †

THE WISHING BOX
(Self-Concept Development Activity No. 9)

Objective: To provide children with an opportunity to think about something that is really important to them.

Level: Primary

Materials Needed: A brightly wrapped gift box with ribbon or bow

Procedure:

1. Discuss "special gifts." Ask the children to describe a special gift they received and tell why that gift was important to them. (The teacher/counselor should be prepared to share information about his/her special gift also.)

2. Talk about prized possessions. What makes them so special. (Children will no doubt share information such as the special person who gave them the gift, the gift itself, the special meaning behind the gift, etc.)

3. Show the gift wrapped package to the class. Have them think about it. Then say "If this gift box was for you, what would you like it to contain?"

4. Provide time for the children to share their wishes, or if you prefer, write a brief paragraph or draw a picture of their special wish.

5. Use the material for a bulletin board by attaching the box to the bulletin board and putting slips of paper with the wishes on them in a circle around the box.

Evaluation: Children will identify something that is very important to them and will be able to tell the class why that item/thing/person is important to them. Each child should have the opportunity to tell at least one other person what would be in his/her "Wishing Box."

Variation: Have each child make their own "gift box" from a small milk carton and draw or write on a piece of paper what their special gift would be.

† † †

WHAT WOULD YOU BUY?
(Self-Concept Development Activity No. 10)

Objective: To enable children to participate in a decision making activity based on their personal values.

Level: Upper Primary and Intermediate

Materials Needed: Mail order catalogs, pencils, and paper

Procedure:

1. Display a mail order catalog and tell the children that some people call them "wish books" because they wish they could have certain items.

2. Ask the children if they have ever looked through a catalog and wished they could have certain items.

3. Explain that the class is going to pretend that each of them has $300.00 to spend and that they are to prepare an order from the catalog not to exceed their $300.00.

4. Allow sufficient time for the children to make decisions based on their own personal values.

5. Provide time for the children to share their orders with the class if they wish.

6. Take time to discuss differences in likes, values, and interests.

Evaluation: Children will complete a "wish list" of items not to exceed $300.00. Following the activity, questions to be posed might include:

1. How did you make decisions about what things were important to you?

2. Did anyone go over the $300.00 and have to eliminate something? If so, how did you decide what to eliminate?

3. Can you think of something you might want that money can't buy?

Variations:

1. Limit the children to a number of items from the catalog rather than a specific price figure (Although the dollar figure provides some math reinforcement, also.)

2. Have the children work in dyads and share the information with a partner rather than with the entire class.

✝ ✝ ✝

MY FAVORITE PLACE
(Self Concept Development Activity No. 11)

Objective: To provide an opportunity for the children to identify a place which has a special meaning to them.

Level: Intermediate

Materials Needed: Shoe boxes, construction paper, various other scrap materials, cotton for clouds, twigs for trees, etc., paste and scissors.

Procedure:

1. Ask the children to close their eyes, relax, and picture in their minds their very favorite place.

2. While the children are relaxing and thinking about this favorite place, ask them to think about why they like that place and what are some things that make it special.

3. Encourage the children to tell the class something about their favorite place.

4. Give each child a shoe box and provide time for them to make a diorama to show their special place.

5. When they have completed it, suggest that they make construction paper people that we might see if we visited their ideal place. (If they paste a bent drinking straw on the backs of their people, they can stand them up in the diorama.)

6. Display the completed dioramas.

Evaluation: The children will each complete a diorama which shows a place which is special to them. They also should be able to tell the class why the place is special to them.

Variation: *If the dioramas seem a bit time consuming, the same project may be completed by having the children draw pictures of their favorite place and writing a brief narrative to go along with it.*

† † †

WISHING ON A BIRTHDAY CAKE
(Self-Concept Development Activity No. 12)

Objective: *To have the children identify things which are important to them in their lives.*

Level: *Primary and Intermediate*

Materials Needed: *Construction paper, crayons, markers, scissors, and paste.*

Procedure:

1. *Provide each child with a large piece of construction paper (to make a birthday cake) and several small strips (for making candles).*

2. *Explain to the children that they are to cut out the cake and cut out one candle for each year of age.*

3. *Ask the children to make one wish for each candle and write the wish on the candle.*

4. *Instruct them to paste the candles on their birthday cake.*

5. *After the children have completed the activity and shared their wishes, discuss the different kinds of things for which people wished.*

   a. *Did some people wish for things which would benefit others rather than themselves?*

    b.   Were some of the wishes for things that are non-material?

    c.   Do you think any of your wishes will ever come true?

6. Use the cakes for an interesting decorative bulletin board.

Evaluation: Children will be able to identify their own personal wishes for each candle on their birthday cake and give a brief explanation as to why the particular wishes are important to them.

Variations:

1. Use the theme of "Wishing on a Star" to have the children think of things for which they would wish.

2. Use the idea of a magic genie who gives three wishes. Have the children describe their three wishes.

† † †

THINGS I'M GOOD AT
(Self-Concept Development Activity No. 13)

Objective: To assist children to identify their strengths.

Level: Intermediate

Materials Needed: Paper and pencils

Procedure:

1. Talk about things people are good at doing. Have several children share something about their strengths as they see them.

2. Discuss the fact that each person has different strengths; some may be academic, some physical, some social, but everyone is good at something.

3. Provide children with a sheet of paper and ask them to list their strengths. Tell them they may list as many as they wish, but they must have at least 3.

4. Collect the papers and put them in folders for a marking period.

5. Review the papers at the end of each marking period (or at least four times a year.) Have the children add at least one thing to their strength list each time.

6. Make note of changes in children's attitudes towards their personal strengths. Commend them for being more positive about themselves.

Evaluation: Each child will identify at least three personal strengths during the initial activity and will be able to evaluate and identify at least one additional strength at a subsequent review with the teacher/counselor.

Variation: Have each child identify something he/she can do and would be willing to help others learn to do better. Then make a classroom helper list:

1. If you want help with math facts, ask _____ .

2. If you want to learn to run faster, talk to _____ .

3. If you want to keep a neater desk, ask _____ for some tips.

✝ ✝ ✝

HOW WOULD THEY DESCRIBE YOU
(Self-Concept Development Activity No. 14)

Objective: To encourage children to describe themselves as they think significant persons in their life would describe them.

Level: Intermediate

Materials Needed: *Paper with lists of descriptors on them, paper, scissors, and paste*

Procedure:

1. Ask the children to think of three people who are important to them.

2. Instruct them to divide their paper into four columns and write the name of their significant persons at the top of three columns and their own name at the top of their fourth column.

3. Provide each child with a list of descriptors such as:

neat	popular	friendly	uncooperative
pretty	unpopular	generous	unfriendly
sloppy	intelligent	stingy	unpopular
ugly	stupid	handsome	strong
courteous	weird	cooperative	weak
			honest

4. Suggest that the children decide how each of the three persons would describe them and how they would describe themselves. They may feel free to use the same word more than once and to add their own words.

5. Indicate that they should use at least three descriptors under each person's name.

Evaluation: *Children will be able to identify at least three adjectives which they feel significant persons in their life would use to describe them.*

Variation: *Instruct children to label the four columns as follows: Teacher, Parent, Best Friend, Self. Utilizing the same list of descriptors, have the children complete the activity again. Watch for positive versus negative descriptors.*

† † †

THINGS I LOVE TO DO
(Self-Concept Development Activity No. 15)

Objective: To provide children with an opportunity to evaluate things which are important to them.

Level: Intermediate

Materials Needed: Pencil and paper

Procedure:

1. Discuss with the children some of the things they like to do. Explain that in this activity they will be evaluating some of these things in terms of how important they are to them.

2. Provide children with a sheet of paper and ask them to list at least 10 things that they really enjoy doing.

3. Then ask the children to label their choices by answering the following items:

   a. Which two activities are your very favorite? (Put a star behind them.)

   b. Which two are your least favorite? (Put a question mark behind them.)

   c. Which ones cost money? (Put a dollar sign behind them.)

   d. Which ones are things that your whole family enjoys? (Put an F standing for family behind them.)

   e. Which ones do you enjoy doing by yourself? (Put an A behind them).

4. When the children have completed the activity, ask them if they learned anything about themselves from this activity. (Permit time for sharing.)

5. Suggest that the children keep these lists and reevaluate them from time to time.

Evaluation: The children will be able to identify at least 10 things which they enjoy doing and will be able to analyze these activities according to cost, type of activity, etc.

Variations:

1. Have children divide their paper into four sections and label each section with one of the four seasons. Then direct them to write at least five activities which they enjoy during each season of the year. Complete this activity by discussing the limitation of certain activities by the weather.

2. Have children divide their paper into 3 sections and label them: Alone, With Friends, and With Family. Then describe five activities under each column. Discuss and evaluate.

✝ ✝ ✝

MY VALUES JOURNAL
(Self-Concept Development Activity No. 16)

Objective: To assist the children to consider what types of things they value in their life.

Level: Intermediate

Materials Needed: Paper and pencil, construction paper, crayons, markers, and stapler

Procedure:

1. Talk about and define values. Provide time for the children to share information about something they value.

2. Give each child a large piece of construction paper and ask them to fold it and decorate it as a cover for their values journal.

3. Have the children make their booklet by stapling five pages inside their cover.

4. Instruct the children to put the following headings on their five pages.

   a. My goals for this year.

   b. My goals for the future.

   c. Things that are important to me.

   d. Something about my family that I value.

   e. Current problems in my life.

5. Provide more specific direction for some children if necessary, but most will be able to complete the activity based on the titles provided.

6. Assure children that information is personal and need not be shared with classmates if they choose not to do so.

Evaluation: Children will complete a confidential values journal which identifies current and future goals, problems, and values.

Variation: Have the children keep a journal for a period of 1 to 2 weeks on the following topics:

1. Important things that happened to me today.

2. My feelings about these things.

✝ ✝ ✝

SETTING PRIORITIES—TAKE A STAND
(Self-Concept Development Activity No. 17)

Objective: To help children state a position based on their beliefs and values.

Level: Primary and Intermediate

Materials Needed: Unfinished stories for discussion and reaction, chalkboard, and chalk

Procedure:

1. Talk with the children regarding decisions they have made. Ask them to think about why they made the specific decisions. Point out that our own personal values help us determine how we will act in a situation.

2. Explain that the class is going to participate in a decision making activity based on their values.

3. Write the words "Yes," "Not Sure," and "No" high on the chalkboard and spaced about 5 to 6 feet apart.

4. Present a dilemma such as the following to the class. "You know that your best friend tore a page out of a library book, but the teacher is blaming someone else." Would you tell what you know?

5. Choose 5 to 6 children to "Take A Stand" on the issue by going to the chalkboard and standing under the word that describes what they would do. Provide discussion time for children to give reasons for their choices.

6. Continue with the activity until all children have had an opportunity to participate. Some additional types of situations are as follows:

   a. John gave you a cookie at lunchtime. Now he says you owe him a favor and he wants to copy the answers from your math paper. Would you allow him?

b. You don't really like Mary very much because she is always talking behind people's backs and saying things to hurt people's feelings. She just called and invited you to be her guest at the amusement park. Would you go?

Evaluation: Children will participate in an activity which requires that they make a decision regarding a specific situation and be able to explain reasons for their decision.

Variation: Have the children "Take A Stand" on various items such as the following: (Place the letters a, b, and c on the chalkboard for choices.)

1. You just had a birthday and got your very favorite gift. Was it

   a. a bicycle,

   b. a portable T.V. for your room, or

   c. your very own telephone?

2. You received a surprising gift of $100.00. Would you

   a. have a party and invite your friends,

   b. put it in the bank, or

   c. spend it on something you really want?

3. Which is most important in a friendship:

   a. loyalty,

   b. generosity, or

   c. honesty?

✝   ✝   ✝

A PIECE OF MY LIFE
(Self-Concept Development Activity No. 18)

Objective: To enable the children to consider and evaluate how they spend their time each day.

Level: Intermediate

Materials Needed: One large (12" diameter) circle, pencil, and ruler for each child.

Procedure:

1. Explain to the children that they are going to be making a "pie" to show how they spend an average day.

2. Provide a chalkboard example of a typical day in your own life by drawing "pie" slices to show time approximations.

3. Be sure the children understand that their circle stands for a 24 hour day and they are to divide it into sections to show how their time is spent. (Explain that if they sleep 8 hours, that accounts for 1/3 of the circle.)

4. Instruct each child to make a daily pie to show how their time is spent. Provide directions such as asking "How many hours do you spend

   a. sleeping,

   b. going to school,

   c. playing outside,

   d. watching T.V.,

   e. doing homework or reading,

   f. with family (including mealtime), and

   g. doing chores?"

5. Provide time for the children to share their pies. They may find the results very eye-opening.

Evaluation: The children will be able to identify how they spend their day in terms of a total 24 hour period of time.

Variation: Ask each child to keep a diary of a day in their life based on a 24 hr. time schedule beginning with the time they got out of bed. Give an illustration such as the following:

7:00-7:30	Got up and got ready for school
7:30-8:00	Ate breakfast
8:00-8:45	Watched T.V.
8:45-9:00	Walked to school
9:00-11:45	Morning school subjects
11:45-12:30	Lunch etc.

✝ ✝ ✝

WHO ARE THESE PEOPLE
(Self-Concept Development Activity No. 19)

Objective: To assist children in identifying other persons who make a significant impact on their life.

Level: Intermediate

Materials Needed: Paper and pencil

Procedure:

1. Guide the children to develop a "Who Are Those People" worksheet in the following manner:

   a. Draw a circle (about the size of a half dollar) in the center of your paper. Put your name in the center.

b. Draw 7 more circles (about the size of a quarter) in various places on the paper. Under each of these circles, write the following labels:

(1.) Parent
(2.) Best Friend
(3.) Favorite Aunt
(4.) Favorite Uncle
(5.) Grandparent
(6.) Important Teacher
(7.) Other Important Person

c. In the center of each of the circles write the name of each person you have described.

d. Think of why these 7 people are important in your life.

2. Provide some time for the children to share information about the special people in their lives.

3. Have the children describe what kinds of things they enjoy doing with their special persons.

Evaluation: The children will consider how several significant persons in their lives affect their day to day living and identify at least one way that each person is special.

Variation: Ask the children to draw portraits of each of their seven people and to place them in the setting they most enjoy being with these persons.

✝ ✝ ✝

WHAT I CAN DO WITHOUT
(Self-Concept Development Activity No. 20)

Objective: To provide an opportunity for children to make some decisions on the importance of certain needs in their daily lives.

Level: Intermediate

Materials Needed: Pencil and Paper

Procedure:

1. Talk with the children about things they do daily in their life such as sleep, eat, watch T.V., play, go to school, argue, do homework, etc.

2. Ask children to make a list of 10 things which they do everyday.

3. When their list is complete, suggest that they evaluate their list and decide what one thing on that list they could do without for three days.

4. After children have decided, ask them to try doing without that item for three days and be ready to report on their progress after the experiment.

5. Follow up with a discussion of the experiment. Be sure to cover the following types of questions.

   a. Were you able to do without the item for three days?

   b. Was it difficult to do without your particular item?

   c. If you gave up, how did you feel about it?

Evaluation: The children will be able to experience "doing without" important items in their life and will be able to share the effect of this experience on their day to day life.

Variation: Suggest that the children as a group decide on one thing they would like to do without for a week. (No, it can't be Math class)   This might provide an excellent opportunity to have the class try to stop arguing or tattling for a week. At the end of the week, point out all of the positive benefits of the experiment.

† † †

IDEAL LIVING PLAN
(Self-Concept Development Activity No. 21)

Objective: To assist the children in examining their lifestyle and consider what things are important to them.

Level: *Intermediate*

Materials Needed: *Pencil and paper, construction paper, and markers*

Procedure:

1. Ask the children to close their eyes and picture what their room would look like if they could have it exactly as they wanted it.

2. Provide time for a brief discussion of some of the types of things children would put in their ideal room.

3. Give the children a piece of paper and ask them to describe:

   a. The types of furniture they would have.

   b. Accessories needed, i.e., pictures, plants, etc.

   c. Any other things that they would like to have in their ideal room.

4. When this has been completed, give the children a piece of construction paper so they can draw the floor plan for their ideal room.

5. Display floor plans on the bulletin board.

Evaluation: *Each child will complete an ideal living plan which identifies at least 4 to 5 items which he/she feels would be essential to a "perfect" room.*

Variation: *Provide some decorative catalogs and home improvement magazines with pictures of room settings. Have the children cut pictures from these magazines to create their ideal room in terms of color schemes, decorator touches, etc.)*

† † †

HARVEST OF SKILLS
(Self-Concept Development Activity No. 22)

Objective: To encourage children to evaluate their skills in terms of strengths and weaknesses.

Level: Intermediate

Materials Needed: List of skills, paper, and pencil

Procedure:

1. Discuss strengths and weaknesses. Point out that everyone has some things that they are very good at doing and some things that they need to improve. Suggest that children give some thoughts to some of their skills and some things they need to improve.

2. Have children brainstorm some of the things that may be on the various lists of children their age. List all of the items mentioned on the chalkboard. Some possibilities include:

   a. playing kickball
   b. sewing
   c. swimming
   d. riding a bike
   e. doing chores
   f. drawing
   g. handwriting
   h. helping with cooking
   i. babysitting
   j. spelling
   k. multiplication tables
   l. making friends

3. Give children a piece of paper and instruct them to draw two baskets on the paper for harvesting their skills.

4. Then suggest that they fill one basket with 5 to 6 special skills or strengths. (This can be done by drawing apples, pumpkins, etc., in the basket and writing the skill on the object.)

5. The other basket should contain at least 3 things which children feel they need to improve.

6. Provide time for group sharing of their harvest basket of skills.

Evaluation: Children will each be able to identify at least five individual strengths and three weaknesses.

Variation: This activity can be done by having many different baskets—each with a skill on it. Students who feel they have that skill will put their name on a slip of paper and put it in the basket.

✝ ✝ ✝

UNFINISHED SENTENCES
(Self-Concept Development Activity No. 23)

Objective: To provide children with an opportunity to increase self awareness and feelings of self-worth.

Level: Primary and Intermediate

Materials Needed: List of unfinished sentences for sharing

Procedure:

1. Arrange the children in a large circle.

2. Explain to them that today they will be thinking about themselves, their strengths, their feelings, and their relationships with others.

3. Ask the children to number off by 5s so that there will be several number 1s, number 2s, etc.

4. Begin with the first unfinished sentence and indicate who will respond, i.e., "I would like all number 4s to complete this statement."

5. Use statements similar to the following:

    a. I am very good at . . . .

    b. I get angry when . . . . .

    c. My friends like the way I . . . .

    d. If I were the teacher I'd . . . .

    e. One of my favorite things is . . . .

    f. Something that is hard for me to do is . . . .

    g. I feel jealous when . . . .

    h. I would like to go to . . . .

    i. My favorite school activity is . . . .

6. When the children have completed the activity, discuss similarities and differences.

Evaluation: The children will be able to participate successfully in the activity by completing the unfinished sentences provided.

Variation:

1. Divide the class into small groups and give a list of unfinished sentences to each group. Children share information within their group.

2. Provide each child with a slip of paper with one unfinished sentence on it. When the child's turn comes, he/she completes the sentence, then chooses 3 other children to complete it.

✝ ✝ ✝

"ME" SHIRT
(Self-Concept Development Activity No. 24)

Objective: To encourage children to share information about things that make them special persons.

Level: Primary and Intermediate

Materials Needed: Large piece of construction paper, crayons, markers, paste, yarn, old magazines, scissors, glitter, etc.

Procedure:

1. Discuss T-Shirts. They usually have a picture or some type of special decoration on them. Provide a few minutes for the children to tell the class about their favorite T-shirt.

2. Explain to the children that they are going to make a "me" shirt to tell the class about themselves. Some of the things they may want to draw on their "me" shirt include

   a. family members,

   b. pets,

   c. a favorite place to visit, and/or

   d. favorites—food, sport, color, TV show etc.

3. Give each child a large piece of construction paper and instruct them to draw a large T-shirt on the paper and cut it out.

4. Provide ample time for students to complete the decorations on their "me" shirt to show things about themselves.

5. Display the "me" shirt on the classroom clothesline.

Evaluation: *Each child will complete a "me" shirt which identifies at least 5 special characteristics or qualities.*

Variation: *Provide instructions for the children, but have them complete their "me" shirt at home. Hang them on the classroom clothesline and ask class members to guess which shirt belongs to which child.*

✝ ✝ ✝

BIBLIOGRAPHY

Beane, J.A., Lipka, R.P. & Ludewig, J.W. (1980). Synthesis of research on self-concept. *Educational Leadership*, Vol 38.

Borba, M., & Borba, C. (1978). *Self-esteem: A classroom affair*. Minneapolis: Winston Press.

Borba, M., & Borba, C. (1982). *Self-esteem: A classroom affair*, Vol. II. Minneapolis: Winston Press.

Clemes, H., & Bean, R. (1981). *The key to your child's well-being*. New York: Keystone Publishing.

Clemes, H., & Bean, R. (1980). *How to raise children's self-esteem*. San Jose: Enrich Div./Ohaus.

Davis, D.E. (1977). *My friends and me*. Circle Pines, MN: American Guidance Service.

Dinkmeyer, D., & Caldwell, E. (1970). *Developmental counseling and guidance: A comprehensive school approach.* New York: McGraw-Hill.

Eldridge, M.S., Wittmer, J.M., Barakowski. R., & Bauer, L. (1977). The effect of a group guidance program on the self concepts of EMR children. *Measurement and Evaluation in Guidance*, Vol. 9.

Farnette, C., Forte, I., & Harris, B. (1977). *I've got me and I'm glad.* Nashville, TN: Incentive Publications.

Farnette, C., Forte, I., & Harris, B. (1979). *People need each other.* Nashville, TN: Incentive Publications.

Knight, M., Graham, T., Juliano, R., Miksza, S., & Tonnies, P. (1982). *Teaching children to love themselves*. Englewood Cliffs, NJ: Prentice Hall.

Morgan, C., & Jackson, W. (1980). Guidance as a curriculum. *Elementary School Guidance and Counseling*, Vol 15.

Reasoner, R.W. (1982). *Building self-esteem*. Palo Alto, CA: Consulting Psychologists Press.

Simon, S.B. (1974). *Meeting yourself halfway*. Niles, IL: Argus Communications.

Wrenn, C.G. (1980). The importance of believing in yourself or building a more positive self image. *The School Counselor*, Vol. 27.

CHAPTER **10**

DIMENSION
OF COGNITIVE
DEVELOPMENT

Much of each elementary child's school experience is spent on the development of cognitive skills because many teachers think that this is the most important skill to be emphasized within the educational system. While this is true to some extent, we promote the idea that cognitive development is just one of the five dimensions which needs to be addressed. The dimension of cognitive development must be combined with those of social, physical, career, and self-concept development if children are to achieve to their optimum potential.

RESEARCH ON COGNITIVE DEVELOPMENT

In order for children to become more capable of dealing effectively with their environment, certain abilities must be strengthened. These include such factors as effective use of thinking skills, ability to process information effectively, development of better listening skills, and improvement of decision making ability.

According to Thompson and Rudolph (1983), four blocks are in the development of children's thought processes. They are

1. egocentrism block—shown by the inability to see another's point of view,

2. centration block—shown by the inability to focus on more than one aspect of a problem,

3. reversibility block—shown by the inability to work from front to back and back to front to solve problems, and

4. transformation block—shown by the inability to put events in proper order. (p. 19)

In attempting to work through these blocks, children must receive assistance in the form of structured activities. Wirth (1977) suggested that such activities which are aimed at improving academic achievement must integrate affective components in order to be most successful. This belief is also supported by Kaczkowski (1979) who stated that "a basic skill area like arithmetic or reading can be used as a vehicle not only for remediating a child's skill but also for enhancing his or her level of self-concept and level of aspiration" (p. 50).

Activities which are provided on the next several pages have been designed to strengthen specific cognitive abilities. This seems to be a critical factor in helping each child to achieve maximum potential. Piaget (1965) reinforced this belief when he stated that "cognitive competence is the child's chief mainstay to reality and hence the chief bulwark of his general emotional stability" (p. 29).

NEEDS TO BE ADDRESSED

1. The need to be able to motivate oneself to achieve a goal

All children need to be able to develop self motivation skills. This can be achieved through goal setting activities where children can self monitor their progress.

2. The need to express oneself both verbally and in writing

Very early in each child's school experience, the need to be able to express oneself becomes very apparent. Children need repeated opportunities for such expressions.

3. The need for variation in skill building activities

When building specific skills, much drill and practice is necessary. However, too much of any kind of drill becomes boring for children. For this reason, use a variety of activities when developing a particular skill.

4. The need to be aware of how one approaches learning

While most children learn best within a structured environment, many of them are not aware of their own personal learning style. They need opportunities to look objectively at personal style, habits, and behavior.

5. The need to look critically at one's own performance and evaluate progress

Most children rely heavily on input and feedback from teachers to determine their rate of academic progress. To be most successful, however, children must be able to utilize self evaluation techniques and strategies.

SKILLS TO BE DEVELOPED

1. Listening Skills

Although children should be utilizing listening skills throughout the school day, few of them receive much practice in developing good listening skills. Activities which are fun, yet promote listening skill-development are provided at the end of this chapter.

2. Thinking Skills

Higher order thinking skills such as analyzing, reasoning, and problem solving are necessary for children to be successful in school. Thinking skills should be developed from the simplest through the most complex. An excellent source for information on classifying these skills is the *Taxonomy of Educational Objectives Handbook* by Benjamin S. Bloom.

3. Processing Skills

Children need to develop the skill of processing, that is, they must be able to translate information received so that it is understandable and useable to them. The skill of processing is most effectively developed through practice.

4. Self-expression Skills

All children must have ample opportunities for self expression in verbal or written form. The "Travel Folder" activity provides a fun opportunity to practice this skill.

5. Goal Setting and Decision-making Skills

While many persons feel that young children aren't capable of setting goals, we promote the idea that goal setting and decision making skills should be introduced in kindergarten. One must keep in mind however, that those goals and decisions should be age appropriate. If children participate in such activities early, the skill will continue to develop as they progress through the educational system.

INTEGRATION OF
COGNITIVE DEVELOPMENT ACTIVITIES

Activities in this chapter have been designed to strengthen the cognitive development areas and can be readily integrated into the curriculum through the use of the Keystone Learning Model. To provide an example of how the activities could be integrated into the curriculum, we would suggest that the "Listening Game" which follows could readily be integrated into any subject area which emphasizes the importance and utilization of effective listening skills. The rules of the "Listening Game" could easily be integrated into any content area as a way of teaching children how to develop and improve their listening skills.

✝ ✝ ✝

THE LISTENING GAME
(Cognitive Development Activity No. 1)

Objective: *To assist children in learning better the importance of developing effective listening skills.*

Level: *Primary and Intermediate*

Materials Needed: *None*

Procedure:

1. *Discuss the importance of listening. Why is it important to listen carefully when participating in a conversation?*

2. *Explain to the children that they are going to participate in an experiment to see how well they listen.*

3. *Ask the children to sit in a circle so that they can see everyone else.*

4. *Introduce a subject of interest to the class for discussion and tell the children that before anyone speaks they must first summarize what the previous speaker said.*

5. *Assign observers to determine if class members are really listening and summarizing.*

6. *Practice this technique for about 10 minutes at least once each week to improve the children's listening skills.*

Evaluation: *Children will show evidence of effective listening skills by being able to successfully summarize the* previous speaker's comments. Those who have difficulty should be given additional practice.

Variations:

1. Play the "I went to the store" game to increase listening skills. (First child says, "I went to the store and bought milk." Second child says, "I went to the store and bought milk and oranges." Third child says, "I went to the store and bought milk, oranges and soap" etc. Continue until the list becomes too long for the children to remember.)

2. Use the previous activity to help children remember each other's names at the beginning of a new school year.

† † †

MYSTERY BOX
(Cognitive Development Activity No. 2)

Objective: To help children develop effective thinking and listening skills.

Level: Primary and Early Intermediate

Materials Needed: A mystery box with an object inside, chalk and chalkboard (for scorekeeping)

Procedure:

1. Show the children the mystery box and explain that they need to solve the mystery of what is in the box by asking questions about it. The following rules will apply:

   a. They may ask a maximum of 20 questions.

   b. If a child can guess what is in the box in fewer than 20 questions, that child is the winner and will have an extra special fun activity.

c. They must listen carefully and try to remember what has been said.

d. The child who guesses what the content is may bring in the next item for the mystery box.

2. Appoint a scorekeeper to tally the number of questions and someone to make sure everyone gets a turn to ask a question.

3. Continue with the game until the 20 questions have been asked or the content of the mystery box has been guessed.

Evaluation: Children should be able to identify the contents of the mystery box within the 20 question time limit. Although this may not happen initially, effective questioning strategies should begin to appear as the game continues. To assess individual skills, the activity can be done on a 1 to 1 basis in classroom teams.

Variations:

1. Rather than using a mystery box, have a child think of something he/she sees on the way to school and write it on a slip of paper. The children try to guess the mystery item.

2. Use colors, numbers, songs, etc., for this activity.

✝ ✝ ✝

BEHAVIOR CONTRACTING
(Cognitive Development Activity No. 3)

Objectives:

1. To help children learn the importance of commitment to a goal.

2. To encourage children to work to improve one or more aspects of their behavior.

Level: *Primary and Intermediate*

Materials Needed: *Specific behavior contracts based on individual child needs*

Procedure:

1. Decide upon the behavior which needs to be improved; it may be a social behavior such as encouraging a child to participate more fully in classroom activities; a learning behavior such as studying multiplication tables, or a specific behavior such as staying in one's seat.

2. Work with the child to develop the specifics of the contract—be sure to state the behavior in very specific terms, i.e.,

   a. Complete all daily math assignments.

   b. Raise your hand to speak.

3. Prepare the contract which contains the desired behavior; the consequences for not meeting the behavior and the rewards for successful attainment of the desired behavior (see example under variations).

4. Have the child and counselor/teacher both sign the contract.

5. Duplicate a copy of the contract and have the child take it home.

6. Review the contract with the child on a regular basis.

7. Reward the child with praise and encouragement.

Evaluation: *The children will successfully complete terms of their behavior contract. For those who do not, it would be advantageous to review the contract and set more attainable goals.*

Variations: Develop a group behavior plan based on classroom rules. A sample is provided below.

SAMPLE: Assertive Discipline Behavior Plan

Rules:

1. *Follow directions first time.*
2. *Work quietly, no calling out.*
3. *Leave seat only at appropriate times.*
4. *Walk quietly through the halls.*

Negative Consequences:

First Time—Name on Chalkboard

Second Time—Check behind name—10 minutes time out (in room)

Third Time—Check behind name—20 minutes time out (in room)

Fourth Time—Check behind name—sent to time out for 30 minutes with academic work to be completed.

Fifth Time—Check behind name—sent to principal and make call to parents.

Positive Consequences:

1. *One bean in jar each time that no names go on chalkboard.*
2. *One bean each time hall behavior is quiet.*
3. *Special visits to principal for sticker.*
4. *Two happy grams per day.*

If the class has 35 beans in jar by the end of the week they may choose one of the following:

1. *Popcorn Party*
2. *Special class visitor*
3. *Extra game time*
4. *Special art project*
5. *Lunch with teacher*
6. *VCR Cartoon or story*

✝ ✝ ✝

REINFORCEMENT FOR READING—BOOKWORMS
(Cognitive Development Activity No. 4)

Objective: To motivate children to achieve better reading skills and complete reading assignments.

Level: Primary and Intermediate

Materials Needed: Construction paper circles 3 inches in diameter, scissors, paste, crayons or markers

Procedure:

1. Explain to the children that they are going to make a "bookworm" to show how well they do in their reading work.

2. Ask each child to take a colored circle and make the head of his/her bookwork—each time a paper is completed in reading, children will add another segment (circle) to their bookworm. When a child has added 10 segments to the bookworm, he/she receives a special treat such as a sticker, a certificate, happy gram, etc.

3. Have segments added to the bookworm for perfect spelling papers and other reading related assignments.

Evaluation: Each child will have at least 10 segments on his/her bookworm.

Variations: This technique can be used with any academic subject and many different types of accounting procedures can be used. Examples include:

1. Color the pieces of bubble gum in the gumball machine.

2. Put a dot on the ladybug.

3. Place a leaf on the tree.

4. Color the eggs in the basket.

† † †

CREATIVE WRITING—DESIGN A TRAVEL FOLDER
(Cognitive Development Activity No. 5)

Objective: To enable children to have an opportunity to express themselves while improving their writing skills.

Level: Intermediate

Materials Needed: Samples of travel brochures, 8½ x 11 inch paper, crayons, pens or pencils

Procedure:

1. Talk about places the children have visited. Ask them to tell something they liked about their favorite place.

2. Show samples of travel folders. Discuss the kinds of things that are presented in the folder that make people want to visit the place. Also talk about illustrations and their purpose.

3. Ask the children to close their eyes and picture in their minds the perfect vacation spot.

4. Provide time for the children to develop a tri-fold travel brochure for their perfect "make-believe" vacation spot. The brochure should include:

   a. name of the place,

   b. description that tells why it would be a good place to visit,

   c. some illustrations of interesting things to see, and

   d. directions for travel to the make believe place.

5. Encourage the children to use their creativity in developing their brochure.

6. Provide time for sharing.

Evaluation: *Children will complete a travel folder and be able to describe it to the class.*

Variations:

1. Have the children work in groups and utilize larger paper to develop a travel brochure.

2. Provide various other "make-believe" scenarios for creative endeavors. What would children do if they could

   a. live underwater?

   b. live in the year 2050?

   c. have a rhinocerous for a pet?

   d. live a day it rained jellybeans?

3. Allow the children to develop their own make believe titles.

✝ ✝ ✝

MATH BALL GAME
(Cognitive Development Activity No. 6)

Objective: *To encourage children to learn math facts so that they can quickly state the answer to a math fact as presented.*

Level: *Primary and Lower Intermediate*

Materials Needed: *Large ball, tags with the numbers 1 and 2 on them*

Procedure:

1. Explain to the children that they will be playing a game to see which team knows the most math facts.

2. Instruct the children to sit in a circle. Provide number tags for the children in alternating order, i.e., 1 - 2, 1 - 2, etc. Have the children attach numbers to the front of their shirt with masking tape.

3. Explain that each time a child answers a fact correctly, his/her team gets a point. If he/she misses the person on his/her right has an opportunity to earn a point for his/her team.

4. Give the ball to a child on Team 1 and tell him/her to roll the ball to a child on Team 2 along with a math fact. The child says "Mary what is 8 times 9?" (or 5 minus 4) or (2 plus 1), etc. By the time the ball reaches Mary, she must provide an answer. If she is unable to do so, the ball goes to the person on her right who has an opportunity to get a point for his/her team by giving the correct answer to the fact.

5. Have the person, who correctly answers the question, roll the ball to another person on the opposite team and play continues.

Evaluation: Each child will know enough facts to successfully participate in the game. (Those who have difficulty may benefit from a peer tutor.)

Variations:

1. Use a large spinner for random choices following the same format.

2. Utilize this same type of activity for a fun drill with spelling words, language usage, etc.

† † †

STUDENT SURVEY OF STUDY HABITS
(Cognitive Development Activity No. 7)

Objective: To have children look objectively at their personal study habit behaviors.

Level: *Intermediate*

Materials Needed: *Survey sheet and pencils*

Procedure:

1. *Explain to the children that they will be completing a survey to determine the effectiveness of their study habits. Ask them if they feel they use good study habits.*

2. *Provide a brief survey to the children utilizing an Always, Sometimes, Never choice format. The following types of questions may be helpful.*

   a. *Do you set aside a certain time period each day for studying?*

   b. *Do you budget your time for each different subject?*

   c. *Do you study every weekend?*

   d. *Is it quiet in your study area?*

   e. *Are you away from TV, radio, or other distractions?*

   f. *Do you keep an assignment notebook or record of assignments?*

   g. *Do you have someone at home who will help you if you get stuck?*

   h. *Do you have a special place to study?*

   i. *Do you have the materials you need, i.e., pencils, eraser, etc.?*

   j. *Do you try to keep up to date on homework assignments?*

3. *Discuss the children's responses. Have them rate their study habit behaviors.*

4. Have a brainstorming session to prepare a list of 8 to 10 tips for developing good study habits.

5. Prepare a handout for the children to take home and share with their parents.

Evaluation: The children will each complete the survey and discuss it with their teacher/counselor. At the completion of the discussion, each child should choose one area for study skill improvement and develop a plan for individual growth.

Variation: Allow the children to develop skits to show good study habits. Provide time for them to present their skits to the class.

† † †

GOAL CHARTS
(Cognitive Development Activity No. 8)

Objective: To have the children evaluate objectively their progress in a specific area.

Level: Primary and Intermediate

Materials Needed: One goal chart for each child, crayons or markers for charting progress

Procedure:

1. Discuss the term "goal." Share with the children some personal goals and what was done to achieve them.

2. Ask the children if they have a goal they would like to work towards. Suggest some things, such as

   a. remembering to do homework each night,

   b. learning addition facts to 10,

   c. being at school on time each day,

   d. not missing any days of school, and

   e. improving grades on spelling tests.

3. Aid the children in preparing goal charts:

    a. For primary age children, a happy-sad face chart may work well. (If you achieve your goal this week, color the happy face. If not, color the sad face.)

    b. For older children a thermometer type chart is effective because the children can show upward (or downward) progress from week to week.

4. Have the children mark their goal chart for several weeks and praise them for effort and achievement.

5. Send a note home to their parents when they have attained their goal; provide a "good work certificate" for the child.

Evaluation: The children will discuss their goal attainment success with their teacher/counselor at the conclusion of the specified time limit.

Variations:

1. Have the class set a goal which they work toward as a group. Such goals as the following can be quite motivating.

    a. Walking quietly through the hall.

    b. Improving classroom attendance on a weekly basis.

    c. Improving class math test grades.

2. Have the class members work toward a specific goal for a special reinforcement, i.e., pizza party, special movie, extra kickball time. etc.

3. Have the class members chart steps as they move toward something they want to achieve, thus they can actually see whether they are progressing toward their goal.

✝ ✝ ✝

STUDENT SORTING
(Cognitive Development Activity No. 9)

Objective: To enable children to sort themselves into groups using good listening skills.

Level: Primary

Materials Needed: Slips of paper with Song Titles written on them (4 different titles with each title on 6 to 7 separate sheets of paper)

Procedure:

1. Explain to the children that they are going to participate in a game that involves practicing good listening skills.

2. Have each child select a slip of paper, look at it to see the title, and put it in their desk without showing it to anyone else.

3. When each person has a paper, tell them that when a signal is given they are to sing their song and move through the group trying to identify others who are singing the same song.

4. As the children identify others in their group, have them circulate through the class until they have separated themselves into four separate groups.

5. Explain to the children that each group will form a team for subsequent classroom activities.

Evaluation: The children will be able to find their group through effective listening skills. When they are all sorted into groups, suggest that they discuss as a group ways that helped them sort themselves into groups. Such questions as the following may be helpful:

1. How did you "turn off" the other sounds?

2. What did you do to "key in" on the particular sound you were listening for?

3. What did you do to communicate your sound to others?

Variations:

1. Utilize animal sounds, letter sounds, nursery rhymes, or other distinctive noises for the sorting activities.

2. Complete the activity by having individual children do the classroom sorting. Time the children to see how quickly they can accomplish the task.

✝ ✝ ✝

FUN MATH COMPUTATIONS
(Cognitive Development Activity No. 10)

Objective: To help the children use math skills to learn things about their classmates.

Level: Intermediate

Materials Needed: Pencil and paper

Procedure:

1. Explain to the children that they are going to be doing some math problems as a way of finding out more about their classmates.

2. Provide the class with a list of questions or problems.

   a. Find the total number of eyes and ears in the classroom.

   b. What is the total of brown eyed children?

   c. Find the total number of June birthdays.

d. Find the sum of the ages of all children in the room.

e. What is the total number of those children who have green as their favorite color?

3. When class members have completed the activity, compare answers and discuss how the children arrived at their solutions.

4. Point out that the children not only solved math problems, they learned a lot about their classmates as well.

Evaluation: The children will be able to answer all of the questions on the sheet by using math skills. At the conclusion of the activity, pose questions such as:

1. What did you learn about your class that you didn't know before?

2. How did you go about the process of finding answers to the questions?

3. Can you think of other ways that you use math skills in everyday life?

Variation: Have the children make up their own fun math problems for a "rainy day review" at some future time.

† † †

TUTORING PROGRAMS
(Cognitive Development Activity No. 11)

Objective: To provide the children with academic assistance in areas of need.

Level: Primary and Intermediate

Materials Needed: *Textbooks, papers, pencils, worksheets, and flash cards*

Procedure:

1. Talk with classroom teachers to identify those children whom they feel would benefit from services of a tutor.

2. Obtain tutor volunteers (Some possibilities are high school students, parent volunteers, senior citizens, retired teachers, or even high achieving students in the same grade).

3. Prepare a list of tutoring hints for volunteer tutors. Remember: In most cases volunteers are not trained teachers and will need some guidelines so they can be most effective during the time provided.

4. Carefully select and match tutor-child pairs. (Evaluate programs and compatibility frequently in the beginning of the program.)

5. Set aside a specific time period once or twice each week for tutoring services.

6. Reward progress of each child through the use of notes to parents, happygrams, phone calls, etc.

7. Maintain close contact with tutors and let them know how much you appreciate their efforts and dedication.

Evaluation: The children will show progress in the academic area for which the tutoring was provided. This will be determined through careful analysis of test data, child and teacher subjective comments, etc.

Variations: Provide information to present to parents in a booklet or handout format so that they will be able to help their children at home. Topics which may be helpful include

1. tips for studying spelling words,
2. math drills can be fun,
3. overcoming the homework battle at home, and
4. how to maintain your sanity while helping your child with schoolwork.

✝ ✝ ✝

BINGO (WORDO-MATHO) VARIATION
(Cognitive Development Activity No. 12)

Objective: *To provide the children with an opportunity for learning facts through use of a gaming format.*

Level: *Primary*

Materials Needed: *One bingo card for each child, and markers.*

Procedure

1. *Explain to the children that they will be learning a new game; if they know certain facts (words, sounds), they may win a prize.*

2. *Show the methods by which a person may win the game (Any 5 spaces in a row or 4 spaces plus the center FREE space will be a winner).*

3. *Have the children fill in their cards with spelling words, numbers, letters, or whatever is appropriate for the facts to be learned.*

4. *Play the game until several children have won the game.*

5. *Provide "prizes" such as stickers, certificates, etc., to children who win the games.*

6. *Reinforce the idea that if children know their words, sounds, math facts, etc., it will be easier to win the game.*

Evaluation: *The children will be able to successfully participate in the matho game. Those who still experience some difficulty may need a peer tutor for additional reinforcement.*

Variation: *The "bingo" format may be used in a variety of ways and is limited only by the creativity of the teacher/counselor.*

† † †

FAVORITE WORK FOLDER
(Cognitive Development Activity No. 13)

Objective: *To help children to realistically evaluate their own schoolwork to determine quality work.*

Level: *Intermediate*

Materials Needed: *One folder for each child, construction paper, crayons, and markers*

Procedure:

1. Ask the children to look through a small sampling of their completed assignments and choose the best paper.

2. Talk about what kinds of things one must consider in evaluating his/her own work:

   a. grade received or number correct,

   b. neatness of writing,

   c. margins, spacing, and/or

   d. lack of erasures or smudges.

3. Allow the children to decorate a folder for their good work papers. They may decorate it any way they wish.

4. Each week, allow the children to choose up to five papers to place in their favorite work folder.

5. Send favorite work folders home at the end of each month.

Evaluation: *Each child will be able to select at least ten examples of favorite work to be included in the folder which is sent home to parent.*

Variation: *Have the children make a "Seal of Approval" or stamp to use on papers which they feel are of high quality. If they feel the paper fits the standard they have set for quality, they put their seal or stamp on it when they hand it in.*

✝ ✝ ✝

MY NAME BEGINS WITH
(Cognitive Development Activity No. 14)

Objective: To provide an opportunity for children to identify items in the classroom that begin with the same letter as their name.

Level: Primary

Materials Needed: None

Procedure:

1. Have the children sit in a circle.

2. Ask each child to introduce himself/herself to the class saying name and telling all of the items in the room that begin with the same letter.

3. When everyone in the class has had a turn, ask the children to see how many of their classmates' names they can remember.

4. Utilize this activity on a subsequent day and have each child choose a classmate, say the person's name, and tell all of the things he/she can think of that begin with the first letter of the classmate's name.

Evaluation: The children will successfully identify at least five items in the classroom that begin with the same letter as their name (first or last depending on the difficulty of the letter).

Variations:

1. Ask the children to group their classmates according to the first letter of their names.

2. Have the children use each letter of their name and identify items that begin with each of the letters.

✝ ✝ ✝

FOLLOWING DIRECTIONS ACTIVITY
(Cognitive Development Activity No. 15)

Objective: To assist children to find the hidden picture if they listen carefully and follow directions.

Level: Primary

Materials Needed: One "hidden picture" sheet and pencil for each child.

Procedure:

1. Provide each child with a worksheet that looks something like this.

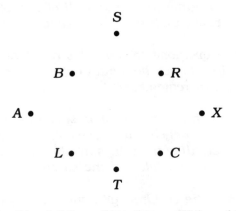

2. Explain to the children that they will be able to find the hidden picture if they follow directions carefully. Remind them that each direction will only be given once.

3. Give slowly the following directions:

   a. Draw a line from B to C,
   b. Draw a line from L to S,
   c. Draw a line from C to S,
   d. Draw a line from R to L,
   e. Draw a line from B to R, and
   f. Color the picture "Yellow."

4. Check to see how many children followed directions and were able to complete the hidden picture.

5. Provide a special reward, i.e., sticker for each child who followed directions correctly.

Evaluation: Each child will be able to follow directions in such a way that he/she is able to find the hidden "star" in the picture.

Variations:
1. This type of activity can be used as a "fun" drill in following directions. Pictures can be made increasingly more difficult as the children become better at following directions.

2. For older children have them start with a blank paper and follow directions to make specific abstract figures. Have the children compare their pictures to see if directions were clear and that each person followed them.

   Example:

   a. Make 1 inch horizontal line in the center of the paper.

   b. Make 1 inch vertical line on the right side of the horizontal line.

   c. Make a 2 inch horizontal line to the right side of the paper.

   d. Draw a circle at the left end of the 2 inch line.

✝ ✝ ✝

BIBLIOGRAPHY

Bergmann, S., & Rudman, G.J. (1985) *Decision making skills for middle school students.* Washington, DC: National Education Association.

Borba, M., & Borba, C. (1978). *Self-esteem: A classroom affair.* Minneapolis: Winston Press.

Borba, M., & Borba, C. (1982). *Self-esteem: A classroom affair, Vol. II.* Minneapolis: Winston Press.

Dinkmeyer, D. (173). *Developing an understanding of self and others.* Circle Pines, MN: American Guidance Service.

Farnette, C., Forte, I., & Harris, B. (1979). *People need each other.* Nashville, TN: Incentive Publications.

Farnette, C., Forte, I., & Loss, B. (1977). *I've got me and I'm glad.* Nashville, TN: Incentive Publications.

Farnette, C., Forte, I., & Loss, B. (1977). *At least 1000 things to do.* Nashville, TN: Incentive Publications.

Gibbs, J., & Allen, A. (1978). *Tribes: A process for peer involvement.* Oakland, CA: Center Source Publications.

Grimm, G., & Mitchell, D. (1977). *Mostly me.* Carthage, IL: Good Apple.

Johnson, E.W., & McClelland, D.C. (1984). *Learning to achieve.* Glenview, IL: Scott Foresman.

Kaczkowski, H. (1979). Group work with children. *Elementary School Guidance and Counseling,* Vol. 14, No.1.

Knight, M., Graham, T., Juliano, R., Miksza, S., & Tonnies, P. (1982). *Teaching children to love themselves.* Englewood Cliffs, NJ: Prentice Hall.

Piaget, J. (1965). *Insights and illusions of philosophy.* New York: Meridean Books.

Reasoner, R.W. (1982). *Building self-esteem.* Palo Alto: CA: Consulting Psychologists Press.

Simon, B. (1974). *Meeting yourself halfway.* Niles, IL: Argus Communications.

Smith, A., Cooper, J., & Leverte, M. (1977). *Giving kids a piece of the action.* Doylestown, PA: TACT.

Thompson, C.L., & Poppen, W.L. (1975). *Guidance for the elementary school.* Springfield, TN: Robertson County Board of Education.

Thompson, C.L., & Rudolph, L.B. (1983). *Counseling children.* Monterey, CA: Brooks/Cole.

Williams, S., & Mitchell, R. (1976). *Career awareness.* Monterey, CA: Creative Teaching Press.

Wirth, S. (1977). Effects of a multifaceted reading program on self-concept. *Elementary School Guidance and Counseling, Vol. 12,* No. 1.

CHAPTER

DIMENSION OF CAREER DEVELOPMENT

Although career education has been strongly promoted in the elementary school for the past 25 years, many persons still view career education as the domain of the secondary school. For this reason, we have provided a somewhat lengthier review of the research on career education in the elementary school.

RESEARCH ON ELEMENTARY SCHOOL CAREER EDUCATION

When many people think of career education in the elementary schools, they perceive a specific unit of study which is separate from the actual curriculum. This perception, however, is in total contradiction to what actually should take place in a career education program.

One of the most important elements of a successful career education program is that it must be considered an integral part of the curriculum and not an added unit of study. Another important aspect is that a good program of career education consists of much more than learning about careers and occupations. The program involves creating an awareness of self and a broadening of self perceptions.

In looking at some of the elements of an elementary career education program, we can actually identify three major areas of focus: self awareness, career awareness, and awareness of the decision-making process.

Self-Awareness

Much of the activity in the primary grades consists of self awareness. Children begin to identify their strengths and weaknesses, feelings, interests, and personal characteristics in relation to the world of work.

Career Awareness

Career awareness starts in the primary grades when the children begin to notice the many different jobs found within the school and local community. Awareness activities also highlight the importance of family and community in addressing a wide range of occupations available to children. Within the context of career education, teachers and counselors have a responsibility to all children in dispelling all types of stereotypes, thoughts, and behaviors which limit children's world view when it comes to exploring all areas of the world of work. This necessitates a variety of experiences which show men and women in non-traditional careers.

Awareness of the Decision-Making Process

As the children begin thinking about tentative career choices, they need to gain an awareness of the decision making process. Many opportunities must be provided for the children to learn decision-making skills.

GOALS OF CAREER EDUCATION

To further broaden the scope of elementary career education, an essential component is to identify some goals which an effective program would attempt to attain. Children need to do the following six things.

1. Observe how current learnings relate to future work experience.

Hoyt, Pinson, Laramore, and Magnum (1973) stated that "education must be seen as a preparation for something—both as a preparation for living and a preparation for making a living" (p. 3).

As teachers and counselors, we have frequently heard the often repeated cry of the children, "Why do I have to learn this?" We can and must help children identify, for example, how the math they are learning now, will help them function both now and in the future. The children who are able to see this connection will also see learning as being more relevant.

2. Identify interests both for possible careers and leisure activities.

As early as kindergarten, the children are able to identify things they enjoy doing. Kindergarten is not too early to begin identifying careers which include such interests. Also at this time children need to begin to consider leisure activities and how their interests may generate into hobbies which might be pursued during their leisure time.

3. Recognize the interdependence of workers.

All of us realize that "no man is an island." This is especially true in many careers where people depend on each other so that things can run smoothly. We can start with young children to assist them in identifying such interdependence among workers.

4. Consider and identify reasons why people work.

Most children never stop to think of why people work. An important part of career education is providing opportunities for the children to consider this puzzling question of why people work.

5. Classify jobs according to working with people, ideas, or things.

As the children become more aware of all of the career opportunities available, they can be helped to extend this awareness to include the circumstances in which certain careers exist. A good place to begin is to have the children learn to classify careers into the three basic groups of people, things, and ideas.

6. Attach worth or value to all work.

Many children see value in the so called "prestigious" jobs, but not in the everyday routine ones. The children must expand their horizons so that they become aware of the worth and dignity of all jobs.

INVOLVEMENT OF OTHERS

Role of the Counselor

A critical factor in a career education program is the role of the elementary counselor. The counselor, according to Hoyt (1976), has three major roles in a school career education program:

1. **Providing professional leadership.** Most counselors readily accept the fact that they must provide leadership and coordination within the program. Often they see themselves in the role of the "teacher of teachers" but will quickly stress that they are not the "boss" of the career education program.

   In their leadership role, counselors coordinate the scope and sequence of the program, provide suggestions regarding curriculum infusion, conduct needs assessments, develop evaluation measures, and aid in interpreting evaluation results.

2. **Helping teachers in career education.** Counselors can be a great assistance to teachers by supplying creative ideas and resources, working with the teachers in the classroom, and serving as consultants/coordinators in identifying and organizing community resource persons.

3. **Working directly with children.** Individual and group counseling with children are ways in which counselors provide direct services to children. These sessions aid the children in clarifying values and identifying their strengths, weaknesses, and interests. However, counselors also have direct contact with children in teaching specific career education activities and in planning for and accompanying children on career education field trips.

Involvement of Teachers

Possibly the most important person in the career education program is the classroom teacher. Probably the teacher is the one who first overhears the children's career aspirations as they tell their friends, "I'm going to be a pro quarterback when I grow up." and the teacher is the one who will have the most consistent contact with the children in their career education experience.

Oftentimes, children will have unrealistic career choices in the early elementary years, but to challenge them at this time is not necessary. When they are 12 to 14, most of them will begin to understand and become more reality oriented in their thinking about possible career options.

Schmidt (1976) made the following suggestions to teachers for successful implementation of a career education program:

1. Teachers and counselors should work together to implement the program.

2. Children need to be made aware that their own values and career choice may change many times during their life.

3. Each career choice should be viewed in terms of the life style it creates for the worker.

Hoyt (1976) described several benefits to teachers from career education activities. First of these is that such activities provide opportunities for teachers as well as students to learn. This helps teachers realize that as a result of this additional learning they become better teachers and develop more understanding of the total community in which they live.

A second benefit is that these activities help teachers understand the children more completely. This not only makes the teacher more aware of the children as individuals, but it also carries over to the entire teacher/child relationship.

Third, career education activities provide a natural vehicle for sharing with other teachers. Through career education activities, teachers have indicated that they become better acquainted with their fellow teachers and have developed increased respect for their peers.

An additional benefit for teachers is that an increase occurs in community understanding and support. This happens when resource persons come into class to talk with the children about their jobs. With these visits come an increased community awareness and respect for the tremendous challenges facing today's teachers.

Fourth, teachers begin to see the entire community as a learning lab. This has multiplied the opportunity for adding variety to the teaching/learning process.

Involvement of Community

Career education as defined by Hoyt et al. (1973) is

> the total effort of public education and the community aimed at helping all individuals to become familiar with the values of a work oriented society, to integrate these values into their personal value systems, and to implement these values into their lives in such a way that work becomes possible, meaningful and satisfying to each individual. (p. 1)

The inclusion of community in the definition emphasizes the importance of community involvement in a total career education effort. Such involvement is evidenced through

1. community support and participation in providing field trip experiences,

2. community support in school/community advisory committees, and

3. community representatives as resource persons for classroom presentations.

Norris (1963) indicated that the choice of a career is one of the most important decisions a person makes in a lifetime because to choose a career is to choose a way of life. Since career development begins in childhood, occupational experiences are as essential to elementary school children as they are to high school students.

NEEDS TO BE ADDRESSED

1. The need to be aware of self

One of the first levels of career education in the elementary school is self awareness. Children must be able to be aware of self in terms of strengths, weaknesses, likes, dislikes, etc. These needs can be addressed through the self-concept activities which were described in Chapter 9.

2. The need to be aware of the wide range of occupations

When elementary school children are asked "What would you like to be when you grow up?" their answers are pretty predictable, i.e., nurse, teacher, doctor, lawyer. This may be because these are the only occupations of which they are aware. Elementary school children can and must be aided in gaining an awareness of the myriad of occupations which are available. This can begin simply with information on "Jobs in our School" and move into very specific areas such as "Music Careers".

3. The need to relate current education to careers

This can be done quite simply through a question such as "How does math help us live our lives now as we are growing and developing?" Once the children begin to realize the importance of math and numbers in the way they and others live, they may view math with a little more interest and respect.

4. The need to be aware of the importance of leisure time

While most of us think of leisure time as something we never have enough of, children need to be aware of the value of developing leisure time interests. This is particularly important in view of recent information which suggests that occupations of the future will leave more time for leisure pursuits.

5. The need to be aware of the interdependency of occupations

The idea that "no man is an island" is certainly apparent when we begin to view the interdependency of occupations. Children, however, do not see these relationships as readily as adults. Time must be provided for the children to consider and discuss these relationships.

SKILLS TO BE DEVELOPED

1. Self-description Skills

In reviewing this last section of activities, we gain a clearer picture of the interrelatedness of the five dimensions. Although we have alluded to the self-description skills in previous chapters, they are equally crucial in the area of career development.

2. Decision-making Skills

The decision-making skills, which were developed in previous domains, will be utilized to a great extent in career education activities. Children will not only use these skills in their current school experience, but will depend heavily on them in the future when further educational and/or occupational choice becomes a reality.

3. Career Awareness

Elementary school children must have opportunities to become aware of the wide range of careers available to them in the future. If this doesn't happen in the elementary school, children will enter junior and senior high school ill prepared to make decisions regarding future educational directions. Although we realize that today's workers may have several careers throughout a lifetime, the process of career awareness must begin in the elementary school.

4. Interest Awareness

Children need opportunities to consider and to investigate various areas of interest during their elementary school years. Such opportunities can be readily provided through activities such as the Hobby Days presented later in this chapter.

5. Leisure Awareness

Although elementary school children can usually name several favorite leisure time activities, they need to develop a sense of leisure as being something they will have throughout their lifetime. The Hobby Day activity described in this chapter also will promote leisure awareness for children.

INTEGRATION OF
CAREER EDUCATION ACTIVITIES

The following activities have been designed to be infused into the curriculum in several different subject areas and should be presented using the Keystone Learning Model. An example of curriculum infusion would be the integration of Hobby Days into the Language Arts curriculum. The children could write invitations and thank you notes to the presenters, write a description of the hobbies for the school newspaper, etc.

✝ ✝ ✝

HOBBY DAY
(Career Development Activity No. 1)

Objective: *To help children to develop a better awareness of the importance of leisure time activities.*

Level: *Intermediate*

Materials Needed: *Pencils and paper*

Procedure:

1. Discuss the term "hobby." A hobby is something that we do because we enjoy it. Ask the children if they know anyone who has an interesting hobby.

2. Develop a list of resource persons and their hobbies based on children's suggestions. Also be ready to add some suggestions of your own. (Fellow teachers, teachers aides, and other school staff members often have very interesting hobbies that they would be willing to share.)

3. Have the children decide on 10 to 12 hobbies that they would like to have represented at a Hobby Day. (Be sure to try for a good variety to catch everyone's interest.)

4. Work with the children to develop an invitation letter to be sent to the resource person.

5. When "yes" responses have been received, schedule a Hobby Day as follows:

   a. Try to get each resource person to prepare a 20 minute presentation on their hobby and leave 10 minutes for questions.

   b. Schedule 3 to 4 presentations at one time in different locations. Allow the children to choose which one they will attend. Schedule 3 different half hour sessions, 9 to 12 different resource persons in all. (Each child will see a total of 3 presentations.)

   c. When the children have returned to the classroom following the presentation, take time to discuss. Children generally will be very enthusiastic about what they have seen.

d. Have the children write "thank you" letters to presenters.

6. Follow up with a Hobby Day where the children in the
class share their hobbies.

Evaluation: Each child will be able to identify at least three
leisure time activities which are of interest to him/her.
Following the Hobby Day activity, children will be able to
describe, in some detail, one hobby which is of particular
interest to them.

Variation: As a follow up to the Hobby Day activity, have
children investigate how certain hobbies can relate to
different careers. Stress the idea that "a job should be
something that you really like to do." Example: A person who
likes taking pictures may want to investigate the possibility of
a career in photography.

✝ ✝ ✝

HATS AND TOOLS
(Career Development Activity No. 2)

Objective: To assist the children in identifying some of the
equipment associated with various occupations.

Level: Primary

Materials Needed: Various hats and tools related to specific
careers

Procedure:

1. Discuss how one can determine what jobs people do
by their hats or tools. Ask children to think of some that
immediately come to mind.

2. Present several examples of hats and tools that have
been collected.

3. Allow time for discussion and guesses as to the occupations.

4. Discuss the fact that some tools are often used in many different occupations. A ruler, for example may be used by a teacher, a carpenter, a draftsman, etc.

5. Ask the children to bring in a hat or tool that someone they know wears/uses at work and see if the class can guess what their job is.

Evaluation: Children will be able to participate in the activity and correctly identify at least two hats or tools and the associated career. As a follow up, each child will bring to the classroom one "tool of a trade" (or a picture of it) for a subsequent activity.

Variations:

1. Invite guest speakers in to talk about their jobs. Ask them to wear the uniform of the job and bring along samples of equipment used.

2. Play "What Job Do I Have." Have children describe the tools of a job and allow the class to guess what job the child is describing.

† † †

CAREER INTERVIEWS
(Career Development Activity No. 3)

Objective: To increase the children's awareness of some important aspects of various careers.

Level: Intermediate

Materials Needed: Prepared list of interview questions

Procedure:

1. Following a discussion of careers, ask the children to think of a job they would like to know more about.

2. Discuss interview techniques as a way of discovering more about jobs.

3. Suggest that the children choose a person they know who has a job they would like to know more about and ask if they may interview that person.

4. Provide each child with a list of possible interview questions or have the children develop a list of questions. Some of the questions might include the following:

    a. Do you need any special training or schooling to do your job?

    b. What is the beginning hourly wage for this job?

    c. What are some of the benefits of this job?

    d. Is the work mostly done indoors or outdoors? With other people or alone?

    e. What equipment or special tools are needed to do this job?

    f. What are some disadvantages of this job?

5. Provide class time for the children to share information from their interviews with the other members of the class.

Evaluation: Each child will complete a career interview and report the information to the class in a two minute report.

Variations:

1. Invite guest speakers into the class and allow the children to interview them in panel format so they can see the differences in various jobs.

2. Have the children role play interviews to share information they have learned about specific occupations. Example: One child role plays a carpenter and another child interviews him/her using the list of interview questions.

† † †

JOB TREE
(Career Development Activity No. 4)

Objective: To increase children's awareness of the interdependency of jobs.

Level: Intermediate

Procedure:

1. Discuss the idea of a family tree. Provide an example using the name of one of the children in the class.

2. Tell the children they are going to develop a "Job Family Tree" to show how different jobs are related in some way.

3. Prepare a chalkboard model or sample of a personal job tree. If school jobs are used, be sure to include all of the jobs in the school and show how they are interrelated. This would include principal, secretary, teacher, teacher aide, counselor, nurse, speech therapist, cafeteria worker, custodian, etc.

4. Ask the children to prepare a job tree of "People Mom/Dad work with."

5. Place completed job trees on the bulletin board to illustrate the interdependency of jobs.

Evaluation: Children will complete a job tree for display and discussion. The discussion questions which may be helpful include the following:

1. Before doing this activity, did you realize how many different jobs were involved?

2. Were you surprised at some of the jobs in the "job family?"

3. Can you think of any jobs that are not related in any way to at least one other job?

Variations:

1. Make an "interest" job tree by writing the interest (e.g., sports) on the trunk and all of the different possible jobs (pro athlete, coach, announcer, sports reporter for newspaper, equipment manager, run a sporting goods store, manufacture sporting equipment, etc.)

2. Make a Careers in _____ family tree. For example, a Careers in Health family tree would include such things as Doctor, Nurse, Lab Technician, X-ray Technician, Nurses Aid, Respiratory Therapist, Dentist, etc.

✝ ✝ ✝

SEASONAL CAREERS
(Career Development Activity No. 5)

Objective: To assist children in becoming more aware of the seasonal nature of many occupations.

Level: Intermediate

Materials Needed: List of questions to promote discussion

Procedure:

1. Promote thinking about seasonal careers by preparing a list of questions and place them on the chalkboard. Some good motivators include

   a. What do department store Santa's do in July?

   b. What do lifeguards do in the winter?

   c. What do the grain farmers of the mid-west do in the winter?

   d. What do ski instructors do in August?

   e. What do people who work at outdoor amusement parks do in the winter?

2. Provide time for the children to do some discussing of these and other seasonal careers.

3. Divide the children into groups of 3 to 5 and allow them to develop "Mystery Occupations" which are seasonal.

4. When the groups are brought back together, use 15 to 20 minutes for presentation of the "mystery occupations." Suggest that children present clues to their occupation—Example:

   Clue No. 1—I work very hard from July to January.

   Clue No. 2—I wear a uniform with a number on it.

   Clue No. 3—My job is to play a game once each week.

   Clue No. 4—If I am very good at my job, I may go to the Super Bowl.

   Mystery Occupation—Pro Football Player

Evaluation: The children will become aware of the fact that some jobs are very seasonal in nature. At the conclusion of the activity, each child will be able to identify at least three "seasonal" jobs.

Variation: Encourage the children to consider the fact that many people, because of the seasonal aspect of their occupations, have more than one job. Suggest that the children interview other teachers in the building to see what they do in the summer.

† † †

JOBS IN A SCHOOL
(Career Development Activity No. 6)

Objective: To help children become more aware of the different jobs that make their education possible.

Level: Primary and Intermediate

Materials Needed: Chalkboard, construction paper, crayons, paper punch, and yarn

Procedure:

1. In a discussion of school, ask the children to name all of the jobs they can think of that can be found in school. In addition to the ones that are readily apparent, have the children also consider such jobs as the equipment repair people, audio visual delivery persons, milk and food delivery persons, etc.

2. Ask each child to choose a school job that they would like to draw and then place in a booklet entitled "Jobs in Our School." Be sure to include enough different jobs that every child can do a different job.

3. When the pictures are completed, assemble them into a booklet and tie it with yarn.

4. Display the booklet in a place where it is easily accessible for the children to look through when they have free time.

5. Share the booklet with other classes.

Evaluation: The children will be able to identify at least seven jobs that play an important role in making their education possible. (This may be done either individually on paper or in a small group discussion following the activity.)

Variation: Using the same technique, have the children develop booklets for other jobs areas, such as: Jobs in a Bank, Jobs in a Hospital, Jobs in a Restaurant, Jobs in a Shoe Factory, or Jobs in a Police Station.

† † †

MY CAREER NOW
(Career Development Activity No. 7)

Objective: To increase children's awareness of the importance of current schooling as a preparation for a future career.

Level: Intermediate

Materials Needed: Notebook or folder for each child, pens, crayons, or markers

Procedure:

1. Ask the children if they can think of any way that their schooling now is preparing them for the future. If they do not see the connection, give an illustration such as math will help you be able to balance a checkbook when you grow up and have a job; reading will help you be able to read directions when you need to do so.

2. Provide each child with a notebook or folder which is to be divided into three sections "My School Career," "My Home Jobs," and "My Leisure Time."

3. *Suggest that children use illustration to show how school and home work are related to "real" jobs.*

4. *Have the children draw several pictures with captions in each of the three sections.*

5. *Permit time for the children to share their folders.*

Evaluation: *The children will have completed a folder to show the interrelatedness of current schooling to a future career. In the follow-up discussion of folders, a helpful procedure is to point out the fact that each subject can be connected in some way to our future careers or leisure pursuits.*

Variation: *Have the children take a look into the future by labeling the three sections "My Career Now," "My Career in 10 Years," and "My career in 20 Years."*

† † †

PEOPLE AT WORK
(Career Development Activity No. 8)

Objective: *To increase children's awareness of different tasks performed in various occupations.*

Level: *Intermediate*

Materials Needed: *Inexpensive cameras, film*

Procedure:

1. *Ask the children to think about where and when they see people working. Discuss.*

2. *Tell them that they will have an opportunity to take pictures of people at work.*

3. *Have an inexpensive camera and film available for the children to take turns using to take pictures of*

people at work. (Depending on money available for film, it may be necessary to limit each child to 2 or 3 pictures each.)

4. When the film is developed, create a collage of pictures and place on a bulletin board entitled "People at Work." (Children are usually very enthusiastic about activities involving picture taking. This is one they really enjoy.)

Evaluation: Children will have had the opportunity to take photos of "people at work" and to share these photos with the class. Once the photos are all in place, discussion could center around such questions as the following:

1. What was it about the job you took a picture of that particularly interested you?

2. Did the person in your photo talk with you about his/her job?

3. Do you think you would like to do that job?

Variation:

1. If funds aren't available for film, do this activity by having children cut pictures from newspapers or magazines to show people at work. Use these pictures to create the collage.

2. If camera, film, or money are not available, have children draw pictures of people at work.

† † †

ORGANIZE A "SUPER BOWL"
(Career Development Activity No. 9)

Objective:

1. To have children become more aware of the inter-relatedness of tasks in organizing a special activity.

2. To help children gain an increased awareness of the importance of careful planning.

Level: Intermediate

Materials Needed: Paper and pencils

Procedure:

1. Discuss the Super Bowl. What other jobs are involved in the Super Bowl besides the athletes and coaches? Remind the children not to forget such people as souvenir salespersons, food vendors, TV cameramen, analysts, newspaper photographers, etc.

2. Tell the class members that they are going to be working to organize their own class Super Bowl.

3. Divide the group into several smaller groups to handle all of the different tasks. There should be committees for Publicity, Teams, Food, Half-time Entertainment, Souvenirs, Field Preparation, and Clean Up.

4. Have each group write a plan for their committee, indicating all of the tasks that their group will have to complete in order for the Super Bowl to run smoothly.

5. Allow the children to share their reports with the class and permit additional suggestions from other children.

6. If possible, stage a game with another class so the children would have an opportunity to carry out their plans to see if, in reality, they do run smoothly.

Evaluation: Children will have organized an activity in such a way that they have become aware of the interrelatedness of jobs involved in bringing the activity to fruition. Because they have developed a written plan, they will have experienced an important element in preparing for the smooth operation of an activity. Following the activity, the discussion should center on such things as successes, problems encountered, suggestions for improvement, etc.

Variations: This idea can be implemented in planning a variety of activities and might include the following:

1. Plan a birthday party.

2. Plan an end of the year party.

3. Organize a fund drive for charity.

4. Organize an entertainment program for a visit to a retirement home.

✝ ✝ ✝

JOB POSTERS
(Career Development Activity No.10)

Objective: To encourage children to investigate a career of their interest.

Level: Intermediate

Materials Needed: One 24 inches x 36 inches piece of poster paper for each child, markers, old magazines, paste, scissors, paper, pens and pencils, letters, patterns and stencils

Procedure:

1. At the culmination of a unit on careers, ask children to choose an occupation that they would like to investigate more thoroughly.

2. Explain that this is to be their final project for the unit and that it is important for them to do their very best work.

3. Provide each child with a piece of poster board and the instruction that they are to develop a poster on their chosen occupation. The poster should contain the following:

   a. The name of the occupation in large letters.

b. Several pictures of persons working at the occupation.

c. A one page report to describe the occupation.

4. Set a time limit of 2 to 3 weeks for completion of the project.

5. Allow time for each child to show his/her poster and give a 2 to 3 minute report to the class.

6. Display the posters in the hall for other children to see.

Evaluation: The children will each complete a career poster and give a 2 to 3 minute report on his/her chosen career.

Variation: Allow the children to work together in small groups to complete their posters. In this way the tasks can be delegated to take advantage of class members' strengths and interests; for example, the good language child can write the report, the artist can do the lettering, the verbal member can present the report, etc.

† † †

WORKERS IN OUR COMMUNITY
(Career Development Activity No. 11)

Objective: To assist children to identify workers that they see each day in the community.

Level: Primary

Materials Needed: Large sheets of mural paper, crayons, or markers.

Procedure:

1. Discuss with children some of the workers that they see in the community each day. Point out that several are easily identifiable by their uniforms.

2. Continue discussion until the children have success-fully named a large number of occupations they see each day.

3. Divide the class into groups of three or four and give each group a large piece of paper for a mural.

4. Ask each group to choose one aspect of community jobs and develop their mural around that theme. Examples of some of the possible mural titles include

   a. jobs in our school,

   b. city workers who help us,

   c. people who work in factories, and

   d. people who provide services for us.

5. Display the completed murals around the classroom for all to see.

Evaluation: Each child will be able to name and describe at least five occupations which can be found in the community.

Variations:

1. If the children have not yet developed the cooperation skills to work successfully in groups, utilize the different topics and ask each child to prepare an individual drawing for display in a booklet entitled "Workers in our Community."

2. Invite various community workers in to discuss their occupations with children.

✝   ✝   ✝

JOBS WE SEE ON T.V.
(Career Development Activity No. 12)

Objective: To create children's awareness of the large number of occupations represented by various T.V. programs.

Level: Primary and Intermediate

Materials Needed: Pencil and Paper

Procedure:

1. Ask the children to name their favorite T.V. programs. Discuss some of the programs mentioned to point out the wide variety of occupations which are represented on T.V. programs. Usually children will have to think a bit before they are able to identify all of them.

2. Tell the children that they are going to have a T.V. - watching homework assignment. Then ask them to spend at least one hour per night for three nights watching T.V. During that time, they are to write down all of the different jobs that they see portrayed on the various shows.

3. Have the children share the information at the end of the three nights. Tally the results to see how many different occupations were represented.

4. Discuss each occupation as portrayed on the T.V. shows. Is it pretty much the way you think that job is in real life? Talk about exaggeration for entertainment value in many cases.

Evaluation: The children will be able to describe a current T.V. show and identify occupations portrayed by characters on the show. As part of the evaluation discussion, a helpful procedure is to have children consider questions such as the following:

1. What kinds of things did you see the worker doing that surprised you?

2. Can you compare the way the T.V. star portrays the job with someone you know who has that same job? What similarities/differences do you see?

Variation: Make a list of a number of occupations and ask the children to watch T.V. to see if they can identify a T.V. character that has that occupation on a show. Tally the class results. For example, show how many T.V. "doctors" they are able to identify.

✝ ✝ ✝

PEOPLE WHO HELP US HAVE FUN
(Career Development Activity No. 13)

Objective: To promote children's awareness of the wide variety of careers in the entertainment field.

Level: Primary and Intermediate

Materials Needed: Pictures of persons involved in jobs that entertain us or in some way help us have fun.

Procedure:

1. Begin by discussing leisure activities. What are some things we do to have fun?

2. Ask the children if there are others involved in helping us have fun. Direct the discussion to include such jobs as lifeguard, park ranger, clowns and other circus performers, and persons who run the rides at the amusement parks.

3. Develop a bulletin board heading entitled "People Who Help Us Have Fun" and ask the children to bring in pictures of people in occupations that help us have fun.

4. Discuss the fact that many people really have jobs that we would consider fun things to do and they make a living doing them.

5. Relate this to a discussion of interests and strengths as being major factors in helping us choose our careers.

Evaluation: Children will be able to identify a personal leisure activity and describe at least one "fun" career related to that interest.

Variations:

1. Play a variation of "What's My Line?" in describing occupations that help us have fun.

2. Invite some people who have "fun" jobs in to talk to the class.

† † †

JOBS NEEDED TO MAKE A _____
(Career Development Activity No. 14)

Objective: To help children identify the interrelatedness of jobs.

Level: Primary and Intermediate

Materials Needed: Objects for consideration, 3 x 5 slips of paper

Procedure: Note: When children have been studying jobs in industry, the following activity creates a good deal of interest and enthusiasm.

1. Place an object such as a shoe or a purse on the shelf for consideration along with the sign entitled "Jobs Needed to Make a Shoe (Purse, Umbrella, etc.)."

2. Have available a supply of 3 x 5 slips of paper for children to write the names of jobs that relate directly to the producing of the article.

3. Allow two or three days for the children to write names of related jobs and place them in or near the object.

4. Read each child's suggestion to the class and discuss how each is related to production.

5. Place another object on the shelf the following week and continue the activity in the same manner if children's interest remains high.

Evaluation: Children will be able to name at least three different jobs which are involved in the production of a specific item. If they have difficulty, provide an example such as the following:

Loaf of Bread

1. Farmer who grows the wheat
2. Baker who makes the bread
3. Manufacturer of plastic bag to keep the bread fresh

Variation: Develop large charts to show the steps involved in the production of various objects. In the production of a chair, for example, the steps would begin with the lumbering process and would conclude with the varnishing or finishing of the completed chair.

† † †

THE MATCHING GAME
(Career Development Activity No. 15)

Objective: To assist the children to match equipment, clothing, and products associated with specific occupations.

Level: Primary

Materials Needed: Cards with pictures on them for matching workers with tools, clothing, and products

Procedure:

1. Prepare a set of cards to show equipment, clothing and products associated with specific occupations. Examples:

   a. Musician—record, musical instrument, microphone

   b. Doctor—stethoscope, thermometer, blood pressure cuff

   c. Cook—dishes, pans, food, chef's hat, apron

   d. Beautician—hair rollers, dryer, comb, scissors

e. *Cowboy—boots, hat, lasso, saddle, horse*

f. *Pro-Football Player—ball, uniform, helmet, shoes*

g. *Teacher—books, pencils, paper, crayon*

2. Permit time for the children to play the matching game. This can be done by small groups of children during free time, by individuals, or by the entire class.

3. Reinforce children for good thinking if, during the course of the activity, they note that some equipment is used by persons in different occupations.

4. Leave the cards on the shelf along with other "free time" activities that children may choose at a later time.

Evaluation: The children will match at least 80% of the items with the appropriate occupation. Children who are unable to do this may profit from time spent in a game format with a peer helper.

Variation: Have each child develop his/her own set of cards for one occupation. Put all of the cards together to make one large class matching game.

† † †

CAREER ABC'S
(Career Development Activity No. 16)

Objective: To assist children to gain an awareness of the wide variety of occupations.

Level: Primary and Intermediate

Materials Needed: Pencil and Paper

Procedure:

1. Ask each child to think of at least one occupation for every letter of the alphabet. Example:

a. artist
b. bookkeeper

    c. *carpenter*
    d. *doctor*
    e. *engineer*

2. Go over the various lists in class and see how many different occupations were mentioned for each letter. Compile into one master list.

3. Place a blank a,b,c, chart on the wall and ask the children to add others as they think of them. Make a game of it to see which letter has the most occupations at the end of a specified period.

Evaluation: The children will be able to identify an occupation beginning with a letter of the alphabet for at least 20 of the 26 letters of the alphabet.

Variations:

1. Divide the group into smaller groups with the instruction that they are to think of as many jobs as they can for each letter of the alphabet.

2. Assign a specific letter to each child with the same procedure as described above.

† † †

FAMILY CAREER TREE
(Career Development Activity No. 17)

Objective: To help children become aware of the number of different careers represented in their family.

Level: Intermediate

Materials Needed: One piece of 12 x 18 construction paper for each child, fine line markers

Procedure:

1. Instruct the children to draw a large tree with many branches on it. On the trunk of the tree they should write their name.

2. On the first level of branches, they should write either mother or father, plus any aunts' and uncles' names.

3. On the second level of branches they should write grandparents and on the third level, they should write great grandparents' names (two sets) example:

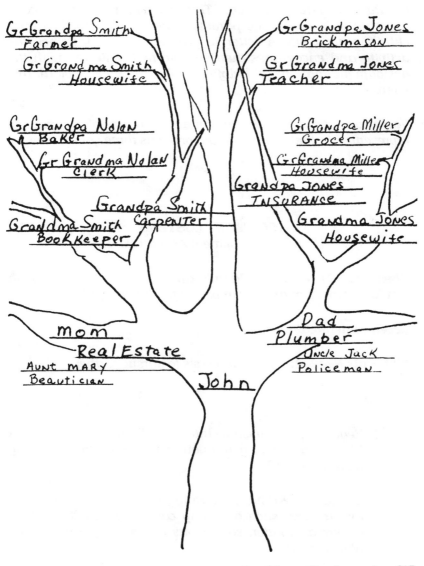

4. Instruct the children to write the name of each person's occupation beneath their name.

5. Permit time for sharing of Career Family Trees.

Evaluation: The children will be able to complete a family tree which identifies occupations of various family members for three generations. Note: This activity presents a good opportunity to encourage parents to become involved in their child's schoolwork. A letter to parents which describes the activity and encourages them to help their children with the assignment may be a helpful public relations tool at this point.

Variation: Ask the children to make a collage of occupations represented in their family for the previous three generations.

† † †

COMMON CLUSTERS
(Career Development Activity No. 18)

Objective: To create children's awareness that people with similar interests may work in very different occupations.

Level: Intermediate

Materials Needed: List of interests to pursue further

Procedure:

1. Begin by discussing interests. What would be an interesting job for you if you were interested in working with children?

2. Spend some time discussing jobs that would relate to this interest such as: camp counselor, teacher, school cafeteria monitor, school bus driver, day care worker, librarian, etc.

3. Provide the children with a list of 7 or 8 interest areas and ask them to think of three different jobs for each interest. Example of interest areas to get them started may be such things as

   a. interest in growing plants,

   b. interest in horses,

   c. interest in drawing pictures,

   d. interest in working with money, and/or

   e. interest in making things out of wood.

4. Allow time for discussion and sharing of ideas at the conclusion of the activity.

Evaluation: The children will be able to identify at least three jobs related to each interest area presented on the list.

Variation: Have the children write an interest area on a piece of paper. Collect papers, put them in a hat and allow each child to draw out an interest area and match three jobs to that interest.

† † †

CAREER RIDDLES
(Career Development Activity No. 19)

Objective: To help children to describe various aspects of an occupation in riddle form.

Level: Intermediate

Materials Needed: Pencils and paper

Procedure:

1. Talk about riddles—"Everyone likes to use riddles with their friends—Let's see if we can make up some riddles about jobs."

2. Start the children off with some samples.

Every morning when you come to school I'm at my post. Your safety is what concerns me the most. Who am I?

School Crossing Guard

I try to keep you up to date on what has happened all day long, I'm on T.V. but I don't sing a song. Who am I?

T.V. News Reporter

3. Divide the group into smaller groups and ask members to make up some riddles about jobs. They don't need to rhyme but sometimes that invites a little extra creativity.

4. Allow the children to present their riddles to the entire class.

Evaluation: Each small group will be able to prepare at least one career riddle and share it with the class at the completion of the activity.

Variation: Suggest that the children make other game type activities about careers. A word find puzzle or a scrambled word game generates a good deal of enthusiasm.

✝ ✝ ✝

CAREER COAT OF ARMS
(Career Development Activity No. 20)

Objective: To encourage children to give special attention to a specific career interest area.

Level: Intermediate

Materials Needed: Large sheet of construction paper for each child, crayons or markers, and scissors

Procedure:

1. Explain to the children that each of them time is going to develop a Career Coat of Arms for his/her chosen occupation. If questions occur about what a coat of arms is, spend some time in discussion.

2. Provide examples of shapes and designs for a coat of arms. Let each child select and complete a design on construction paper.

3. Instruct the children to divide their coat of arms into six sections. Each section will tell something about the career of their choice.

4. Suggest that the six sections be used for pictures or descriptions of the following information:

   a. description of the job,

   b. skills needed,

   c. education necessary,

   d. tools which are used,

   e. special dress or uniform, and

   f. location of the job.

5. When the projects have been completed, display them on a bulletin board or other prominent place for viewing by the children.

Evaluation: The children will each create a Career Coat of Arms to describe a chosen career in terms of the six areas presented in the activity.

Variation: Have the children make a "career scrapbook" and collect as much information as they can about their chosen career. Allow them to share their scrapbooks with classmates in small groups.

✝ ✝ ✝

LOOK INTO THE FUTURE
(Career Development Activity No. 21)

Objective: To encourage children to consider similarities between current chores and possible future careers.

Level: Intermediate

Materials Needed: Pencil and paper

Procedure:

1. Discuss "jobs" the children have now. Ask them how these jobs might be similar to future occupations.

2. Work with the class to make a list of children's jobs. These could include

   a. caring for pets,

   b. delivering newspapers,

   c. drying dishes,

   d. making beds,

   e. setting the table, and

   f. mowing lawns.

3. Ask the children to think about how these jobs could lead into a future career, such as

   a. caring for pets—veterinarian,

   b. making beds—maid service in a hotel or motel, or

   c. setting the table—working as a waiter/waitress.

4. Make a matching game for the children by listing a series of "Now Jobs" and a series of "Future Careers." Have the children draw a line to match the "now job" with the "future career."

Evaluation: *The children will be able to name a current chore and identify a possible occupation which relates to that chore.*

Variation: *Have the children write an advertisement for a job they do now. In preparation for this activity, suggest that they review the newspaper "want ads" to see what kind of information should be included.*

† † †

MY CAREER CHOICE
(Career Development Activity No. 22)

Objective: *To create children's awareness of the possibility that career choices sometimes change as one grows older.*

Level: *Intermediate*

Materials Needed: *Pencil and paper*

Procedure:

1. *Ask the children to identify a job they feel they would like to have when they grow up.*

2. *Discuss reasons for their choices.*

3. *Ask what are some things that might happen that would cause them to change their mind at some future time. Such reasons might include*

   a. *not wanting to commit to additional schooling for training,*

   b. *no opportunities in career choice areas,*

   c. *working conditions not what they expected,*

   d. *injury or inability to do job, and/or*

   e. *learning about something more interesting.*

4. Have the children identify other job possibilities that may interest them.

Evaluation: The children will be able to identify at least two reasons why a person may wish to change careers at a given point in his/her lifetime.

Variation: When discussing the reality that sometimes persons change jobs several times during a lifetime, ask the children to interview relatives who have changed jobs and ask them to identify some of the reasons for job change. Provide a classroom listing of the reasons people change jobs.

✝ ✝ ✝

BIBLIOGRAPHY

Borba, M., & Borba, C. (1978). *Self esteem: A classroom affair.* Minneapolis, MN: Winston Press.

Farnette, C., Forte, I., & Loss, B. (1977). *At least 1000 things to do.* Nashville, TN: Incentive Publications.

Hoyt, K.B., Pinson, N., Laramore, D., & Magnum, G. (1973). *Career education and the elementary school teacher.* Salt Lake City: Olympus Publishing.

Hoyt, K.B. (1976). *The school counselor and career education.* Monographs on Career Education. U.S. Department of Health, Education, and Welfare.

Hoyt, K.B. (1976). *K-12 classroom teachers and career education monographs on career education.* US Department of Health, Education, and Welfare.

Knight, M., Graham, T., Juliano, R., Miksza, S., & Tonnies, P. (1982). *Teaching children to love themselves.* Englewood Cliffs, NJ: Prentice-Hall.

Norris, W. (1963). *Occupational information in the elementary school.* Chicago, IL: Science Research Associates.

Schmidt, J.A. (1976). Career guidance in the elementary school. *Elementary School Guidance and Counseling, Vol, 11,* No. 2.

Thompson, C.L., & Poppen, W.L. (1975). *Guidance for the elementary school.* Springfield, TN: Robertson County Board of Education.

Woal, S.T. (1977). *Self awareness—Career awareness in your curriculum.* Paoli, PA: INSTRUCTO: McGraw Hill.

PART III

ELEMENTARY SCHOOL COUNSELING: CHALLENGING THE FUTURE

PART III

ELEMENTARY SCHOOL COUNSELING: CHALLENGING THE FUTURE

The theme presented throughout this book is that successful elementary school counselors are leaders, managers, political activists, and service providers. They are people of vision and action. Their programs do not exist in a vacuum, but are designed to meet developmental needs of children and address societal issues that impact significantly on the teaching/learning process.

For elementary school counselors to be successful in orchestrating such a proactive endeavor, they must have a clear sense of where their counseling programs have been, where their counseling programs are now, and where they want their counseling programs to be in the future. Counselors must be leaders who are prepared to challenge the status quo, inspire a shared vision of the future, enable others to participate in that vision, model action in working toward that vision, and provide the necessary encouragement and recognition of others as they support that vision.

In Chapter 12, *Planning the Future*, is stressed the importance of the counselor's role as leader in challenging the future and offers a practical model and suggested activities for accomplishing that end.

In Chapter 13, *Future Programs and Future Professional Issues*, are explored five elementary school counseling programs with a future. Each program presented addresses specific issues and future directions to be studied when applying the leadership model and suggested activities for challenging the future as presented in Chapter 12. The chapter concludes with a brief description of the counselor's future roles as leader, manager, political activist, and service provider in creating tomorrow's world today (the future).

PLANNING THE FUTURE

Planning can be a thought provoking process at best when applied to the present, let alone trying to comprehend and plan the future. The future, for most people, represents that which is to be or a time that will come to pass. The future for some people is viewed as fixed and determined. Little or nothing can be done to change the course of destiny. For those who aspire to this belief, the future of counseling is already cast in stone and all that can be done is to try to forecast the future and prepare for the inevitable. Others view the future as being totally unpredictable, fluid, everchanging, and uninfluenceable by man. People who hold to this view of the future often perceive themselves as victims and at the mercy of all which influences that which is to come. To accept this view of the future means that people must adapt in the best way they can to all that is good as well as bad. And still for others, the future is a gigantic game of chance. The future is full of many possibilities, none of which are predictable and none of which can be influenced in any particular direction. People take their chances and hope for the best where their own lives are to be affected by the outcomes.

None of the mentioned scenarios regarding the future are very satisfactory if counselors expect to address the future of elementary school counseling in any meaningful way. And so counselors are left with some very penetrating questions to ponder. Can the future be predicted or influenced in some constructive manner? What does the future hold for elementary school counseling? How can counselors bridge the gap between the present and the future?

FUTURE vs. FUTURISM:
IS THERE A DIFFERENCE?

When discussing the concept of future, little disagreement occurs as to its meaning. The future represents that which lies ahead of the present and is not directly observable. While most people purport to prepare for the future, these same individuals tend to view the future as something that will come to pass and yet is uninfluenceable from their perspective.

Futurism, by comparison, is a relatively new concept that has emerged with new understandings about the future. Futurism, according to Inbody (1984), involves more than just an interest in the future. Futurism shatters the conceptual understanding that the future must be accepted as inevitable and challenges people to do more than just prepare for the future but to create it as well. Futurists define futurism as a disciplined process of deciding what kind of future is wanted and then how to go about influencing that future in a positive and constructive manner.

The good news is that futurists have helped people to recognize how decisions of the past have created those futures which continue to impact so significantly on their lives today (medical breakthroughs, irresponsible disposal of contaminated waste, the invention of the automobile).

As professionals from all walks of life, people have the moral and ethical responsibility of shaping the present and at the same time being evermindful of how what they do today charts the future (their present) for those who will come after them. "Thus futurism was born from the realization that earlier decisions had strong unforeseen effects on later generations" (Inbody, 1984, p. 216). Hopefully this lesson has taught people that futurism must represent a carefully thought out process that teaches them to look beyond the present when determining how their life choices will change, for better or worse, their tomorrows. Kauffman (cited in Toffler, 1970) stated, "the purpose of futuristics [futurism] is not to predict but to improve the understanding of alternatives and the role of choice in achieving or avoiding any futures" (p. 13).

In further defining the concept of futurism and the potential impact that it can have on shaping our tomorrows, Inbody (1984) offered the following summary:

1. What we do today will have an impact on the quality of the world in which we and our descendants must live.

2. Scientific methods can be used for anticipating the various futures we could create unknowingly.

3. There is no longer just one future that awaits us, but many different possible futures, depending on what we choose today.

4. There is a moral urgency in our responsibility to future generations.

5. Mankind, in this age of powerful technology, is responsible for the future in a way that was already inconceivable even a century ago.

6. Prior to unleashing the power of an idea on the earth and its population, an extensive study of the future impact of that idea must be maintained. (pp. 216-217)

HELPFUL UNDERSTANDINGS ABOUT FUTURISMS

Hays and Johnson (1984), in their discussion about counseling in the 21st century, supported the notion that counselors need to become aware of the essential understandings that embody futurism in their quest to understand and apply the concept in inventing the future. Most futurists basically believe, among other things, that the future is unpredictable, that it may be viewed as a concept of quality, that the future may be expressed as a concept of time, and that some basic postulates help to shape the future.

The Future is Unpredictable

According to Amara (1981), the future is not predictable. One can not forecast what will be on the basis of incomplete, inaccurate, and often unverifiable information. And even if complete, accurate, and verifiable data were available, people do not completely understand the process of change nor can they anticipate the direction that the future may take given the variability and impact of choice on possible outcomes.

Even though the future is not predictable, nothing stops people from shaping alternative futures, even if ever so slightly, by exercising the element of choice (decision making) in response to their perception of reality as they perceive it to be. And while the element of choice contributes to the unpredictable nature of forecasting the future, this very dynamic element is central to the counseling process and responsible for shaping the future. Cornish (1977), in response to this understanding, rejected the notion of future stating that since it does not exist, it can be invented.

Future—Concept of Quality

In response to inventing the future, four futuristic terms describing different types of futures were presented by Fitch and Svengales (1979). The *probable future* is the one that counselors can expect if they do nothing to shape the present. The probable future can be inferred from current trends. The *possible future* is "what may be" and thus encompasses a multitude of scenarios and possible alternatives. Possible futures like possible outcomes in decision making fail to consider the elements of probability and risk when studying the options. Counselors that adhere to developing counseling programs by only examining possible futures seldom consider the management functions of planning, organizing, actuating, and controlling when considering the future of elementary school counseling. *Plausible futures* are those futures that are likely to occur if counselors adhere to program policies based on the management process which includes systems analysis. Of all the futures presented by Fitch and Svengalis (1979), the *preferable future* is the one with which futurists are most often linked. Preferable futures are those which counselors hope for and dream about when envisioning counseling programs of excellence.

The philosophies of elementary school education and school counseling programs reflect what is most desirable and preferable in creating environmental opportunities and conditions that will encourage children to become all they are capable of being. The preferable future is captured in a vision of a world that perpetuates freedom, harmonious living, and responsibility.

The quality of elementary school counseling programs of the future will lie somewhere between the probable and the preferable. And since futures cannot be predicted, but can be created, elementary school counselors and Counseling Program Committees are faced with the challenge of deciding whether they will create their futures or accept those futures which have been created for them. We believe that the future of elementary school counseling programs lies in the counselor's ability and commitment in deciding what kind of future is wanted (preferable future) and how to create that future. Another way of stating this simple message is that elementary school counselors and Program Committees create the future, good or bad, by the actions they take or fail to take today.

Future—Concept of Time

Based on what has been discussed thus far about the future, a logical question to ask is "at what point in time does the future begin?" For counselors to plan for the future, they need to know something about the time frame that will influence their decisions.

According to Joseph (1974), the future has five basic periods. These include an immediate future (the present to five years hence), the near-term future (one to five years from now), the middle range future (five to 20 years from now), the long range future (20 to 50 years), and the far future (50 or more years from now).

Joseph's time periods of the future thus span the gap from the present to time immemorial. Major decisions made today could quite conceivably shape the future one year hence and quite probably five to 20 years from now. Inbody (1984) provided an example of Joseph's model when he noted that four years were required to harness the atom for atomic warfare and yet that very decision continues to impact on the world's military policy even today (40 plus years later). The course of the future, especially the near-term and the middle range future, can easily be influenced in a positive direction by counselors who hold a vision of what can be. "The biggest obstacle between now and the future you want is you" (Hays &

Johnson 1984, p. 208). Stated in yet another way, a counselor's image of the future is the most significant determinant in shaping that person's behavior (Woodell, 1979).

The future is a concept of time which begins with the counselor's view of that which is possible and necessary in meeting children's needs. Counselors have an opportunity, through elementary school counseling programs, to "build a better mousetrap." They can shape the future by looking for better long term solutions in response to perennial societal problems rather than focus on costly temporary and corrective measures which do not satisfactorily address the concerns for which they were designed.

Yes, the future is a concept of time that has its roots in the present. Counselors must become master bridge builders in spanning the gap between what is and what can be. To do this, the tripartite of the child, those behaviors to be learned, and those conditions of the learning environment must be considered in building a future that will address the developmental and societal needs of children. The time to begin is now.

Future—Concept of Connections, Time, and Images

Cornish (1977) presented three tentative postulates that futurists believe shape the future. The first is the *Unity of the Universe* which presents the view that all things are interconnected in the universe. A change in one element will precipitate a chain reaction in all other elements. The universe is constantly changing in response to the decisions and outcomes which shape the environment and all of humanity. Therefore the decisions that counselors make weigh heavily on their responsibility to research the potential impact of their ideas, before they set them in motion.

Second, the future relies on the *Crucial Importance of Time*. "The apparent neutrality of a decision is merely the lag time between the making of a decision and its eventual unintended impact!" (Inbody, 1984, p. 217). Even a gradual change, set in motion over time, can have a significant impact on the future.

Third, the *Importance of Ideas* conveys the significance that ideas and images play on shaping the future. Ideas and images are the pathways to reality and spark the eventual actualization of that which is to be. Counselors and all members of the elementary school counseling program possess the power of creating ideas and images that will eventually spawn the planning, organizing, actuating, and controlling of counseling programs designed to meet children's present and future needs.

FUTURISM—FIVE PRACTICES AND TEN COMMITMENTS AWAY

Futurism has been characterized as a disciplined process in which people can challenge and change the future by deciding what kind of future is wanted and then making it happen. That process (futurism) can only be put into practice by effective leaders. A major distinction between management and leadership is that management connotates the practice of handling things, establishing stability, improving efficiency, making things run smoothly, and other activities designed to control organization processes. Leadership, on the other hand, means to go places and signifies the practices of providing direction; searching for opportunities; challenging the status quo; and seeking ways to improve the organization, it's people, and those who are served by the organization.

Not unlike successful businesses and industries, elementary school counseling programs need both effective leaders and responsible managers. The elementary school counselor is the most likely candidate to move elementary school counseling into the 21st century and therefore must possess leadership and management skills and abilities.

Planning the future and making it happen requires leadership. "In essence leadership appears to be the act of getting others to want to do something you are convinced should be done" (Packard, 1962, p. 170). Kouzes and Posner (1987) suggested that the significance of Packard's quote lies in two words: to want. Leaders must not only have a sense of direction, they must possess the skills and human qualities that move people to action because they are internally moved to do so. A clear distinction exists between getting others to do something and getting others *to want* to do something.

Leaders are people who are credible and they develop that credibility through their actions by challenging, inspiring, enabling, modeling, and encouraging (Kouzes & Posner, 1987). Based on their leadership research, Kouzes and Posner (1987) have identified five practices and ten commitments which represent significant leadership behaviors possessed by most leaders in charting the future. Leaders (counselors) who make a difference (Kouzes & Posner):

Challenge the Process

1. Search for opportunities to challenge the status quo.

2. Experiment and take risks.

Inspire a Shared Vision

3. Envision the future and what the organization can become.

4. Enlist others in the dream.

Enable Others to Act

5. Foster collaboration and build spirited teams.

6. Strengthen others, making each person feel capable and powerful.

Model the Way

7. Set the example for others to follow.

8. Plan small wins.

Encourage the Heart

9. Recognize individual contributions.

10. Celebrate accomplishments. (p. 14)

These same practices and ten commitments can place elementary school counselors and their respective programs on the cutting-edge in creating the very best learning environment that we can offer today's children while at the same time charting a very much needed and significant future for elementary school counseling programs one, five, ten, and twenty years hence. The future of elementary school counseling as with all other futures, is an outgrowth of challenging the process, inspiring a shared vision, enabling others to act, modeling the way, and encouraging the heart. Through these practices, wonderful things can happen from breathing new life into existing school counseling programs—to creating exciting growth-producing learning climates—and to starting brush fires of commitment, challenge, and inspiration in program providers and recipients as they create and are shaped by their own sense of futurism.

Challenging the Process

Counselors must search for challenging opportunities as they revise their programs for change, growth, and innovative potential. They, likewise, must also be willing to experiment, take risks, and learn from their mistakes.

Search for Opportunities. In searching for future program opportunities, the following suggestions are offered:

1. View the counseling program from a fresh perspective. Counselors can gain new insights, as can other program providers, when they pretend that they have just stepped into their elementary school counseling program for the first time. By asking themselves what changes they would make or what they would do differently, some fresh ideas will begin to unfold almost immediately.

2. Counselors should make a list of all the ideas generated from the first suggestion and plan to implement as many as seem possible and reasonable over a planned period of time. All these ideas need not represent major projects, but ones which will move the counseling program forward and give it a new look.

3. Question the things that are done and why they are done that way. Most counseling programs are frought with practices that exist for no apparent reason other than that is the way things have always been done. For

every practice that is listed, ask what purpose does it serve? Does the practice support program growth and innovative development? For every practice that is essential and contributes to the preferable future, keep it. For those that seem to serve no useful purpose, eliminate them immediately. Involve as many people as possible in the elementary school counseling program when engaging in discussions which confront and challenge the status quo.

4. If a hole exists in the bucket, go fix it. All elementary school counseling programs, no matter how innovative and effective they are, can be improved. Counselors need to encourage and teach participants and service providers alike to be critical observers in looking for ways to improve the elementary school counseling program process and product. One way this can be accomplished is by having people take turns doing different activities. People in new experiences often ask questions about the job and the way things are done. They are often quick to point out and support ways in which things could be done better, more cost effectively, and perhaps more efficiently with improved results.

5. Instill excitement, challenge, and adventure into the program. By giving other people responsibility and the opportunity to be innovative and creative, a blanket of high level involvement spreads evenly across the entire elementary school counseling program, thus increasing the potential for continued program development and improvement. Programs that instill excitement, challenge, and adventure are also fun. When parents, teachers, administrators, and community supporters are given opportunities to solve problems, explore new experiences, create new opportunities, and learn new ways of doing things, they have fun investing in themselves, the counseling program, and their future.

Experiment and Take Risks. For counselors and Counseling Program Committees to challenge the process of elementary school counseling in search of change, growth, and innovative opportunities, they must experiment, take risks, and learn from their mistakes. That means that the environment in which they live, learn, and create must be one that supports the freedom to experiment and succeed as well as to fail. Such an environment can be created by doing the following:

1. ***Provide multiple opportunities (formal and informal) to collect innovative ideas.*** Breakfast meetings, suggestion boxes, evaluation forms, brainstorming sessions, good idea clubs, and advisory boards represent a few vehicles for stimulating creative thought and feedback in the elementary school counseling program. Making this process a normal, acceptable, and a regular part of the counseling program helps to remove suspicion and caution that sometimes surfaces when the collection of innovative ideas are connected with yearly program evaluations.

2. ***Solicit innovative ideas.*** Counselors should make idea gathering a part of their weekly planning sessions and ask program providers and recipients each week to discuss the nature of their involvement in the counseling program and how it has helped contribute to their growth. Encourage others to visit school counseling programs, volunteer organizations (YMCA, YWCA, The American Red Cross, etc.), and social service agencies, making it a point to bring back one or two innovative ideas that can be implemented as is, or with modification, into the local school counseling program.

3. ***Encourage experimentation.*** Waiting for good ideas to become fully developed prior to implementation, may serve to "kill off" the idea. Give people enough space to try out ideas on a small scale. Such experimentation encourages controlled risk taking, trial and error learning, and the self-confidence to try new ideas even though some may not work out as planned. Many worthwhile medical and technological advances have evolved out of experimentation.

4. ***Encourage and provide for team renewal.*** All people need stimulating activity and an occasional change of

scenery. Attending conferences, workshops, and professional training sessions help people to keep abreast of new ideas, new ways of doing things, and provides them with the opportunity to build new skills which will make them effective team participants.

5. **Honor risk takers.** Peters (1985) has suggested that every company should create an Innovators Hall of Fame. What a great idea for school counseling. Counselors could utilize a glass case in a prominent location and fill it with pictures, newspaper clippings, trophies, and ribbons belonging to those people whom they continue to honor for having taken a risk in trying something that is new or different for them. Risk takers can and should be honored even if their ideas do not materialize as planned. Well intentioned ideas that do not work out are just as important as the winners. Much can be learned from studying both successes and failures when developing innovative counseling programs.

6. **Model risk taking.** Counselors need to take visible risks as a way of encouraging other team players to do the same. Leaders cannot sit on the sidelines and expect others to want to become involved in planning the future.

7. **Foster commitment, control, and challenge.** Kouzes & Posner (1987) have stated that to build commitment, offer more rewards than punishments. To build a sense of control, choose tasks that are challenging, but within the person's skill capabilities. To build an attitude of challenge, encourage people to see change as full of possibilities. These points represent key issues for counselors to consider when building a volunteer support pool of active participants.

Inspiring a Shared Vision

Visions represent mental images of preferable futures that have a real potential for being achieved. The dream can only become a reality to the extent that the leader (counselor) can breathe life into that vision thus transforming that image into a certainty that is believable, desirable, and possible as perceived by those who will work toward making that vision become a reality. Shearson and Lehman Brothers (1984) stated that "Vision is having an acute sense of the possible. It is seeing what others don't see. And when those of similar vision are drawn together, something extraordinary occurs" (pp. 42-3).

Counselors, if they are to *inspire a shared vision,* must first be able to envision the future and second, be able to enlist the enthusiastic support of others in transforming the dream into new possibilities for elementary school counseling.

Envision the Future. Learning to become a futurist requires that counselors have knowledge about their own past and that of elementary school counseling; are able to express their wants in relationship to the current world view; and are prepared to explore, develop, and communicate positive expectations about the future with those who have a stake in the future of elementary school counseling programs. Here are a few ideas that counselors can use as they envision the future.

1. *Look at the past.* Counselors need to evaluate their own strengths and weaknesses and those of their programs. They need to ask what successes they have enjoyed, and how their successes have occurred. A similar question should be asked about program failures. Counselors also are encouraged to examine what patterns seem to emerge and how these patterns may have influenced the evolution of the school counseling program. If uninterrupted, how might these same patterns (good and bad) continue to shape the future?

2. *Study your wants.* Counselors are encouraged to explore what they want to accomplish during the coming year, the next five years, and twenty years from now. To begin the process of self-exploration, the following questions prepared by Kouzes and Posner (1987) can be used as a catalyst in helping counselors clarify their vision for the future.

   • How would you like to change the world for yourself and your organization?

- If you could invent the future, what future would you invent for yourself and your organization?

- What mission in life absolutely obsesses you?

- What is your dream about your work?

- What is the distinctive role or skill of your organization (department, plant, project, company, agency, community)?

- About what do you have a burning passion?

- What work do you find absorbing, involving, enthralling?

- What will happen in ten years if you remain absorbed, involved, and enthralled in that work?

- What does your ideal organization look like?

- What is your personal agenda? What do you want to prove? (p. 102)

3. **Describe what you did to become a member of the Elementary School Counseling Innovators Hall of Fame?** Counselors reflecting on the preceeding questions, should imagine themselves being inducted into the Innovators Hall of Fame and write an article about their contribution(s) to elementary school counseling as it will appear in the booklet describing the honorees' contributions. This is the counselor's opportunity to showcase dreams, aspirations, and hopes for the future as though they have already occurred.

4. **Write a short vision statement.** Kouzes and Posner (1987) have suggested that counselors write a twenty-five word or less statement, using the ideas generated thus far, in describing their ideal and unique images of the future regarding elementary school counseling programs. Counselors should make the statement short so that they can easily convey the intent of their vision to others. The authors (Kouzes & Posner) then suggested that counselors develop a short phrase or sentence which captures the essence of their vision. They are to use that slogan to keep the vision in the forefront and on everybody's lips. The slogan helps to maintain the focus of the elementary school counseling program and helps to keep the program forward moving.

5. **Act on your visions.** A certain amount of spontaneity and intuition are important variables in moving innovative ideas from dream to reality. Innovation is a process which encourages counselors to look beyond the way things have traditionally been done and to use their quick and ready insight in generating the necessary activity which adds clarity to the vision. Some movement may be necessary before an idea can come into proper focus.

6. **As the vision becomes real, identify what assumptions you have made that either limit or expand the program's opportunity for growth.** Assumptions represent preconceived notions or beliefs about the way things are or must be for success. Counselors should check their assumptions out with trusted supporters. They may turn out to be real or merely founded in myth.

   Counselors have assumptions about the elementary school counseling program, personnel, the way decisions are made, and the amount of counseling program support that exists within the district. Counselors also will find that testing their assumptions through controlled experimentation is of value as well. Reality testing often reveals that counselors and counseling programs have been influenced as much by myth as by truth.

7. **Become a futurist.** Counselors can study the future by turning to books and reports which analyze the forces which shape the future. In 1987, the American School Counselor Association (ASCA) and the American Association for Counseling and Development (AACD) sponsored a "20/20" focus on the Future Conference for school counselors. Attending conferences and programs of this type will help to keep a school district's focus on future trends and issues that need to be addressed. The school district also might develop its own futures committee which can be responsible for conducting research, reviewing research studies, and involving district personnel in futures activities and workshops.

8. *Use mental rehearsal.* A most powerful tool that can be used to usher in the future is imagery. Once counselors' visions have been clarified through the preceeding steps, they can practice visualizing their images as reality. Utilizing mental rehearsal, helps counselors actually see themselves going through steps and planning for the change. They then can convince themselves that they have been successful in selling others their ideas and that their dreams have now become a reality.

Counselors who are able to use imagery and affirmation techniques successfully stand a far greater chance of succeeding in the new endeavor than those who cannot. We used imagery and affirmation techniques when planning for the book (future) and found that we were able to bolster our self-confidence in seeing the book in its completed format before we began to write.

Enlist Others. While counselors must first be able to envision the future for themselves, if the process stops there, little else will happen. Counselors must find a way to communicate their vision to others in such a manner as to attract and excite members of the Counseling Program Committee and enlist their support in working toward a common purpose.

On August 23, 1963, 250,000 people were gathered at the Lincoln Memorial in Washington, D.C. to hear an address by Martin Luther King, Jr. Those who heard the speech watched history in the making and witnessed the future unfold as King uplifted and inspired people all across the nation as he invited them to go to the mountain top with him and dream of a nation united and free at last. That speech, and the manner in which it was delivered, enlisted others in his dream and it continues to do so even today.

While we do not suggest that counselors need to have the speech writing and oratory skills of a Martin Luther King, Jr., we are saying that if counselors are to enlist the support of others, three fundamental qualities of an inspirational presentation are required. Counselors must (1) appeal to a common purpose, (2) communicate expressively, and (3) sincerely believe in what they are saying (Kouzes & Posner, 1987).

Here are a few ideas that counselors can use to enlist the support of others.

1. **Identify the people to be enlisted in the vision.** Make a list of those people and groups (parents, teachers, administrators, schoolboard members, and community supporters) who stand to influence the future and who in turn will be influenced by it. These are the people and groups who stand to gain or lose based on their own actions and those of others.

2. **Identify a rallying point.** Elementary school counseling programs are supported by people of varying interests and backgrounds. Find that common thread or the magnetic field that draws people together because of common interests, shared beliefs, or a specific goal that can represent the rallying point. By talking to people and conducting needs assessments, it is possible to assess what the school and community want for their children. Once that cosmic glue has been identified, use it effectively to cement the commitment and relationships to instill the group to action.

3. **Learn how to present yourself effectively.** Counselors are encouraged to take a Dale Carnegie course or any speech course that will help them to develop their communication skills. Learning to use imagery and illustrations effectively to appeal to common beliefs, to be sincere, to be positive and hopeful, to speak with passion and emotion, and to convey personal convictions about one's dreams, is important.

4. **Develop a short presentation.** Counselors are encouraged to write a five minute, high impact speech that conveys the essence of the vision which can be delivered at a moment's notice to anyone. The speech should be designed to instruct others about the vision and the many opportunities that can be realized through its

employment. Counselors must learn to function successfully as salespeople and as politicians in selling their ideas to others. Using stories, metaphors, analogies, and varying props can help program supporters and customers (program recipients) to smell, taste, feel, and visualize the vision. As leaders, counselors are about the business of sculpturing their vision into a masterpiece of reality that is visible and so desirable that others will want to buy and support what the counselor has to sell.

5. **Be realistic, optimistic, and positive.** The counselor needs to encourage others to act by supporting them in every manner possible as they begin to employ innovative programming. Counselors need to provide words of encouragement, supply information, teach skills, build self confidence, and above all, to be enthusiastic. The future is created by those who can instill in others the *I can* consciousness and the *I will* state of mind. In addition to being highly optimistic, counselors also need to be realistic in acknowledging that there will be hard work and rough spots on the road to success. By helping counseling program supporters focus on the gold instead of the dirt, they will never lose sight of what it is they are trying to accomplish despite the many roadblocks and debris which may have to be moved out of the way in achieving the desired outcome.

Enabling Others to Act

Counselors are leaders and leaders recognize that they cannot build futures without the support and determination of loyal followers. Leaders are team builders who involve others in the planning process. They encourage people to grow by creating self–esteem building environments. Those environments build trust, encourage independence, foster and support team work, and create mutual respect and dignity in all human relationships.

When others feel strong and capable, are trusted and respected, experience love and a sense of belonging, relationships are fostered that serve to sustain extraordinary group effort. Parents, teachers, administrators, school board members, and community supporters hunger for those win-win opportunities in life when they can work together on projects of common interest that support everybody's needs and especially those of children.

The success of an elementary school counseling program is based on the counselor's ability to enable others to act. For this to occur, counselors must learn how to foster collaboration and cohesion among program supporters and to strengthen their positive beliefs in self as significant and contributing members of the elementary school counseling program team. What follows are a number of suggestions designed to foster collaboration and build people's strengths.

Foster Collaboration. Everybody has needs to be met. Counseling Program Committees work best when a spirit of cooperation and collaboration are fostered in the attainment of mutual goals. Team participants are more likely to cooperate with other team players when all members trust each other and discuss openly the benefits to be obtained by a particular course of action. The counselor must not only be task oriented, but also concerned about people and the process of group dynamics and human interactions. Give and take relationships, in addition to supporting collaborative goals, also encourage elementary school counseling team participants to assist each other in attaining personal goals as well. Here are some suggestions that will assist counselors to build collaboration and trust among all team players.

1. ***Always say "we."*** Counselors have always encouraged others to use the personal pronoun "I" when referring to personal accomplishments or behaviors. This helps people take ownership for their actions. However, as leaders, counselors need to take care in using "we" and "our" when describing counseling program goals and successes. No program can be successful without team involvement and shared efforts. Learning to share the credit is an activity that counselors can afford to practice. There is no charge to the institution (the school) for doing so, yet the profits (people efforts and program results) can be extraordinary because the counselor took a few moments to acknowledge and

model positive feedback to those who deserved to be acknowledged.

2. **Create opportunities for interactions.** Counselors, as is true for all team participants, are very busy people. Left to their own volition, they are inclined to become wrapped up in their own activities and gradually isolate themselves from each other. Counselors need to identify and foster a variety of ways to stimulate interactions among teachers, parents, administrators, school board members, and community supporters. Regularly scheduled meetings, problem solving groups, seminars on various school counseling topics, and Friday afternoon mixers provide opportunities for school counseling supporters to discuss the issues and to collaborate on goals they all can support.

3. **Create a climate of trust.** While trust means many things to many people, at the very least, trust communicates confidence and predictability. When a counselor is trusted, that person is believable and predictable based on words and action. A trusting climate is one where people are not afraid to say what they are thinking. They feel comfortable presenting their ideas and sharing their personal points of view because they know that they are loved and accepted for who they are even when their ideas run counter to group opinion. Trusting climates support vulnerability and encourage people to risk.

Counselors who take risks, and stand by others who do the same, pave the way for a supportive climate. A fundamental dimension of trust is delegation. Counselors who are willing to delegate responsibility to others, are demonstrating their trust in themselves and others. They are not afraid to give away their power and share it with others. By helping others get to the top of the mountain, they help to ensure that the counseling program also will attain peak experiences as well. Counseling program innovations must be nurtured in a climate of trust if they are ever to emerge beyond the seed.

4. ***Focus on gains not losses.*** The Counseling Program Committee that focuses on gains is optimistic. *The Committee sees opportunities in every problem, not problems with every opportunity.* They understand that dreams are the gateway to greatness. Before something can happen, people must first have a vision and believe in that vision so strongly that it becomes reality first in the mind and then in the world.

The challenge before all Counseling Program Committees is to cultivate winners, not losers. Counseling Program Committee members are encouraged to work together for the purpose of focusing on a win and to look for compromises, if necessary, to attain the gain. Great ideas often become mediocre advances, because the focus is on protecting the status quo and reducing the losses. When the Counseling Program Committee loses sight of the collective benefits and opportunities to be accrued by all, committee members quickly shift their focus to what they must do to minimize losses for themselves.

5. ***Involve the Counseling Program Committee in planning and problem solving.*** Counselors need to ask themselves who the people are that are involved in the planning and problem solving activities of the counseling program. So very often the counselor is in the situation all alone and does most of the planning and wrestling with the problems. Counselors will find that if they turn to the consumers and providers of counseling services for support in planning and problem solving, that these people, being closest to the action, will have some very practical suggestions to share.

To foster effective collaboration efforts in planning and problem solving, Lawler, III, (1986) has suggested that only those people with working knowledge of the situation be involved. Those people need to be provided with the authority, resources, and standards to be met in meeting the demands of the collaboration effort. Above all else, counselors should tie rewards valued by the group to the performance.

6. *Be a risk taker when building trust.* Counselors can build trust in themselves by being willing to place their trust in others. While we discussed this point earlier, we wish to reemphasize its importance in building peoples' confidence in counselors and in themselves. Counselors need to be open, willing to listen, accepting of other peoples' ideas, support risk taking and creative endeavors, and be ready to praise others for their efforts regardless of whether or not they work as planned.

Strengthen Others by Sharing Power and Information. An old Chinese proverb says that if you want one year of prosperity, grow grain. If you want ten years of prosperity grow trees. If you want one hundred years of prosperity, grow people. Many successful sales organizations have reached their success by growing people. When people grow, sales go up. When people have the information, skills, self confidence, and power to apply what they know best, organizations benefit from this successful mix of attributes. The more people believe that they can influence and control the organization, the greater organizational effectiveness and member satisfaction will be (Tannenbaum, 1968).

Counselors can best influence the future of elementary school counseling by strengthening people and enabling them to act in behalf of themselves and others. Counselors can do this by giving away information, skills, power, and increasing others' visibility in their service to the elementary school counseling program. Strengthening others to act is the process of building new leaders. Some suggested activities follow for counselors to use in strengthening others.

1. *Get to know people.* Don't take people for granted. Spend time getting to know them as people. Schedule informal opportunities to discuss hobbies, interests, talents, hopes, wishes, fears, and the future. The counselor needs to visit with the school staff (bus drivers, cafeteria workers, secretaries, and custodial workers), parents, teachers, and administrators. The counselor needs to develop friendships in the cafeteria, on the playground, in people's homes, and in the hallways. As counselors develop lasting bonds with those

who serve the school and children, they will learn much about themselves, other people, and new ways that they can best meet children's developmental and societal needs.

2. ***Develop team building competence.*** Counselors have the interpersonal skills to interact successfully with others. Those same skills can be used to bring people together and develop team relationships. As professionals, counselors, teachers, administrators, and educational specialists tend to function independent of each other. In so doing no sense of teamsmenship ever develops. While specialty groups are needed to provide unique services, they are all members of the same team when it comes to serving the needs of children and building more effective learning climates. These various groups need the opportunity to learn more about each other and to discuss common interests and concerns. Out of such a climate can grow some new and innovative ideas.

3. ***Use power to serve others.*** A difference exists between using power to help others get what they want and using power to control and manipulate others for the leader's personal gain. Leaders who use their power to serve others ultimately create leaders who in turn also learn to serve others. Leaders use their power to help others perform more effectively in their jobs. These same leaders are liked and respected people. Counselors are encouraged to cultivate leaders, increase their visibility, give them responsibility, and encourage their efforts in support of the elementary school counseling program.

4. ***Enlarge people's circle of influence.*** Counselors, who manage and lead successful counseling programs, involve program supporters in every facet of the program. Volunteers plan, organize, implement, and evaluate. These people have received training from the counselor and other professionals in basic statistical measurement methods, communication skills, decision making and problem solving techniques, and group dynamics. They have been trained and coached and have been given the opportunity and responsibility to perform autonomously.

5. ***Keep people informed.*** Counselors need to become great communicators. They need to keep people informed about the philosophy and mission of the elementary school counseling program. What's more, counselors need to help volunteers understand the importance of their contributions to the total program. Program supporters are more willing to back a program when they understand the critical nature of their efforts in support of their program's success. When people are informed and feel needed, they experience a sense of importance and put 100 percent of their effort into the job that needs to be done.

6. ***Make connections.*** Counselors are familiar with the old adage that says who you know is as important as what you know. The success of elementary school counseling programs is as much based on counseling connections as the counselor's knowledge and skills. The right connections open doors which lead to support in the way of training, money, information, and the backing of important ideas. Connections lead to power and add to the counselor's reputation as a person who can get things done through people. If the counseling program is to flourish, counselors need to introduce program supporters to the people they need to know in order to increase their sphere of influence. Through forming strategic relationships with others and doing the same for counseling program supporters, counselors can empower others in the same manner in which they too gained power.

7. ***Make heroes of other people.*** Another way of strengthening people is to increase their visibility. Counselors can do this by putting the spotlight on others. Glorify the volunteer, the program supporter, and the person with the good idea. Counselors can make use of telegrams, the newspaper, letters to the school board, recognition dinners, trophies, and other methods to focus attention on those who have supported the counseling program in some measure. All people deserve recognition for their efforts as well as their successes. Yet so many people go unrecognized throughout their

lives because no one took the time to focus the spotlight on them even if but for one short glorious moment.

Modeling The Way

The successful leader, according to Kouzes and Posner (1987), functions from a well defined philosophy, a set of statements by which the organization is measured, a value orientation about how children and program supporters ought to be treated, and a set of principles that make the organization (the elementary school counseling program) unique and distinctive.

Leaders create the plans and help design the road maps which highlight the way and guide people toward the desired ends. Leaders help to unravel the bureaucratic entanglements, model the way, and create the opportunities for small wins which lead to major victories. "Leaders know that while their position gives them authority, their behavior earns them respect" (Kouzes & Posner, 1987, p. 187).

Counselors can enhance their credibility as leaders in immeasurable ways if they set responsible goals, proceed with enthusiasm, and practice consistency between their words and actions as they help others attain the high standards by which elementary school counseling programs are measured.

Set the Example. Modeling the way by setting the example is how counselors can make their visions tangible. The counselor's actions become the mirror through which others observe and evaluate their own behaviors in light of values and standards set by the leader which symbolize the credibility of the organization. Counselors therefore need to establish a clear sense of direction and be guided by a basic philosophy and set of values that all program participants can support both personally and organizationally. Counselors shoulder a major responsibility in making sure that everyone connected with school counseling, in whatever capacity, understand the fundamental mission of the program. That responsibility cannot be accomplished in a thirty minute assembly at the beginning of the school year. Counselors must work daily and timelessly through every avenue open to them if they are to point everyone in the right direction when it comes to empowering others to act in behalf of getting the elementary school counseling program where it needs to be. Counselors can become effective example setters by doing the following:

1. **Write a self tribute.** Counselors, if they are to model the way, must first know what they value. Counselors can begin the process by asking themselves on what basis they evaluate the success of their elementary school counseling programs. Once that has been determined, counselors are encouraged to explore and clarify the kind of actions they need to display to communicate their beliefs, values, and ideals to others in support of a successful program. Counselors are asked to imagine themselves being recognized for their contributions to elementary school counseling at a large reception in their honor. Writing 2 or 3 five line phrases that they would like to hear will force them to begin thinking about what they value and hold sacred.

2. **Develop a leadership credo.** Counselors will find the recording of their beliefs and personal ideals useful in establishing a set of guidelines for the elementary school counseling program. An activity used by Kouzes and Posner (1987) asks the organizational leader to imagine being relocated away from the company for several months without any form of communication possible. The leader is permitted to leave only one page of guidelines stating his/her business beliefs, philosophy, values, and credo on how the business should be conducted during the leader's absence. These guidelines would then be distributed throughout the company for employee use. Counselors might imagine a similar scenario and practice writing their own similar set of guidelines. They should take the activity seriously and share their results with several other people for their feedback.

3. **Write a tribute to the elementary school counseling program.** Counselors can ask various program service providers and recipients (parents, teachers, administrators, school board members, and community supporters) to write a testimonial tribute to the elementary

school counseling program. By comparing the testimonial tribute statements, the counselor can begin to understand how the counseling program is perceived by various program supporters and recipients. Counseling programs that do not appear to have a focus or are perceived in ways which run counter to the counselor's credo need to be reviewed. What kind of future is being created for elementary school counseling by those who shape its current existence and future essence?

4. **Publish the credo.** From all data that have been collected, counselors are encouraged to print the credo which best exemplifies the desired future of elementary school counseling programs. Once that future is described from a here and now point of view, the counselor and Counseling Program Committee have that ideal to attain. The credo can be printed on the counselor's business card, the counseling newsletter, printed signs, and posted on the counselor's door. A symbol also can be created which reminds people about the elementary school counseling program and the credo.

5. **Audit actions.** The counselor and members of the Counseling Program Committee are encouraged to record their actions and compare them with what they say and with their printed credo. Actions include what the counselor and committee members say to people, the number of daily contacts they have, the nature of these contacts, and the focus of messages delivered. The purpose of the audit is to scrutinize daily routines, identify habitual patterns of behavior, evaluate behavior under pressure, and compare counseling program messages with the printed credo. Counselors also are encouraged to look at their calendar of appointments and to determine how their behaviors, past, present, and future either support or detract from the philosophy and mission (the future) of the elementary school counseling program.

6. **Evaluate established routines and systems.** Counselors need to evaluate the routines that have been established in the counseling program. Routines represent

established ways of doing things and the systems that have been created which support those behaviors. Some routines and systems are necessary because they help to maintain and support the counseling program's principles and ideals. Those routines and systems can be improved upon while other routines and systems which are less supportive and perhaps destructive can be eliminated. For each function of management (planning, organizing, activating, and controlling), there are routines and systems that need to become firmly established if the future, as described in the credo, is to become more of a reality each year.

7. **Be dramatic.** Sometimes counselors need to stage dramatic events in order to illustrate a point or principle stated in the credo. The challenge before counselors is to devise ways to impress upon counseling program recipients and providers the significance of the counseling program to the educational system and the seriousness of the counselor to get the job done. If counselors wish to establish more risk taking, they will need to emphasize the benefits and minimize the drawbacks through some responsive action that gains people's attention. Sometimes counselors need to use their acting and clowning skills to help people focus on issues.

8. **Be a story teller.** Counselors and Counseling Program Committee personnel have many true stories they can tell to make conversation and to illustrate a standard or value from the credo in action. Program supporters and recipients need to hear, over and over again, the many success stories associated with the elementary school counseling program. These stories, in turn, get repeated by others and the success of elementary school counseling is allowed to expand to a wider audience.

9. **Find teachable moments.** Teachable moments occur during those times in the school day when the counselor identifies and reinforces the positive behaviors and actions of people that support the elementary school counseling program (credo). At other times, the

counselor will want to support others for their valiant efforts, in addition to exploring with them, alternative actions that may yield more desired results. Utilizing teachable moments can be fun for the counselor and can help to illustrate the mission of the school counseling program.

10. **Be emotional.** Most counselors, by nature, are caring, compassionate individuals. That human quality can also be an asset to the elementary school counseling program. Counselors not only care about people, they also must care about what happens to the elementary school counseling program. Counselors must first believe in themselves, second in other people, and third in their program to serve people (program recipients and providers) in a caring and compassionate manner.

Plan Small Wins. "Life is a cinch by the inch and hard by the yard," exemplifies the importance of taking small steps. Many projects look rather discouraging when viewed in their totality. Imagine how anyone would feel if they were to observe all the food that they would ever consume in a lifetime. Such a sight and task would certainly appear to be overwhelming.

The counselor's job is to convince program supporters that what appears to be impossible is possible. The task can be accomplished by planning small wins. As program supporters experience small successes and observe movement toward goal attainment, confidence in the counselor, the counseling program, and in themselves will begin to increase.

Counselors model the way by helping people to change their behaviors, establish new ways of doing things, and create new attitudes regarding what they can accomplish when they plan small wins. Counselors are now ready to plan small wins by exercising the following six ideas:

1. **Make a plan.** Counselors recognize the importance of planning when developing any project. In Chapter 2 are provided guidelines to successful planning which should be followed before any project is implemented.

2. **Make a model.** Before implementing an idea full scale, counselors should identify a location where the model can be field tested. Select a site that is most supportive (physically and psychologically) and capitalize on it. When expanding the project concept to other locations, use the model as an instructional guide and encourage others to adapt and improve upon its application.

3. **Take one step at a time.** Counselors who make use of successive approximation, modeling, cueing, and positive reinforcement principles when planning the project, training the participants, and implementing the project should experience little difficulty in attaining success. Counselors will need to keep focused on the importance of the project, how it reinforces the vision, and the progress being made as it is implemented. Signs can be posted, articles can be written, and people can be verbally praised as means of spotlighting the progress being made.

4. **Reduce the cost of saying yes.** People are reluctant to get involved in those projects about which they know little and lack confidence in themselves to do a good job. For that reason, counselors must make it easy for people to take risks, experiment, and make mistakes with minimal negative consequences to them and the project. Planning small wins begins with the first step. The first step is easier to take when volunteers feel connected to the project, the counselor, and the school counseling program.

5. **Use the natural diffusion process.** Building successful elementary school counseling programs is a change process. Counselors, if they are to be successful in creating a meaningful and positive future for school counseling, must understand the dynamics of change and be able to use them effectively. For example, change is more likely to be supported when people understand the change, when the change supports the mission of the counseling program, when the benefits of change can be substantiated, when the innovation has worked in other settings, and when the people who will implement the

change are committed to the idea and those who are trying to bring it about.

Change can occur in one of two ways. Change can be ordered by those in authority (position power) or it can occur naturally because the groundwork and support for the change has been established (personal power). While personal power and the infusion process usually takes longer to implement, it tends to be the most effective route to take because the support is there to make the project work.

6. *Give people choices and make choices highly visible.*
When planning small wins, counseling program participants need to experience a sense of ownership in the program. A feeling of ownership occurs when people have an opportunity to make choices and to process decisions regarding their participation in the counseling program. When people are told what to do and how to do it, dependence is created and with dependence can come a gradual disinterest in the program. Choices allow for flexibility, independence, creativity, and experimentation. These variables help to stimulate ownership and a sense of pride, challenge, and accomplishment.

Encouraging the Heart

Encouragement is a significant element in the success of any elementary school counseling program. We have discussed the importance of recognition throughout this book, but would now like to focus on ways in which the school counselor can encourage others in their quest for the summit. Whether developing new programs or improving existing programs, counselors and Counseling Program Committees are continually seeking to build more effective delivery systems and better methods for meeting children's needs. Counselors play a significant role in maintaining the courage, enthusiasm, and spirit of program supporters as they commit themselves to the vision. Counselors need to express often and visually their pride in their Counseling Program Committees by using a variety of methods to celebrate team accomplishments.

Counselors can support and recognize program volunteers through thank you notes, kind smiles, awards, public praises, recognition dinners, continental breakfasts, and get togethers after school hours. The recognition of individual and group contributions to the success of every project is critical.

Counselors that have the talent of making their program supporters feel like heroes will help these people to fall in love with the program. Program supporters will experience a sense of family that can only be attained when people care about and for each other. When this happens, everyone benefits—parents, teachers, counselors, children, school board members, administrators, and community supporters. Encouraging the heart can be accomplished by those counselors who actively recognize contributions and celebrate accomplishments.

Recognize Individual Contributions. "Leaders provide people with clear directions, substantial encouragement, personal attention, and feedback. Leaders make people winners, and winning people like to up the ante, raise the standards, and conquer the next mountain" (Kouzes & Posner, 1987, p. 253). Counselors are leaders who have the potential to create environments which can attain the foregoing accomplishments. They can and must learn to express their appreciation in ways that go beyond the formal means of recognition used by their school systems. Spontaneity and creativity are two words that when transformed into action statements, continue to lead Counseling Program Committees and volunteers toward attaining the vision as expressed in the counselor's published credo. For those willing to take the plunge, the following ideas can help forge the way.

1. ***Develop tough measurable performance standards.*** Counseling program standards need to be known and understood by all. Standards also must be stated in such a manner that their attainment, or lack of it, is visible. When standards (What is important to the counseling program and the recipients of services) are clear and attached to goal attainment, recognizing individual and group contributions to project successes become easy.

2. *Install a formal systematic process for rewarding performance.* Many elementary school counseling programs do not have a formal systematic process for recognizing performance. Formal and informal feedback systems need to be instituted. People need to know how they are doing in relation to the performance standards. That means that program supporters not only must be knowledgeable of the standards to be met, but also how they will be measured, how the feedback will be received, and how they stand to benefit from having met the standards.

3. *Be creative about rewards.* Counselors need to discuss the matter of recognition with school board members and administrators. For a small monetary investment, many recognition ideas can be instituted, other than pay raises and promotions, which will please the recipients and increase productivity.

4. *Let others help design nonmonetary compensation systems.* While counselors have been singled out as those individuals most responsible for recognizing individual contributions, various individuals and volunteer groups may choose to show off their own skills and talents. For example, a group of teachers may have developed a special self-esteem building program in their school and choose to showcase their efforts through the local newspaper, the display of projects in a downtown store window, and through a radio interview describing the project. These same teachers could be supported by the local district to present their project at a state conference and to write an article for a national journal. These successes in turn can be recognized.

5. *Make recognition public.* Not everything that people do has to be honored publicly. However public recognition does bolster self-esteem, develops self-confidence, supports desired behaviors, and builds enthusiasm. The Boy Scouts and Girl Scouts of America provide numerous opportunities for young people to be recognized for meeting program standards. Those awards are visible and are given at public recognition ceremonies. Our own

military system operates quite successfully on a formal recognition program that awards ribbons and medals ceremoniously.

6. **Go out and find people who are doing things right.** Many elementary school counseling volunteers go quietly about their business doing a good job but are never recognized for their work. When counselors go looking for people to celebrate, they are looking for positive behaviors. They also are forced to think about their credo (vision) and the standards to be met in their quest for excellence in action. When program supporters are identified who are meeting program goals, they need to be told in a very specific and clearly stated manner why they are receiving a particular recognition. "Mary, you were selected as the parent volunteer of the week because you made five presentations this month at social service agencies about our parent volunteer program. That is the kind of activity that makes you a valued friend of elementary school counseling and supports our mission of increasing our parent volunteer corp. Thank you for your contribution." This kind of recognition also gives other parent volunteers another example of a valued activity endorsed by the counseling program.

7. **Coach.** All professional sports teams coach their players before, during, and after the season is over. Coaching is also a process that guides people throughout their participation in the elementary school counseling program. Counselors (coaches) spend time with program supporters (players) listening to them, talking to them about program strategies, and providing them with feedback about their efforts. Through successive approximation and continuous feedback, program supporter participation is gradually shaped into program successes. As the fundamentals of effective participation are learned, the values and the vision of elementary school counseling programs emerge with ever increasing awareness and clarity. Recognition and celebration are thus linked to the coaching experience because both activities signal program achievements and victories.

Celebrate Accomplishments. In addition to being leaders, counselors must also become cheerleaders of accomplishment. Kouzes and Posner (1987) have stated that celebration is based on three key principles: (1) focusing on key values, (2) making recognition publically visible, and (3) being personally involved.

Focusing on key values requires all personnel to know what those values are and to tie all celebrations to the accomplishments of those values. Everything about a celebration must occur with purpose. And one of the major purposes of celebrating key values is to have a positive impact upon the behavior of all program supporters. When Amway, Mary Kay, or similar organizations get together, they plan seminars which celebrate people in relation to the key values of the organization. These organizations build people, inspire a shared vision, enable others to act, model the way, plan small wins, encourage the heart, and celebrate team accomplishments regularly and proudly.

Public ceremonies, as we have discussed, communicate the seriousness of the organization in cherishing and accomplishing its stated values. By visibly demonstrating the importance of attaining program goals, the act of celebrating fosters commitment and a team spirit that binds elementary school counseling supporters together. People learn that the way to get to the top is based on helping other people get what they want. So often the lesson is learned incorrectly with people clammering over each other in hopes of being first. People who work for organizations like Amway and Mary Kay, recognize that their success is tied directly to the success of everyone above and beneath them on the corporate ladder. This lesson is also true for elementary school counseling as well. Counselors must make use of seminars, rallies, and public celebrations used by other successful organizations to accomplish similar ends.

Personal involvement of the counselor is important when celebrating team accomplishments. When parents, teachers, children, administrators, school board members, and community supporters are asked to share their impressions about the school counselor and the counseling program, how is that person and program characterized? The counselor's behavior and program visibility, or lack of it, communicate much about how the elementary school counseling program is viewed. If counselors are unaware of how they and their programs are characterized, then the time for them to become personally involved is now, in a planful way, in creating and celebrating tomorrow's vision today. Celebrating team accomplishments can become a reality by practicing the following four suggestions.

1. **Schedule celebrations.** While many celebrations ought to be spontaneous, others can be scheduled on the calender. Counselors and the Counseling Program Committee should identify the key values of the elementary school counseling program and then schedule dates on the calender to recognize all those people who have contributed to the program's success. Counselors should plan to recognize everyone at sometime during the year for at least one major contribution that they have made. Perhaps the following celebrations can be scheduled:

   a. **Founders Day.** The beginning of elementary school counseling in the school district.

   b. **Parent Volunteers Day.** A day to celebrate all those parents who contribute to the success of the counseling program.

   c. **Project Pride and Respect Day.** A day to celebrate pride and respect of those people and children who have accomplished a milestone (academically, physically, socially, environmentally) during the year.

   d. **Community Support Day.** A day to recognize various community organizations, groups, and individuals for their contributions to the school counseling program.

   Perhaps one day a month could be set aside by counselors to publicize and recognize key supporters and special counseling programs. The special days that are celebrated each year can change as desired.

2. **Be a cheerleader the counselor's way.** Counselors are all individuals and will have their own unique way of

leading a cheer. How the recognition is made is less important than doing something. Sincerity and genuineness are most critical variables when celebrating. Counselors are encouraged to use their imaginations, borrow ideas from other people, and experiment with new ideas of letting people know that the school counseling program cares. When money is a major problem, involve various groups in the school to share their talents and creativity in making different recognition tributes. T-shirts, plaques, flowers, cards, and coffee and donut breaks can become rewarding methods for communicating the thought that "this team" has helped the counseling program achieve another milestone in meeting the vision of what elementary school counseling hopes to become.

3. **Secure a social network.** Counselors are faced with developing two major networks. They need to build strong social support between and among members of the elementary school counseling team and they need to secure their own personal social network which may include team members but usually extends beyond the immediate work group.

Counselors function in jobs that demand a social support system consisting of friends, close colleagues, mentors, and sponsors. These people can lend an open ear, provide honest feedback, offer suggestions, provide a needed source of strength during periods of distress, and be there to share in joys and accomplishments.

Counselors, if they are to cultivate a social support system, cannot wait until a crisis occurs and hope to secure that needed assistance. They need to determine what their network looks like right now. What people, clubs, organizations, associations, and political and religious groups do counselors belong to and support actively? Counselors should ask themselves which of their relationships are solid, which ones can be bolstered, and which ones need to be renewed? With those questions and responses in mind, the next logical step is to build a plan for getting in touch with these potential supporters and implement the plan today. Counselors that are interested in developing and managing pace setting elementary school counseling programs with a future must rely on the support of many people and organizations in achieving and celebrating meaningful wins in the here and now.

4. **Stay in love.** Counselors need to stay in love with who they are, what they do, and with the people with whom they work and serve. Leaders that are successful, love their work and all that it entails. They know what they love to do and incorporate that love into their work. Counselors may find that taking a refreshing pause from their busy routines will give them an opportunity to question whether or not their current activities support their vision and what they love to do. Counselors who are unhappy with their jobs can choose a leadership journey described by Molitor, account executive at Regis McKenna, Inc. (cited in Kouzes & Posner, 1987).

> When I get back to RMI (or School District)
> These are lessons
> I'll try to fly.
>
> Challenge the process
> Push the status quo
> Try new ideas
> Don't say no.
>
> Share a vision
> First foot on the way
> Enlist in a dream
> Its rewards begin today.
>
> Provide other the tools
> Let them draw from within
> Remove the path's barriers
> Shout praise over the din.
>
> Do as I do
> Do what you may
> If I listen to you
> You'll show the way.

Celebrate history
Awake for a loss
Life is a journey
Venture is the cost.

Never let it be said
"If only I had. . ."
Time's too short
Inaction is sad.

First step outward
With friends gathered round
Envision the future
Feet on the ground. (p. 276)

BIBLIOGRAPHY

Amara, R. (1981). Imperatives for tomorrow: Images, institutions, involvement. *World Future Society Bulletin, 15,* 1-4.

Cornish, E. (Ed.). (1977). *The study of the future.* Washington, DC: World Future Society.

Fitch, R.M., & Svengalis, C.M. (1979). *Futures unlimited* (Bulletin 59). Washington, DC: National Council for the Social Studies.

Hays, O.G., & Johnson, C.S. (1984). 21st century counseling. *The School Counselor, 31,* 205-214.

Inbody, N.M. (1984). Futurism: Philosophy and procedures adapted to counseling. *The School Counselor, 31,* 215-222.

Joseph, E. (1974). What is future time? *The Futurist, 8,* 178.

Kouzes, J.M., & Posner, B.Z. (1987). *The leadership challenge: How to get extraordinary things done in organizations.* San Francisco: Jossey-Bass.

Lawler, E.E., III. (1986). *High-involvement management: Participative strategies for improving organizational performance.* San Francisco: Jossey-Bass.

Packard, V. (1962). *The pyramid climbers.* New York: McGraw Hill.

Peters, T.J. (1985, February, 13). Developing distinctive skills. Presentation to the Executive Seminar in Corporate Excellence, Santa Clara University.

Shearson and Lehman Brothers. (1984, June, 4). Vision Business Week, pp. 42-43.

Tannenbaum, A. (1968). *Control in organizations.* New York: McGraw-Hill.

Toffler, A. (1970). *Future shock.* New York: Bantam Books.

Woodell, G.D. (1979). Images of the future: Some questions for study. *World Future Society Bulletin, 13*(3), 1-6.

FUTURE PROGRAMS AND FUTURE PROFESSIONAL ISSUES

Elementary school counselors can have their greatest impact on the future, not by attempting to predict what will be, but by planning the preferable future as described in Chapter 12. As a concept of quality, the preferable future represents what school counselors, school personnel, and community supporters dream about when envisioning educational programs of excellence for all children. While Chapter 12, *Planning the Future*, describes a process for transforming dreams into realities, Chapter 13 explores some of the programs, issues, and directions that will need to be addressed by elementary school counselors as they develop programs that will encourage and support freedom, harmonious living, and responsibility. The readers of Chapter 13 thus are encouraged to use this chapter as a model for exploring additional topics of interest and need and then use Chapter 12 and the ideas presented there as means of making program dreams come alive.

We will explore five topics which we believe will continue to play an important role in shaping children's futures. Our purpose is not to discuss these topics in depth, as numerous publications are available for resources. Our intent is to explore some of the yet unresolved issues associated with these topics and to stimulate the reader's thoughts by presenting some future directions to consider when creating preferable futures. The five topics which we have chosen are

1. microcomputers in counseling and human development,

2. multicultural education,

3. living in a nuclear age,

4. children's rights, and

5. living a wellness lifestyle.

The last half of the chapter will explore and expand upon the role of school counselor as leader, manager, political activist, and service provider and the importance of these key ingredients for getting things done in shaping successful elementary school counseling programs.

MICROCOMPUTERS IN COUNSELING AND HUMAN DEVELOPMENT

Most people would agree that computers have an exciting and productive future in elementary school counseling. Nelson and Krackover (1983) suggested six areas of computer usage that are valuable for elementary school counselors. They include (1) learning from computers via drill, practice, and tutorials; (2) learning with computers via simulation, games, and data collection or interpretation; (3) learning about computers via computer literacy and programming languages; (4) learning about thinking with computers using educational computer languages such as LOGO and PILOT; (5) learning about management and school management programs; and (6) using the computer as a reinforcer. Many counselors are likewise familiar with the computer applications described by Alpert, Pulvino, and Lee (1985) regarding the storing of records, conducting needs assessments, managing counseling program research, instituting counselor accountability procedures, assessing needed data from various information services, automating effective educational placement programs, creating and promoting efficient public relations efforts, and using counseling simulations and computer-assisted training programs.

The microcomputer is quickly becoming as common as the chalkboard in our nation's schools (Dinkmeyer & Carlson, 1983). Computers and software manufacturers have created a competitive multibillion dollar business for themselves. The sale of computers and software has increased dramatically in the past five years in part due to the vast coverage which computers have received as management and educational aids. Counselors, teachers, parents, and children have had the importance of being computer literate impressed upon them to the extent that survival in a computer age is believed to be directly proportional to one's knowledge and skills in computer use.

Microcomputers will continue to increase in numbers because they are small, relatively inexpensive, easily maintained, and are user friendly. In addition, numerous, easy to use, and relatively inexpensive software packages are available which will allow counselors to do the many things previously described. With its relative, recent, and fast paced emergence on the educational scene, microcomputer technology has the potential to augment as well as to undermine those potentialities for which the technology was designed (Sampson & Pyle, 1983).

The aim of any computer application in counseling and human development is to assist children in meeting their needs. Although the needs of children and counselors will vary, three central factors are critical in contributing to the responsible use and future of computers. They are (1) selecting a computer application that has demonstrated capability of meeting the user's needs, (2) implementing the system within the constraints of the environment for which it was designed, and (3) recognizing the potential and limits of the resources as outlined by the developer in realizing desired user outcomes (Sampson, Jr., 1984). The potential benefits of using computer applications are greatly limited when these factors are applied to their use (Sampson, Jr., 1984).

Issues and Problems

In addition to being knowledgeable about the potential of computer technology, counselors also must consider the problems and issues that have or are likely to occur if they are not used responsibly. Childers, Jr. (1985) has identified 11 issues that have ethical implications for counselors and the counseling profession.

Confidentiality. Computers present their own unique problems when maintaining children's right to privacy in terms of access and collection of data without family permission. While maintaining confidentiality has always been a concern of counselors, addressing this issue, in response to the use of computers in record collection, maintenance, use, and release, needs to occur.

Data Storage. Because data storage has become easy and cost effective when maintaining large amounts of data, standards need to be established which guard against the indiscriminate collection of information on children and their families that have little or no direct value in the delivery of effective counseling services.

Another issue to be addressed is the length of time that various data should be maintained. Some states provide minimum guidelines for retaining certain types of information while calling for the periodic purging of other data.

Software Issues. Inadequate software is cited as the single greatest impediment to the computer revolution (Benderson, 1983). Benderson stated in 1983 that 95% of the available software on the market was not worth having. While software packages have improved since that time, counselors share a major responsibility with other educators in selecting high quality software programs that are valid, reliable, useable, and meet children's needs in a most responsible manner.

Counselors also are faced with updating computer software programs which have outlived their usefulness. Those that can not be easily updated, should no longer be used. Unless someone with the appropriate background and skills has been assigned to periodically review outdated software packages, the irresponsible dissemination of misinformation is likely to become a significant ethical problem.

Counselor-assisted Software Programs. Many counseling program software packages have been designed to be used by counselors and children working together. When children are left to operate these programs independent of adult supervision and guidance, much of their intended values can be lost.

Client-screening Procedures. While computers serve a useful purpose, they can become a vehicle of frustration and pain. Children need to be taught how to use the computer and software packages and not be placed in situations that demand more of them than they are capable of delivering. Some children also are more anxious than others and may become overly stressed when using the computer or certain software programs. All children should be screened for appropriate knowledge, skill, and self confidence before being placed in an independent situation with a computer.

Use by Affluent Versus Poor Clients. A potential problem exists with the use of any technology. The affluent are more likely to have access to the technology than those who are less well off. With the passage of time, the gap is likely to widen between those with the computer information, skills, and self confidence and those who are lacking in this strength. If society continues to move in the direction of high technology, people who are more familiar with the technology and its use will have greater job opportunities, more freedom, and better education than those who do not. Perhaps as more computers are purchased and easy access to their use improves with time, the potential societal problem of the "haves" versus the "have nots" will not take place.

Sexism. Becker (1983) reported that a smaller percentage of girls were electing to take computer classes in high school. We believe that with the introduction of computers in the elementary school grades (K-6), that the trend identified by Becker is changing. We have mentioned the sexism issue because we believe that counselors must insure that both sexes have an equal opportunity to learn about and use computers throughout their years in school.

Computer Literacy with Poor Socialization Skills. Computer literacy is an important skill for children to have. However, that skill should not be attained at the sacrifice of other equally important skills. As long as counselors, teachers, and parents monitor children's use of the computer and provide for the attainment of socialization skills, they will achieve a responsible balance in developing a variety of interactive skills. For some children, however, the concern of self-imposed isolation is a reality. Children who are very shy, those lacking in interpersonal skills, those who have been rejected by their peers, and those who are psychologically addicted to gadgetry are likely candidates to spend an excessive amount of time at the computer.

External Locus of Control. Children with an external locus of control tend to believe that what happens to them is based on the control of powerful others, luck, fate, or chance (Joe, 1971). They do not attribute what happens to them as being based on their own behavior, capacities, or attributes (internal locus of control). Children with an external locus of control may perceive the computer as possessing the power to make decisions and to provide correct responses and therefore be less inclined to assume personal responsibility for their own actions in supplying the data which leads to the solution. Children need assistance in understanding how computers function and to assume personal responsibility for their own choices.

Left-brain Thinking. Computer technology and many related programs tend to reinforce thinking (logical, rational, and digital thinking) to the exclusion of developing right hemispheric activity (intuitive, metamorphical, and analogical thinking). Counselors will need to develop strategies that will insure the development of the whole person and more specifically enhance and validate right brain thinking.

Counselor Preparation. The American Association for Counseling & Development (AACD) and the American School Counselor Association (ASCA) recognize the importance of counseling training in computers. Both organizations have provided training in computers, developed publications, and have established guidelines in their use. However, much still remains to be done. Many counselors probably still lack formal training in computers and yet they are faced with having to make decisions about software and computer applications. Counselors graduating from the different counselor education institutions are, no doubt, receiving quite a variation in computer training.

The future of computers is solidly grounded, what is not is the most appropriate, responsible, and effective uses of computers to meet children's needs. The counseling profession is now at the crossroads of computer technology. Their potential and some of the problems associated with their use are obvious.

Future Directions

The goal of the School for Individual Education (SIE) in Merritt Island, Florida is to develop in children the four R's of responsibility, respect, resourcefulness, and responsiveness (Mastroianni, 1983). The extent to which the four R's can contribute to the development of computer education is unlimited when serving as a guide for creating those opportunities designed to meet children's needs.

Responsibility. The goal of responsibility is to develop in children a sense of independence and self sufficiency. Children are provided with the information, skills, and self confidence they need to function in the environment on their own. The challenge of school and community personnel is to identify and implement only those educational and computer based programs that facilitate and reinforce the concept of responsibility.

Respect. Children are taught to value themselves, others, and their environment. Respect is also synonymous with teaching right from wrong, ethics, and morality. Helping children to understand and utilize computers in the context of developing responsible and respectful human interactions between and among people; serving the environment in positive and growth producing ways; and upholding human rights, ethics, and morality will help to insure that the technology is used to advance the interest of mankind.

Resourcefulness. Providing children with the capability of devising ways and means of challenging new situations with their own resources (information, skills, self confidence) is the goal of being resourceful. Teaching children how to use computers and packaged software without them understanding and being able to comprehend the use of the technology to solve their own problems means that educators have fallen short of the mark of teaching resourcefulness. Teaching children to become effective problem solvers using computers is a resourceful application of the technology.

Responsiveness. The goal of responsiveness is to teach children to act appropriately and empathetically to another person's needs. Children should be taught computer applications as a human activity (process) that reinforces cooperation between and among people in the service of others. Children must understand that all computer transactions eventually affect people's lives. And while the process of computer manipulation is mechanical, those who are responsible for and who are affected by those manipulations are people with feelings and needs.

Developing a computer program for children that meets the four R's and is responsive to the many issues and potential problems discussed requires the construction of a road map in

1. determining the district's philosophy of computer education,

2. creating general and specific goal statements,

3. determining how computers will be used based on the philosophy and goals,

4. determining which model and brand will best meet the district's goals (consider available software and its compatability with specific hardware),

5. determining optimum number of computers necessary to carry out the recommended program,

6. determining which children or grade levels should be included,

7. creating a scope and sequence of activities for the district,

8. recommending postponement of major purchases until the above planning has been completed, and

9. screening and coordinating purchases. (Wilmoth, 1983, p. 49)

Counselors and educators who follow the preceding course of action when implementing a comprehensive computer educational program with a four R's emphasis will help to insure an important place for computers in the curriculum.

Meeting children's needs, be they developmentally or societally focused, must be the single most determining factor in deciding what behaviors children are to learn. Computer technology provides society with another useful tool for meeting human needs and should be taught in schools for as long as that purpose continues to be served.

MULTICULTURAL EDUCATION

Multicultural education shows much promise for enhancing the working-living climate of the school; reducing tensions between and among ethnic, racial, religious, and national origin groups; and in establishing a positive direction for families, communities, and the media in emulating and implementing multicultural programs which will permeate all dimensions of society. The need for continued efforts in developing and implementing responsible multicultural education programs has never been greater in our most recent history than it is right now. Racism and racial tension continue to be major problems and represent serious barriers to whites and nonwhites alike as they attempt to maximize their own economic, psychological, and social growth (Lee, 1982). Increased educational measures must continue to be taken by the schools in order to foster more positive attitudes and favorable behavioral changes among the diverse segments of a vast multicultural population.

Counselors will continue to play a significant role in helping to create teaching/learning climates which address the needs of all children. A major threat to the disruption of children's education is an environment which does not support cooperation, harmonious living, and acceptance of all people. In an effort to establish and maintain an environment which supports these attributes, a review of some of the major issues confronting multicultural education needs to be addressed.

Issues and Problems

While the literature varies in its accounting of the various problems and issues that need to be addressed when establishing a sound multicultural education program, these are a few that continue to surface. As we present these issues, we encourage the counselor and the Counseling Program Committee to explore and respond to all multicultural education issues which need to be addressed prior to establishing a viable program.

Negative Attitudes. Many school districts are reluctant to measure children's attitudes toward minority groups because they believe that doing so in itself will give rise to inbread negative attitudes. Kehoe (1983) has stated that no evidence exists that supports this claim. Rather, the advantage of assessment will allow educators to focus their attention on problems that do exist.

Effective Programs. Ramsay, Sneddon, Grenfell, and Ford (1982) compared a number of schools with multiethnic populations and found that schools with the lowest truancy, vandalism, antisocial behavior, and the potential for higher levels of achievement among minorities were from those schools with a clearly articulated multicultural philosophy.

Racism. Contrary to what many people would like to believe, evidence of racism still permeates major institutions in the United States and the public schools are no exception (Lee, 1982). Evidence of racism in teacher expectations, special education assignments, class placement practices, career counseling activities, textbook content, and supervision practices does exist in varying degrees in many school districts throughout the Unites States.

Racial Problems. According to Kehoe (1983), a major reason cited by some school districts for rejecting multicultural education programs is that they do not have any racial problems in their schools and so why respond to problems that don't exist. While effective multicultural programs show promise for reducing tensions among diverse ethnic, racial, religious, and national origin groups, such tensions need not exist for multicultural education programs to serve a useful purpose. Multicultural education is also designed to teach respect and understanding, to instill a sense of cooperation between and among all people, and to create an atmosphere of acceptance which celebrates diversity and individuality.

Ethnic Minorities. Another widely acceptable reason for rejecting multicultural education by members of some school districts is that they don't have any ethnic minorities attending their schools. While a school district may not have ethnic minorities, that does not mean that these children have not, or will not, come in contact with minority groups at some time during their lifetime. These young children also will continue to form varying perceptions about those who are different from them which will shape their attitudes and behaviors in relation to any subsequent multicultural experiences they may have. Children living in environments with no or limited opportunities to interact with ethnic minorities are often influenced in their understanding about such groups by people and groups who are equally uninformed. Children and adults need the opportunity to recognize the contributions and achievement of all people to the richness of American society (Lee, 1982).

Teacher Training. Multicultural studies cannot be addressed successfully until trained teachers are available to integrate pluralistic materials into the curriculum of all classrooms, regardless of whether ethnic minorities are present or not. "Not only are teachers needed, but also guidance counselors, school psychologists, and school administrators are needed who are comfortable with and accepting of themselves and others, cognizant and proud of their own cultural heritage, and knowledgeable and respectful of the cultural heritage of others" (Lee, 1982, p. 406).

Multicultural Materials. While considerable multicultural materials exist, a significant need also exists for schools to avail themselves of highly reliable, valid, and useable curriculum guides, textbooks, films, and other multimedia classroom aids in providing children with a broad, rich, and meaningful multicultural experience.

Examination of Goals. In addition to training a cadre of school personnel, and having available for their use the necessary resource materials, the school will likewise need to examine the goals and objectives selected to produce the desired affective, cognitive, and behavioral outcomes. A balanced program calling for the infusion of curriculum materials;

appropriate teacher, administrative, and student performance; and a positive and conducive climate are needed to support a successful multicultural educational program.

Community Support. The issue of community support is partially critical to the success of multicultural education programs. Schools have a vital role to play in support of multiculturalism, but they can not do the job alone. Parents, community members, organizations, governmental agencies, and media likewise must play significant roles in shaping multicultural education. For these groups to attain the desired multicultural educational goals, a school and community coalition designed to meet those ends is highly suggested. The school must play an active role in establishing the necessary networks and in organizing the training efforts. They must sponsor workshops, town meetings, and make active use of various minority group consultants in spreading the word to community groups and individual citizens about the goals, objectives, and benefits of multiculturalism.

National Unity. Another issue being raised by some people is that, if educators encourage multiculturalism, they will threaten national unity (Friesen, 1985). The fear is that various multicultural and ethnic groups will become more solidly entrenched and will support a separatist policy of existence in staking out their territories.

The fear that people describe, who share the belief of a loss of national unity, is more likely to occur in an environment which denies cultural diversity and supports unhealthy competition among those who are "different." Such environments are created when people are not provided with the opportunities to learn about and practice cooperation, harmonious living, and acceptance of all people.

Future Directions

Despite some of the issues and problems that need to be addressed when establishing a multicultural education program, no doubt exists about the need for future programming in this area. While the elementary school counseling program should not be solely responsible for multicultural education, it has a significant role to play in helping to create a teaching/learning climate which supports multicultural pursuits.

As elementary school counselors, teachers, and administrators plan the future of multicultural education, one of their most critical tasks will be to decide which concepts, generalizations, and content are to receive priority attention. A potential solution to this problem can be derived by following a set of overall objectives which are designed to foster a moral and responsible citizenship. Those objectives consist of the development of (1) critical thought, (2) competency for enlightened citizenship, and (3) the growth of intercultural understanding and harmony (Freedman, 1984). Eight foundations formatted by Freedman (1984), if followed, will support these three objectives and a multicultural/multiethnic educational program which will yield positive results. These eight foundations hopefully will assist young people to make constructive life choices that will promote their own personal growth and will shape public policy which will lead to intergroup harmony and cooperation on the planet.

Clarify Definitions. Terms like ethnicity, culture, race, religion, and nationality are not clearly understood by a vast majority of the population. In addition, much printed material likewise continues to perpetuate the imprecision with which these terms are used. If children are to benefit from a sound multicultural educational program, educators will need to select materials which use the terminology correctly and they in turn will need to take care in establishing an accurate use of vocabulary in creating intercultural perceptions.

Information. Educators need to be as far reaching as they can in securing, organizing, and making readable a substantial quantity and variety of information. The information ought to cut across a variety of disciplines (anthropology, sociology, psychology) dedicated to the understanding of humankind. The information presented should provide insight into human behavior rather than characterize a particular group by presenting a series of isolated events and then leaving the children to draw their own and often inaccurate conclusions (Martin, 1975).

Understanding Group Differences. Multicultural programs need to enable children to understand and perceive, in a nonthreatening manner, various group characteristics and differences. Teaching children about group differences is not to be shied away from, or denied, but addressed in a very positive and reassuring manner. As differences are acknowledged, children can be taught to comprehend and understand the multifaceted, historical, social, and psychological forces which produced them, thereby challenging the mythology and stereotyping which has contributed to the judgment, persecution, and condemnation of various cultural, ethnic, racial, and religious groups. According to Glock, Wuthnow, Piliavin, and Spencer (1975), "cognitive sophistication" is the cultural factor that distinguishes relatively unprejudiced students from prejudiced ones.

Origins of Stereotyping. Exploring the origins of stereotyping and dispelling them will help children to become consciously aware of the erroneous assumptions that have influenced their thought and governed their behaviors. Such knowledge can help children assume responsible control over those previously unrecognized forces which have motivated their irresponsible thoughts and actions. Freedman, Gotti, and Holtz (1981) found in their studies that the examination of the sources of stereotypes constituted an important variable in helping young people to counter ethnic stereotypes.

Place Ethnicity, Race, and Religion in Perspective. The ethnicity, race, and religion of a person is often oversimplified as a cause for their behavior. Blacks, Irish, Jews, and others have had their actions attributed to an aspect or dimension of their background. The fact is that all people are members of numerous groups (socioeconomic, geographical, educational) as well as racial, ethnic, and religious ones. "Awareness of human complexity is a requisite to addressing the philosophical question of how individuals and groups should relate to multiethnicity/multiculturalism" (Freedman, 1984, p. 202).

Values Clarification. Imposing others' values on children in order to promote an understanding of little known cultures is not a very desirable action to take for any reason. However, learning about the values of others from culturally different backgrounds is vitally important. As children learn about their own values and those of others and how values affect thoughts and actions, they will be less likely to judge those actions in a negative way. Instead they will come to recognize those thoughts and actions as a reflection of morality or that which is properly based on that person's perceptions at the time of action. Again, Martin's (1975) findings substantiate that children who understand that cultures are organized systems of behavior become less ethnocentric than those who lack such teachings and understandings.

Persecution of Victims. Children need to become acquainted with some of the infamous persecutions in world history and the physical and psychological damage suffered by victims. By teaching children about the atrocities suffered by various religious, racial, and ethnic groups and how those persecutions materialized, the hope is that the likelihood of similar demonstrations of brutality will be minimized if not eliminated altogether. Some evidence exists to suggest that this hope has a strong element of reality associated with it.

Benefits and Costs of Group Identification. Educators need to explore with children, the benefits and costs associated with the identification of any given racial, ethnic, and/or cultural group. Freedman (1984) reported that scholars at a 1975 B'nai B'rith conference on Pluralism in a Democratic Society agreed that both positive and negative consequences do ensue from substantial association with ancestral groups. The point of exploring the value judgments of people regarding the "good" or the "bad" of group identification and outcomes is to help children fully comprehend what it means to be a part of any group and to make informed choices as they shape their own life style.

LIVING IN A NUCLEAR AGE

Violence is very much a part of children's environments today. Television programs, video games, movies, and graphic pictures in daily newspapers and magazines portray crimes of violence, threat of nuclear annihilation, and the environmental destruction of the planet earth. Helping children address their fears of separation, injury, and death and responding to the conflicting views they hear about these topics is absolutely necessary. Children express many doubts about their future and often feel powerless in changing the more negative causes of events which have already been set in motion.

Research conducted by Beardslee and Mack (1983); Chivian, Mack, and Waletzky (1983); and Myers-Walls and Fry-Miller (1984) reinforce the intense fear that many children already experience when they hear terms like nuclear power, radiation, nuclear explosion, environmental destruction, and nuclear war. These words conjure up feelings of anxiety, thoughts of death, and being very scared and are likely to precipitate nightmares and feelings of isolation.

While counselors, teachers, parents, and community supporters are not in a position to protect children from all the environmental forces that expose them to violence and fears of destruction, nor should they be. They are in a position to help children identify and address their fears in a responsible manner. Such action calls for the spotlighting of those issues and problems which threaten human existence and the challenging of irresponsible and unjustifiable reporting of unreliable, unverifiable, and inaccurate information which serves only to intensify children's fears.

Issues and Problems

As school districts prepare children to live in a nuclear age, they must provide them with the information, skills, and self confidence to address their fears and to take responsible action in their own behalf and that of mankind to resolve our planetary problems. So as not to compound children's fears when developing programs to help them understand and address planetary issues that are of grave concern to all of us, considering some of the issues and problems associated with curriculum development in this area is imperative.

Influences of Fear. According to Piaget (1954), several characteristics of thinking between the ages of 3 and 6 influence children's fears. Young children easily confuse reality, dreams, and fantasy: they attribute human or lifelike qualities to inanimate objects; they are in the process of learning about cause and effect relationships; and they often feel helpless and out of control in regard to helping themselves. Armed with this knowledge, adults need to monitor children's exposure to events which could precipitate undue fear, be there to discuss and answer questions about fearful events, and not place children in fearful positions in which they can exercise little or no control.

Inaccurate Information. Many of the fears that children experience regarding nuclear war and environmental destruction are often based on inaccurate, unverifiable, and unreliable information. Children need to understand that their thoughts about nuclear war and environmental destruction are frightening, however very capable people are working hard to insure that nuclear war does not occur and that a safe clean environment in which to live will be present.

Children also must be exposed to accurate information about people from many different cultures and their interest in preserving world peace. Children have been taught to fear people from different countries and to view them as evil and the enemy. Such beliefs do not spawn cooperation and non-combative methods of conflict resolution and understanding.

Lack of Control. Children's fears are likely to be intensified when they experience being out of control or powerless to influence their own life circumstances. Children can be taught creative ways to express their fears; be given opportunities to participate in activities which shape public policy (write letters to public officials and register their opinions and attitudes); participate in multicultural activities that expose them, in positive ways, to people from other lands; and learn power skills such as goal setting, decision making, and conflict resolution. Children also will experience a sense of control when they are told the truth and given accurate information in response to their concerns and questions about such issues as nuclear war, environmental planetary destruction, and all forms of human violence. Children need stability and a sense of predictability in their lives that can only come from developing a trusting relationship with people of influence who can convey a sense of hope through their own positive actions.

Conflict Resolution. Children are our future. How and what we teach children about themselves and their world will serve as the models they will use in responding to tomorrow's problems. If children receive the idea that the way people deal with conflict is through war and other forms of violence, positive and nonviolent forms of responding to conflict will not be viewed as viable options.

Children have many more concrete ideas about war and violence than they do about peace making activities. One place to begin is to teach children peace making skills in managing their peer relationships; and as they grow older, to use these same skills in responding to larger political, social, and environmental issues. Caldwell (1977) has suggested that our society needs to work toward strengthening altruism in children by emphasizing helpfulness and cooperation as highly valued behaviors. "Learning nonviolent behavior both requires and supports self acceptance, the development of empathy, respect for others, and the learning of effective techniques for expressing opinions that do not involve violence" (Myers-Walls & Fry-Miller, 1984, p. 30).

Negative Role Models. The environment is full of role models that perpetuate violence, environmental misuse and abuse, and criminal activity. While we do not support the banning of books, movies, comic strips, war toys, and games which glorify these activities, we do advocate parental and teacher intervention strategies designed to monitor and guide children's play and the shaping of their belief systems in reality oriented and responsible ways.

Denial of the Threat. While many children and adults respond to the concept of nuclear war by denying its possibility, others view nuclear war as inevitable and likely to occur during their lifetime. Both points of view serve to perpetuate a lack of responsibility and personal control over one's own destiny. Nuclear education programs (K through 12) however, have been developed in the last few years that are designed to be infused into the curriculum. These programs teach children about various issues of nuclear war and help them to sort out their own attitudes, feelings, and beliefs (biases) about the topic.

Nuclear education is a controversial topic in that mixed feelings exist as to whether or not the topic should even be addressed in the schools. For those interested in pursuing the topic, we recommend *Bibliography of Nuclear Education Resources*, edited by Susan Alexander (1984) and *Dialogue: A Teaching Guide to Nuclear Issues* developed by Educators for Social Responsibility (1982).

A threat of equally devastating proportions, which people have yet to come to fully realize, is the environmental destruction of planet earth. The ozone layer is threatened which protects the planet from deadly cancer causing ultra-violet rays, the land and water is ravaged by the disposal of medical wastes and deadly chemical toxins, and the air is heavy with deadly chemical gases which threaten our very existence. Carbon dioxide, methane, and chloroflurocarbons in the atmosphere also are contributing to a phenomenon known as the greenhouse effect which is resulting in the gradual warming of the earth's atmosphere. As this occurs, the delicate life sustaining balances between and among our air, water, and land systems will gradually deteriorate resulting in an unin-habitable planet ravaged by violent storms, intense heat, drought, and the flooding of our coastal cities brought on by the melting of the polar ice caps. The planet has already begun to experience some of these changes. The problem is a planetary one which needs immediate attention less we experience an irreversible condition. The psychological, social, political, legal, and educational ramifications from this major threat have yet to be fully accepted or understood. Counselors, teachers, parents, and community leaders worldwide will have a major responsibility in stopping the pollution and in changing people's lifestyles in order to save their home (the Earth).

Influence on Personality. The teenage years are a period when identity and ideas about future roles become a major developmental task (Erickson, 1963). Reifel (1984) has stated that "Attitudes about what the world has in store for us can shape our expectations about the future and be an important influence in personality formation" (p. 77).

Escalona (1965) stated that the greatest impact on young people when threatened by nuclear disaster was not the knowledge of danger, but the lack of positive adult role models in responding to that danger. She stated that a sense of adult helplessness is conveyed to young people in the way that adults ignore nuclear issues and in their failure to act or improve upon those dangerous conditions that confront mankind. Escalona (1965) has further agreed that the danger of nuclear war has undermined adolescents' "pull to maturity" in that they fail to see a future in which they can fulfill their life's dreams. Research by Schwebel (1982), Beardslee and Mack (1982, 1983), Mack (1982), and Winter (1986) supports the research findings of Escalona that threats of nuclear disaster and an uncertain future do have a significant influence on adolescents' feelings, thoughts, and actions. They tend to feel helpless and pessimistic about improving conditions for the future and are inclined to make more here-and-now life decisions.

While the research cited has been in reference to the threat of nuclear war, we believe that the same kinds of conclusions can be drawn about any perceived threat (real or imaginary) to national or international security.

To what degree will the psychological stresses (helplessness and powerlessness) associated with potential worldwide disasters affect suicide rate, school drop out rate, teenage pregnancy, substance abuse, and other forms of personal destruction when contemplating life decisions that are limited in scope to the present? One can only guess that some youth will give up, others will rebel, and still others will seek to attain whatever life pleasures they can grasp for the moment without bothering to address the consequences. Elementary school personnel, parents, and the community in particular, must take an active lead in discussing the societal issues and dangers that confront us. They must provide children with hope and a sense of power by becoming effective role models in shaping a future that offers a promise for a brighter tomorrow.

Future Directions

When contemplating shaping the future in response to those critical life threatening issues faced by children and adults living in a nuclear age, the task seems overwhelming, if not impossible. However, a choice does not exist concerning whether or not actions need to be taken, but rather what actions.

In October, 1984, the National Congress of Parents and Teachers resolved to support the inclusion of nuclear education programs in the schools. The programs were designed to enable young people to learn about nuclear issues for the purpose of addressing their concerns and fears and responding to the realities of nuclear development with accurate information, critical thinking, and full ethical considerations (Winter, 1986). Large school districts including San Francisco, Pittsburgh, Milwaukee, New York City, and Dade County, Florida have sought to develop appropriate peace education curricula that have involved parents, teachers, and community members in their development. Likewise, nuclear age initiatives have been introduced by state legislatures of Connecticut, California, Maine, and Oregon which clearly indicate a movement in the right direction (Winter, 1986).

In reviewing many publications and studying the complexities associated with developing an educational curriculum appropriate to the nuclear age, Winter (1986) identified a number of characteristics and themes that continue to appear in the literature. Among them are

> a holistic approach that includes facts, values, and feelings; a tolerance for diversity; cooperation instead of competition; a reexamination of underlying concepts and assumptions; concretizing theoretical ideas into practical strategies; honoring differences while looking for a common ground; interdependence and interrelationship as characteristic of interpersonal, national, and international relationships; a realization that there are no infallible experts, no single right answers; perceiving the solving of complex problems as an ongoing process; an optimistic attitude; creation of a common body of knowledge and a common language with which to talk about a subject heretofore shrouded in myth and mystery; development of critical thinking skills; contextualizing information; evolution of ethical principles; an approach that is active instead of passive; exercise of the imagination; assumption of individual and group responsibility; encouragement of innovation and improvisation; and the active involvement of parents, teachers, and community members in making educational decisions. (pp. 30-31)

Keeping Winter's (1986) ideas in mind, elementary school counselors can have a significant role in helping children respond to their fears and to shape their own futures by consulting with teachers, parents, and community leaders in developing curriculum programs and materials that will help children to

1. separate the realities from the myths when learning about such topics as nuclear war, violence, crime, and environmental destruction through pollution;

2. find ways in which they can experience a sense of control over their own destinies;

3. learn positive and non-combative ways of responding to conflict; and

4. work actively for world peace, cooperation, and harmony.

The challenge which school districts and elementary school counseling programs face is both exciting and necessary. Developing creative ways for children to explore and understand their fears; to experience public policy involvement; to address conflict positively and nonviolently; and to work actively for peace, disarmament, and environmental wellness are worthy activities for children to experience both inside and outside the classroom.

CHILDREN'S RIGHTS

While few people would debate the importance of recognizing children's rights, not everyone agrees on what basis children's rights should be recognized nor what those rights should be. Teachers, counselors, administrators, and community supporters need to examine seriously the concept of children's rights and bring some clarity to a subject which heretofore has been frought with ambiguity.

Chisholm (1981) has stated that at least two fundamental reasons exist as to why society should recognize and acknowledge the status of children and youth as persons and citizens. The first she has said deals with the notion of national justice. Because children are members of the human race, they are by virtue of that membership entitled to dignity and respect. Secondly, adults owe it to themselves and the preservation of society to invest in their own future, and the futures of those to come, by teaching and modeling those behaviors which will guarantee the rights and privileges which all Americans have come to expect and enjoy. By attending to rights and entitlements of children now, adults can help to insure that children will come to understand, experience, and appreciate fully what is meant by respecting themselves and the rights of others. For these same children, later as adults, will have their turn in shaping the destiny of those senior citizens who taught them the meaning of human rights.

Issues and Problems

Before embarking upon a program of children's rights or discussing what some of those rights might be, a number of issues and problems to which various authors have alluded need to be addressed. As each point is discussed, we hope that children's rights, as a concept for continual future development, will become a reality and that what we have presented here will help to bring some clarity in establishing a brighter future and a greater respect for children and their rights.

Human Rights Shouldn't Be Taught. Most people would agree that the right to life is a universal absolute right of all human beings as would be any of those rights guaranteed under the Constitution of the United States. So the teaching of human rights should be a pretty cut and dry activity. Wrong! With regard to the right to life issue, does that then mean that abortion should be opposed, that mercy killing is murder, that capital punishment is a crime against the state, that war in all forms is counter to the rights of the living, and that living wills which support people's decisions to terminate their own lives in "hopeless" medical situations are wrong? Human rights do exist in principle and provide excellent guidelines to follow in upholding the dignity and worth of all human beings regardless of their differences. However, in practice, human rights issues are often open to debate and interpretation when attempting to guarantee, regardless of acception, the rights of all people. Does that then mean that the school should avoid teaching children about their rights, protecting their rights, and giving them the opportunity to protect their own rights? No! Counselors, teachers, parents, and related school personnel can address human rights by teaching children about the principles of human rights, modeling respect and dignity for all children, and personalizing some of life's struggles often associated with attempting to guarantee human rights principles in practice. Role plays, case histories, dramatizations, debates, open-ended stories, and actual classroom applications that depict some of the struggles in achieving human rights, protecting them, and interpreting them in practice will help children to value and appreciate the rights that they do have.

Too Big a Risk. No safe rights exist on which educators can speak and teach as long as people (children) live in a nation of gross inequalities and violence. For every human right (child right) that is mentioned, some people will view the topic as too controversial for discussion in the classroom. Teaching children about their rights will undoubtedly spark some controversy in those environments where children's rights are being violated. Teaching, by its very nature, is filled with some danger. "Unless we are willing to accept the fact that our work will involve a bit of danger, we [teachers] will become the servants of systems that do not reflect on or recognize the rights of people [children]; and, we will become individuals who tend machines, administer tests, perpetuate thoughtlessness, and institutional stupidity" (Kohl, 1985, p. 499). Counselors and teachers must take risks in teaching children about those concepts and understandings on which this country was founded and which will lead it into a future of promise, freedom, and the fulfillment of those responsibilities that will guarantee the preservation of human rights.

Parental Control. Another controversial issue associated with children's rights has been society's move to curtail parental power through state laws in those instances when parents place their children at risk (physically and/or psychologically) during the parenting process. Children are entitled to the protection of their rights and when those rights are violated a variety of child welfare services have been developed to give expression to that entitlement (Chisholm, 1981). In recent years, however, the state has likewise learned that its official organizations, departments, and programs, being operated by people, also are prone to failure and that they too must be monitored in their role as surrogate parents. Only when the topic of human rights, and in particular, children's rights becomes a more understood and widely accepted responsibility of everyone in the society, will children become viewed less as property and more as people with guaranteed rights and entitlements of their own as members of the human race.

Fear of Child Anarchy. Two sides exist to most issues and children's rights controversy is no different. Chisholm (1981) has described two camps that have emerged during the past twenty years, the Children's Liberation point of view and the Responsible Children's Rights Position. While between the two camps are many similarities, they part company on a number of issues, the sharpest being that the Liberation group sees children and youth as mini-adults. They have thus transferred to children the rights and privileges of adulthood which for most means assuming responsibilities for which they are biologically and mentally unprepared. The children's Rights camp agrees that children are to have their rights identified and defended, but that one of their most basic rights is the right to be a child and have a childhood (Chisholm, 1981). "That means while adults move to broaden their understanding of what the rights of children are, they also must retain their responsibility, as adults, to care for children and to help set the boundaries for expectation and behavior. Adults must still say no as well as yes" (Chisholm, 1981, p. 50). This means that adults have an important job in balancing children's rights with a corresponding responsibility and obligation to prepare them for assuming those rights when they are developmentally ready to accept them. In the meantime, adults have the responsibility and obligation to protect children's rights until they are ready and capable of managing themselves.

Future Directions

Prior to creating learning environments, academic programs, and counseling activities that focus attention on children's rights, educators must first address the need to establish a theoretical framework which will give some direction to those activities. Farmer (1983) in response to this very challenge, has presented a useful application of Maslow's theory of self-actualization as the framework from which to discuss children's rights.

Maslow's theory is a sequentially organized and hierarchal theory of universal innate human needs which all human beings must fulfill if they are to become fully functioning individuals (mentally, physically, socially, and emotionally). The hierarchy begins with the most basic of human needs, the physiological, and advances to the safety and security needs, belonging and love needs, esteem needs, and self-actualizing needs. The attainment of these needs by children, who are more dependent and vulnerable to harm than are adults, and who are at lower stages of development (physically, cognitively, emotionally) than are adults, demands that adults play a significant role in their evolvement.

A human rights program based on Maslow's self-actualizing theory should focus on those rights that will provide all children with an equal opportunity to grow to their maximum potential as human beings. While Maslow's theory does not provide a list of rights and responsibilities, it does suggest a framework from which specific human rights can emerge. As an example, in Figure 12.1 are listed suggested human rights based on Maslow's (1954) human needs hierarchy.

No theory of personality and human nature holds the promise for developing human potential more than does Maslow's. Teachers, parents, and counselors are encouraged to review children's needs in light of those teaching/learning environments which are designed to meet them. Children have the right to meet their developmental needs and must be given the opportunity to do so. Of course, children likewise have the accompanying responsibility to make good on their rights and to respect the rights of others in meeting their needs as well.

Using Maslow's theory of self-actualization as a guide can help parents, teachers, and administrators to evaluate the teaching/learning climate in identifying effective child right practices, in determining violations of children's rights, and in assessing the capabilities of the social mechanisms to rectify those violations when they do occur. Assuring that all children are provided with the supreme right of having in place, and

Human Needs	Human Rights
1. **Physiological Needs** (The need for food, water, sleep, and exercise)	a. The right to adequate nutrition and medical care b. The right to play and recreation c. The right to be physically healthy and cared for throughout childhood
2. **Safety and Security Needs** (Freedom from fear, violence, and anxiety)	a. The right to live and play in a safe environment b. The right to special care and protection from harm c. The right to grow up nurtured by affectionate parents (guardians) d. The right to be a child and to experience the safety and security of childhood e. The right to freedom from fear of psychological and physical harm or abuse
3. **Belongingness & Love Needs** (Needs for friendship, love, and a feeling of being connected)	a. The right to affection, love and understanding b. The right to develop interpersonal relationships and the freedom to exercise them c. The right to grow in a society (home, school, community) which respects the dignity and life of all people regardless of their differences

Figure 12.1. Suggested human rights based on Maslow's human needs hierarchy.

Human Needs	Human Rights
4. **Esteem Needs** (The need for a positive self-concept and respect from others)	a. The right to develop a unique self identity b. The right to a free education c. The right to learn how to become a useful and contributing member of society d. The right to be educated to the limits of one's capacity
5. **The Need for Self-Actualization** (The need to develop one's innate potentials & talents)	a. The right and freedom to be different from one's parents and teachers b. The right to freedom and opportunity to be one's own person c. The right and freedom to choose one's own values, life-style, and life direction d. The right to gain and utilize self-knowledge for the purpose of self-realization and utilization

Figure 12.1. Continued.

operative, all the social mechanisms necessary to guarantee all other rights in advancing children through Maslow's hierarchy is the most challenging of all challenges.

In developing those teaching/learning climates so necessary in advancing children's growth and development, a quote from Farmer (1983) about children's rights helps to set the topic in proper perspective.

> Merely extending adult legal rights to children is not what children's rights are about. Children's rights are not to make the child completely equal to the adult in civil rights, but instead to guarantee to the child innate human needs, fulfillment opportunities, and to assure the needed special protections children need.
>
> Children's rights does not mean anarchy, rule by children, or a failure to provide needed structure and discipline to the child's world. A concept of children's rights based on Maslow's theory of self actualization has structure. It does not offer a totally exact formula for determining children's rights. It does offer a direction, a framework and a humane bottom line. (p. 88)

LIVING A WELLNESS LIFE-STYLE

Wellness is the building of a life-style based upon a conscious commitment of people to accept responsibility for their own health and the way things turn out in their lives (Koss & Ketcham, 1980). While most people understand the meaning of illness, they do not necessarily understand the meaning of wellness because it is a term that only has recently begun to take on meaning. Wellness, more than anything else, means learning to enjoy life to its fullest by making it a part of one's life-style. Williams (1988), a pioneer of modern health education, introduced the concept that health (wellness) is

> that condition of the individual that makes possible the highest enjoyment of life, the greatest constructive work, and that show itself in the best service to the world. . . Health as freedom from disease is a standard of mediocrity; health [wellness] as a quality of life is a standard of inspiration and increasing achievements. (Hafen, Thygerson, & Frandsen, 1988, p.1)

Wellness may be described as a process of continuous movement toward interpersonal relationships, nutrition, fitness, stress reduction, and other internal and external factors which influence one's ability to live life with total meaning, joy, and purpose. People who choose to live a wellness life-style work toward becoming the best that they can become regardless of their own personal limitations. A wellness life-style represents a multitude of choices and does not call for perfect health to be a participant. Wellness is a matter of learning to self-evaluate, making the necessary life adjustments, and establishing required goals which will enhance one's state of wellness.

"Wellness is a full integration of physical, mental, emotional, social, and spiritual well-being—a complex interaction of the factors that lead to a quality life" (Hafen, Thygerson, & Frandsen, 1988, p. 2). If teachers, parents, and counselors are to take seriously the goal of education stated in Chapter 1 which is to enable youth to acquire the skills and understandings to be competent and responsible people, then elementary school academic and counseling programs must address the need for a sound wellness curriculum.

Issues and Problems

Few people would disagree with the importance of learning to live a healthy life-style. However, few school districts in the United States have developed a schoolwide curriculum with a wellness focus. Many of the reasons cited for not getting involved have been based on inaccurate information and a lack of understanding about the wellness concept. What follows is a discussion addressing some of the issues and problems plaguing the wellness movement.

Wellness Is for the Super Healthy. Many people have been heard to say that unless a person is in top physical condition to begin with, he or she can not participate in a wellness program. Therefore since children's health runs the gamut from illness to healthy, many children would be unable to take advantage of a wellness program. In reality, nothing could be further from the truth. Anyone can live the process of wellness and yet suffer from an illness, be physically challenged, be overweight, or experience any number of conditions. No matter what children's or adults' current states of health are (and few people are in perfect health), they can begin to appreciate themselves as growing and changing people and allow themselves to work toward a happier life and positive health (physically, socially, emotionally, and spiritually). Wellness is a combination of self-awareness, education, and total human growth. All children, regardless of their position on the illness-wellness continuum, can learn to love themselves more and take charge of their lives as they have never done before.

Most Children Are Healthy. Health is a term that people know about, but usually misuse (Ardell, 1982). Most people think of health as a static state that they are in when they are not sick or hurting in some way. Health is almost always restricted in definition to one's physical state and to that which is directly observable or experienced in some way. As long as children and adults are not complaining about bodily symptoms, they must be healthy. Such a narrow definition of health is one that presumes that people are neither responsible for becoming ill nor responsible for getting "well." Illness is a matter of chance and health is a matter of luck and good genes.

While children may appear healthy, without question they live in a culture which supports a life-style that is dangerous to their own well being, that of their peers, and the offspring that they will one day bear unless change occurs. Norms that currently predominate are those which discourage exercise, encourage food practices and sedentary life-styles leading to obesity and dissolution, promote ghastly habits (smoking and substance abuse), support low expectations for positive health and human potential, encourage the dependence on doctors and drugs, and contribute to the environmental abuse and destruction of the planet (Ardell, 1982).

Statistics concerning the destruction of human life and the environment are so grim that they make the headlines regularly. Kuntzleman, in an article by Olson (1985), reported that in a study of 7 to 12 year olds in Spring Arbor, Michigan that 98% of them had at least one heart disease risk factor (e.g., high blood pressure, elevated cholesterol, excess body fat) and that 13% had five or more risk factors. Olson (1982) also reported that less than one-half of public school children get enough aerobic activity to keep their hearts and lungs fit. Hafen, Thygerson, and Frandsen (1988) have likewise reported that a clear 50% of all deaths for people between the ages of 1 and 65 were caused by individual life-styles. Smoking habits, misuse of pharmaceutical and illegal drugs, stressful living, poor nutrition, sedentary behavior, and related life-style factors were listed as the primary causes for permanent damage and the death of people living in the United States. Much more could be said about America's state of health and the destructive life-styles that children and adults are living. However, the bottom line is that our children are victims of cultural norms that continue to perpetuate the destructive life-styles which they are living. If children are to become all they are capable of being and are to contribute to the growth and development of their society, they must learn to assume responsibility for their own growth and development first. Their survival depends on it.

Wellness Programs Are in the School. When people make the statement that wellness programs are already in the schools, they are most often referring to those isolated programs that respond directly to remediation and/or pre-vention issues that have received media attention (drug and alcohol education, suicide prevention, smoking cessation, AIDS education, etc.). While programs like these do serve a purpose, they often are, too little, too late, remedies to very complex problems. Life-style is as directly linked to health and wellness as it is to disease and premature death. If children are to develop healthy life-styles, they must participate in a compre-hensive and sequentially organized wellness plan that cuts across every academic discipline, is aimed at promoting a healthful school environment, and integrates school and community participation. The nation's schools provide an appropriate and necessary vehicle for teaching children how to utilize the information and skills they develop in their academic subject areas in order to make complex life-style decisions that affect their health and well being and the health and well being of the society in which they live. When wellness programs of this caliber are instituted in the nation's schools, many of the separate add-on curriculums designed to address individual societal ills can be eliminated in favor of a more comprehensive and developmental life-style curriculum.

Future Directions

The United States is truly a nation at risk when the children that schools purport to educate do not receive life-style training that is even more basic than the three R's of reading, writing, and arithmetic. Elementary school counselors, teachers, administrators, parents, educational specialists, school staff, and the community must work together in promoting a positive life-style management program that stresses the following five elements (Ardell, 1982):

1. **Self Responsibility**—the element of self responsi- bility is the single most important driving force in a wellness life-style management program. Without an awareness and clarity of understanding and com- mitment to the reality that people (children and adults) are the single most important determiners of their own destinies, they are not likely to pursue knowledge, skills, and self confidence in the practice of the other four ele- ments.

2. **Nutritional Awareness**—the old adage, "you are what you eat" seems to apply here. Children need to understand and practice such things as weight control, understanding food labels, emotional aspects of eating, dietary planning, and food preparation. Children like- wise need to understand the connection between nutrition and those life-style management choices available to them in developing a wellness life-style.

3. **Physical Fitness**—children need to understand and practice a wellness life-style which includes a variety of physical activities designed to promote safe cardio- vascular fitness. Activities which promote flexibility, strength, and endurance and which can be experienced over a lifetime are encouraged.

4. **Stress Awareness and Management**—Ardell (1977) has stated that when people can act in their own best interest, stand up for their rights without fear and anxiety, and express their emotions and still respect the needs of others, they will be able to free themselves from

a great deal of traumatic distress. Stress management teaches children how to use stress positively, how to recognize and cope with distress in a healthy manner, and how to live and work in a stressful environment while keeping distress to a minimum.

5. **Environmental Sensitivity**—environmental sensitivity is the one element in the program which clearly involves a societal interest. Improving the environment is a social, political, and economic problem which affects all people and which likewise requires the involvement of people in achieving the desired solutions. Flynn (1980) has stated that improving health status in this country will require changes in life-style which will reflect a reconciliation of personal and social values designed to encourage new living patterns. Children need to develop an environmental sensitivity and the understandings, skills, and motivation necessary to enhance and sustain a safe and productive environment.

Self responsibility, nutritional awareness, physical fitness, stress management, and environmental sensitivity can be easily incorporated into every facet of the child's academic and extra-curricular activities without the need of adding new courses or programs to an already overcrowded, overdemanding school day. A life-style management emphasis in the school focuses on helping children to understand and utilize what they have learned in school to benefit themselves and their planet. For example in arithmetic, children could be taught the meaning and use of numbers in developing a wellness life-style (understand blood pressure readings, understand serum cholesterol ratings, measure weight control, count calories, compute aerobic proficiency) and the role that numbers and mathematical concepts play in managing their planet effectively.

All other subject matter areas likewise have the same potential for providing children with the necessary information, skills, and self confidence to shape significantly their own lives and to participate actively in addressing those societal forces which shape their destiny. Many children today feel isolated, helpless, and hopeless when faced with those societal forces which impact significantly on their lives because they lack adult role models and the information, skills, and self confidence in understanding how and in what manner they can make a difference in this world. Wellness programs that address self responsibility, nutritional awareness, physical fitness, stress management, and environmental sensitivity will give children that hope because they will have been taught and given opportunities to shape a brighter future for themselves and those with whom they share the planet.

COUNSELORS WHO MAKE A DIFFERENCE: A PROFESSIONAL ISSUE

Elementary school counselors are and will continue to be the key players in determining the future success of elementary school counseling programs across the country. The single most important factor contributing to the success of school counseling is being able to deliver quality human services of the breadth and depth necessary to meet the developmental and societal needs of all children. However, meeting children's needs has become an ever increasing challenge for most school counselors given the numbers of children, parents, and teachers they are expected to serve, the ever expanding role of the position, and the meager budgets on which to finance expanding services.

Elementary school counselors have literally become jugglers in a three ring circus trying to increase the number of balls (activities, projects, & responsibilities) they can juggle with the same two hands. We have found in our discussions with elementary school counselors, that most are skilled as direct service providers. They have been well trained for that role and feel comfortable working directly with parents, teachers, and children. The same counselors, however, are quick to share their frustrations in trying to increase the quantity and quality of their services. They do not have a clear handle on how they can continue to improve their programs given their limited resources of time, money, and personnel.

While the school counselor's role of service provider is very important, that role is also very limiting. Counselors are limited by their own human resources regarding the number of people, programs, services, and activities they can personally administer. We believe, that as critical as the service provider role is to the success of elementary school counseling, too much emphasis has been placed on it. If elementary school counselors are to have a significant role in shaping the future, and we believe they can, then elementary school counselors must function as leaders, managers, political activists, and service providers. These roles can not be separated one from the other in practice, but must function as a whole. However, for the sake of discussion, each role will be presented separately.

Leadership Role

The term leadership has been defined in many different ways by many different people. Common to most definitions however is the idea that leadership connotes a process whereby a person (counselor) influences a group or an organization in the attainment of its goals. Leadership refers to a process and is not necessarily associated with the person who occupies a position of formal power. A person may not hold a position of formal power and yet be perceived as a leader in the group or organization because members either implicitly or explicitly consent to the leader's influence (Mitchell & Larson, 1987). In the case of formal group leader, the organization has given the leader a degree of legitimacy to influence the group. The most successful leaders however are those that have a combination of a personal base of legitimacy as well as that which has been formally ascribed through the position.

Effective leaders give their group direction, coordination, expertise, access to special resources, or other similar benefits that will help the group to achieve desired goals. In exchange the leader gets from the group status, recognition, esteem, compliance, and the potential for greater influence in the future (Hollander, 1978).

The most successful leader, according to Kouzes and Posner (1987), is the one who is successful in getting others to want to do what the leader is convinced should be done. The specific leadership practices and commitments for those interested in accepting the leadership challenge are presented in Chapter 12, *Planning the Future.*

For elementary school counselors, the message is clear. Failure to be viewed by administrators, parents, teachers, and school board members as the person with the professional base of legitimacy to influence the development of the elementary school counseling program will leave the door open to the less qualified, but more influential in determining the future of school counseling. Many elementary school counselors lack the skills and understandings necessary to lead. What is even more tragic is that many counselors function in school systems where school counseling program goals, designs, and practices are influenced more by those (school administrators and school board members) who do not really understand what counselors should be doing (Drury, 1984).

Getting parents, teachers, children, administrators, school board members, and the school community excited about and wanting to participate in a comprehensive and well planned program with a future, requires an elementary school counselor at the helm who practices effective leadership.

> Leaders thrive on change; exercise "control" by means of a worthy and inspiring vision of what might be, arrived at jointly with their people; and understand that empowering people by expanding their authority rather than standardizing them by shrinking their authority is the only course to sustained relevance and vitality. (Peters, 1987, in Kouzes & Posner, 1987, p. xiii)

Management Role

While successful leaders challenge the status quo, search for new opportunities, experiment and take risks, envision the future, enlist others in that vision, model the way, and celebrate accomplishments, managers are necessary to provide a degree of stability and maintenance. Counselors must continue to search for better, more effective, and relevant ways to meet children's needs, but they also must have the management skills necessary to translate counseling program philosophy into a concrete mission statement backed by objective, purposeful, and relevant goal statements.

"Management is a distinct process consisting of activities of planning, organizing, actuating, and controlling, performed to determine and accomplish stated objectives with the use of human beings and other resources" (Terry & Franklin, 1982, p. 4). The management process converts disorganized human and physical resources into a systematic and comprehensive effort in meeting the elementary school counseling program goals. Management skills coupled with leadership capabilities, provide counselors with the capacity of expanding program services. Effective management thus makes human effort more productive in that, as new program goals are defined, the counselor is able to amass and mobilize the resources necessary (people, materials, equipment, methods, money, and locations) to accomplish the desired results within the predetermined constraints of time, effort, and cost (Terry & Franklin, 1982). Effective management practices likewise bring to order those here-to-fore isolated events and practices into meaningful relationships which serve to solve problems and accomplish goals.

As with leadership, many school counselors have received limited, if any, management training. Consequently, they offer services based more on what they like to do rather than on what may be needed. Their services tend to be limited in scope based more on what they can single-handedly accomplish on their own, rather than to provide the nature and scope of services which are needed based on what is relevant and necessary.

Effective managers know how to plan, organize, actuate, and control effective school counseling programs. They continually monitor the environment (school and community) searching for the problems and opportunities facing the elementary school counseling program. They inform and involve the participation of others in responding to program needs. They make program decisions, address and solve unforeseen programmatic disturbances, and participate in the process of determining program priorities and the allocation of resources to support those decisions. And finally, program managers fulfill important interpersonal roles as public relations specialists, as liaisons between and among groups that work with and support elementary school counseling programs (networking), and as motivators and challengers of elementary school counseling personnel to pursue, with enthusiasm, the goals of the program.

Elementary school counselors must never lose sight of the fact that they manage a program that has as its program providers, parents, teachers, children, special service personnel, staff, school board members, and the community at large. A program with this level of potential and commitment, needs an effective manager.

Role of Power and Politics

Power and politics are key ingredients for getting things accomplished in any organization/program. Elementary school counseling programs are no different. Counseling programs, out of necessity, must use power and politics to their advantage. Thus for elementary school counselors to be successful managers, they need to understand and be able to make use of social power and political processes.

While the research and literature on power and politics is extensive and somewhat confusing regarding the conceptual ambiguity of terms as well as in their application, we will never-the-less attempt to clarify the importance of each concept in relation to successful elementary school counseling programs. The topic of *social power* refers to those situations in which one person tries to change or influence the behavior of another person. Counselors, by that definition, must be concerned about influencing the behaviors of administrators, parents, teachers, and community residents in support of their role, the elementary school counseling program, and in providing the necessary resources (people, budgets, supplies, time) to maintain a quality program. Social power, to a large degree, is based on other people's perceptions of the school counselor to provide the valued outcomes as a result of their compliance in accordance with the counselor's desires. To the degree that these people do change their behaviors in the desired direction, the counselor has power.

The degree to which school counselors exhibit social power is based on their available resources. According to French and Raven (1960), these resources consist of rewards, punishments, information, legitimacy, expertise, and referent power. If the person (people) that the counselor is trying to change values the proposed outcomes, values the relationship, and has few other options, then the counselor is likely to be successful in orchestrating the desired change. While power strategies based on coercion may work, they are not often accepted. Power strategies based on expertise, legitimacy, and information are generally more acceptable to most.

Counselors who have a clear understanding of their role, the philosophy and mission of their school counseling program, and have the research data to support their programs will have information power to the extent that they can influence successfully the support of others in maintaining a solid program. Legitimate power has more to do with the counselor's perceived right to make requests. The norms and expectations that have been created surrounding the school counselor's role as leader-manager will help to determine the counselor's success. Counselors must, therefore, exercise due care in establishing their roles and the counseling program in order to create the kind of working relationship and status within the school system which supports legitimate power. Expert power comes by way of training and experience and depends more on the personal attributes of the counselor than on the counselor's formal position within the school's hierarchy. School counselors who are able to demonstrate their expertise in an assertive and tasteful manner are likely to be deferred to for their expertise during a decision.

In contrast to social power, Pfeffer (1981) described **political behavior** as "those activities taken within organizations to acquire, develop, and use power and other resources to obtain one's preferred outcomes in a situation in which there is uncertainty or dissensus about choices" (p. 415).

Mitchell and Larson (1987) have pointed out three important aspects of Pfeffer's definition worth mentioning. First, political activity requires the application of power to obtain outcomes. In this respect, organizational politics and social power are very much alike; the main difference is that in organizational politics the focus is on groups influencing groups while social power refers to individuals influencing individuals. Second, politics occurs in situations of uncertainty.

When a specific direction is supported by all, politics is not necessary. Third, Pfeffer makes no reference regarding the inherent goodness or badness of the process. Rather how the process is used and the outcomes that are sought are open to evaluation.

A natural consequence of most organizations (schools) is differentiation (multiple units: administrative, teaching, human service, and financial) and resource scarcity (money, people, time, supplies, etc). Both of these factors support organizational conflict and political activity in the school as each organizational unit seeks parity with the other. School counselors and the Counseling Program Committee, if they are to develop effective elementary school counseling programs, will need to develop those political strategies that groups use to move their programs forward and to resolve the organizational conflict which may surround the decision-making process. Some of those strategies include compromise, the formation of coalitions, collaboration, domination, avoidance, and strategies designed to dissolve opposition.

For many school counselors, politics is a dirty word and a process that they would prefer to do without. The reality however is that school systems, like other organizations, are frought with political activity. If counselors are to mount support for their ideas and programs, they will need to become masters at developing social power and in engaging in organizational politics in order to expand their programs and to move their ideas from the drawing board to the school board for approval.

Direct Service Provider Role

The role that is most familiar to elementary school counselors is that of direct service provider. The counselor education institutions have done more to promote this role than any other and it is the one which brings the most satisfaction to school counselors and is most applauded by those who receive the services.

The direct service provider role consists of any activity that requires counselor time in meeting the program goal needs of those who receive the counselor's services. Consequently, counselors spend much of their time counseling children individually and in small groups, engaging in classroom developmental counseling activities, meeting with parents individually and collectively, speaking to service organizations, consulting with teachers, conducting inservice workshops, making developmental counseling materials and distributing activities for classroom use, meeting with school boards, preparing reports, and the list continues depending on the energy level of the counselor.

While we applaud elementary school counselors for their high energy levels, their sense of enthusiasm, and their ability and skill to service the needs of others, we are likewise concerned about how school counselors can continue to meet the ever expanding and demanding need for their services. While the developmental and societal demands increase, the number of elementary school counselors hired by school districts and the budgeting allocations to those programs are not likely to increase significantly during the coming years. As long as elementary school counselors go about silently filling their school day with good deeds, their programs are not likely to receive the visibility that they demand.

Successful elementary school counseling programs with a promising future need a strong support base from legislators; need to lobby for their share of school district, community, state, and national funds; and need to enlist the support of families, teachers, administrators, and community volunteers in developing partnerships in the delivery of services to those who need them.

The elementary school counselor must reach out and function first as leader, manager, and politician in order to create exciting, viable, responsible, and relevant program services. Counselors must have a vision of the preferable, the management skills to make the vision a reality, and the power and political skills necessary to support the birth of new ideas and programs. As elementary school counseling programs expand in breadth and depth in a climate which supports such endeavors, the elementary school counselor will have more time, not less, to participate in those school district service activities in which they do so well.

BIBLIOGRAPHY

Alexander, S. (Ed.). (1984). *Bibliography of nuclear education resources.* Cambridge, MA: Educators for Social Responsibility.

Alpert, D., Pulvino, C.J., & Lee, J.L. (1985). Computer applications in counseling: Some practical suggestions. *Journal of Counseling and Development, 63,* 522-523.

Ardell, D.B. (1977). *High level wellness.* Emmaus, PA: Rodale Press.

Ardell, D.B. (1982). *14 days to a wellness lifestyle.* Mill Valley, CA: Whatever Publishing.

Beardslee, W.R., & Mack, J.E. (1982). The impact on children and adolescents of nuclear development. In R. Rogers (Ed.), *Psychological aspects of nuclear developments* (Task Force Report, No. 20). (pp. 64-93). Washington, DC: American Psychiatric Association.

Beardslee, W.R., & Mack, J.E. (1983). Adolescents and the threat of nuclear war: The evaluation of a perspective. *Yale Journal of Biology and Medicine, 56,* 79-91.

Becker, H.J. (1983). *Microcomputers in the classroom: Dreams and realities.* Eugene, OR: International Council for Computers in Education.

Benderson, A. (1983). Computer literacy. *Focus: Educational Testing Service, 11,* 1-32.

Caldwell, B.M. (1977, January). Aggression and hostility in young children. *Young Children, 32*(2), 4-13.

Childers, J.H., Jr. (1985). The counselor's use of microcomputers: Problems and ethical issues. *The School Counselor, 33*(1), 26-31.

Chisholm, B.A. (1981). Children's rights. *Early Child Development and Care, 7,* 45-56.

Chivian, E.S., Mack, J.E., & Waletzky, J.P. (1983). *What soviet children are saying about nuclear war: Project summary.* The Nuclear Psychology Program, Harvard Medical School.

Dinkmeyer, D., Jr., & Carlson, J. (1983). Counselor computer competencies. *Elementary School Guidance and Counseling, 18,* 5-12.

Drury, S.S.. (1984). Counselor survival in the 1980's. *The School Counselor, 31*(3), 234-240.

Educators for Social Responsibility (1982). *Dialogue: A teaching guide to nuclear issues.* Cambridge, MA: Author.

Erickson, E.H. (1963). *Childhood and society.* New York: Norton.

Escalona, S. (1965). The effects of the nuclear threat on childhood development. *Preparing for nuclear war: The psychological effects.* New York: Physicians for Social Responsibility.

Farmer, R. (1983). Children's rights and self-actualization theory. *Education, 103,* 82-89.

Flynn, A. (1980). *Holistic health: The art and science of care.* Bowie, MD: Brady.

Freedman, P., Gotti, M., & Holtz, G. (1981). In support of direct teaching to counter ethnic stereotypes. *Phi Delta Kappan, 62,* 456.

Freedman, P.I. (1984). Multiethnic/Multicultural education: Establishing the foundations. *The Social Studies, 6,* 200-202.

French, J.R.P., Jr., & Raven, B. (1960). The bases of social power. In D. Cartwright & A.F. Zander (Eds.), *Group dynamics* (2nd ed.), (pp. 607-623). Evanston, IL: Row, Peterson.

Friesen, J.W. (1985). Establishing objectives for a multicultural program. *History and Social Science Teacher, 21,* 32-38.

Glock, C.Y., Wuthnow, R., Piliavin, J.A., & Spencer, M. (1975). *Adolescent prejudice.* New York: Harper & Row.

Hafen, B.Q., Thygerson, A.L., & Frandsen, K.J. (1988). *Behavioral guidelines for health and wellness.* Englewood, CO: Morton Publishing.

Hollander, E.P. (1978). *Leadership dynamics: A practical guide to effective relationships.* New York: Free Press.

Joe, V.C. (1971). Review of the internal-external control construct as a personality variable. *Psychological Reports, 25,* 619-640.

Kehoe, J. (1983). Enhancing the multicultural climate of the school. *History and Social Science Teacher, 19,* 65-75.

Kohl, H. (1985). Human rights and classroom life. *Social Education, 49,* 498-99.

Koss, L., & Ketcham, M. (1980). *Building wellness lifestyles.* Branchville, NJ: Frost Valley YMCA.

Kouzes, J.M., & Posner, B.Z. (1987). *The leadership challenge: How to get extraordinary things done in organizations.* San Francisco: Jossey-Bass.

Lee, M.K. (1982). Multiculturalism: Educational perspectives for the 1980's. *Education, 103*(4), 405-409.

Mack, J.E. (1982, March-April). But what about the Russians? *Harvard Magazine,* pp. 21-24, 53-54.

Martin, D. (1975). Ethnocentrism towards foreign culture in elementary social studies. *The Elementary School Journal, 75,* 381-388.

Maslow, A.H. (1954). *Motivation and personality.* New York: Harper and Row.

Mastroianni, M.P. (1983). Computers: More than an academic tool. *Elementary School Guidance and Counseling, 18,* 58-59.

Mitchell, T.R., & Larson, J.R., Jr. (1987). *People in organizations: An introduction to organizational behavior (3rd ed.).* New York: McGraw-Hill.

Myers-Walls, J.A., & Fry-Miller, K.M. (1984). Nuclear war: Helping children overcome fears. *Young Children, 39,* 27-32.

Nelson, C.R., & Krackover, G.H. (1983). Getting comfortable with computers. *Elementary School Guidance and Counseling, 18,* 13-20.

Olsen, E. (1985, October). Is your child fit: Games to grow on. *American Health,* pp. 51-55.

Pfeffer, J. (1981). *Power in organizations.* Marshfield, MA: Pitman.

Piaget, J. (1954). *The construction of reality in the child.* New York: Basic Books.

Ramsay, P.D.K., Sneddon, D., Grenfell, J.S., & Ford, I. (1982). *Tomorrow it may be too late.* Hamilton, New Zealand: University of Waikato.

Reifel, S. (1984). Children living with the nuclear threat. *Young Children, 39*(5), 74-80.

Sampson, J.P., Jr. (1984). Maximizing the effectiveness of computer applications in counseling and human development: The role of research and implementation strategies. *Journal of Counseling and Development, 63,* 187-191.

Sampson, J.P., Jr., & Pyle, K.R. (1983). Ethical issues involved with the use of computer assisted counseling, testing, and guidance systems. *Personnel and Guidance Journal, 61,* 283-287.

Schwebel, M. (1982). Effects of the nuclear war threat on children and teenagers: Implications for professionals. *American Journal of Orthopsychiatry, 52,* 608-618.

Terry, G.R., & Franklin, S.G. (1982). *Principles of Management* (8th ed.). Homewood, IL: Richard D. Irwin.

Wilmoth, L. (1983). Planning an educational computer program. *Elementary School Guidance and Counseling, 18,* 46-50.

Winter, M.L. (1986). Nuclear education update. *School Library Journal, 32,* 22-26.

INDEX

G

Gains
  focus 351
Gannon, M.J. 33, 50
Generalization 156, 158, 166
Gesell, A. 27, 50
Getting acquainted checklist
  social development activity
    212-3
Gibbs, J. 216, 284
Gibson, J.L. 100, 107
Glock, C.Y. 384, 414
Goal charts
  cognitive development activity
    273-4
Goals
  career 30
  career education 288
  child need 64-5
  clarity 45
  cognitive 30
  education 7-8
  establishing priorities 40-3,
    Figures 41 & 42
  examination 381-2
  high priorities 42-3, *Figure* 42
  identifying 18, 26-32
  low priorities 43, *Figure* 42
  needs 42-3
  physical 29
  priorities 18-9
  self-concept 29
  social 29
  statement 28-32
Good deed box
  social development activity
    206-7
Good idea box 150
Goodlad, J. 23, 28, 40
Gotti, M. 384, 414
Graham, T. 184, 216, 258, 284, 325
Great stone face
  physical development activity
    179
Grenfell, J.S. 380, 415
Grim. G. 184, 216, 284
Group differences
  understanding 384
Group identification
  benefits and costs 385
Guidelines
  control 103-6

H

Hafen, B.Q. 399,400, 402, 414
Hall of Fame
  counselor 344
Harris, B. 184, 216, 258, 284, 325
Harvest of skills 221
  self-concept development activity
    253-4
Hats and tools
  career development activity
    297-8
Havighurst, R.J. 10, 23, 27, 50
Hays, O.G. 333, 335, 336, 370
Herr, E.L. 8, 11, 12, 23
Hillman, B.W. 162, 184
Hobbies graph
  social development activity
    194-5
Hobby day
  career development activity
    295-7
Hollander, E.P. 406, 414
Holt, F.D. 130, 152
Holtz, G. 384, 414
How would they describe you
  self-concept development activity
    241-2
Hoyt, K. B. 292, 325
Human development
  microcomputers 372-9
Human needs hierarchy 396,
  Figure 397-8
Human rights 393-4, *Figure* 397-8

I

Ideal living plan
  self-concept development activity
    251-2
Ideas
  collect 341
  importance 337
  innovative 341
Identification
  program goals 26-32
Ilg, F.L. 27, 50
Implement
  corrective action 97-100

N

O

P

Q

R

Race 384
Racism 380
Ramsay, P.D.K. 380, 415
Rationale
    elementary school counseling
      9-12
Raven, B. 409, 414
Reasoner, R. W. 184, 216, 258, 284
Recipients
    program 68-9
Reflection 156, 158, 165-6
Reifel, S. 389, 415
Reinforcement for reading—
  bookworm
    cognitive development activity
      268
Religion 384
Research
    cognitive development 259-60
    elementary school career
      education 287-90
    physical development 161-2
    self-concept development 217-21
    social development 185-6
Resourcefulness 377-8
Resources
    budgetary 66-7
    office 68
Respect 377
Responsibility 377, 378
    self 403
Rights
    children 392-9
Risk
    counselors take 340-2
    honor takers 342
    model 342
    taker 352
Rogers, R. 413
Role
    counselor 290-1
    direct service provider 411-2
    leadership 406-7
    management 407-9
    power and politics 409-11
Role models
    negative 388
Rudman, G.J. 284
Runion, K.B. 162, 184

S

Salvation Army 142
Sampson, J.P. 373, 415
Schermerhorn, J.R. 52, 70, 75
Schmidt, J.A. 291, 325
School
    partnerships 136-43
School counseling program
    actuation 71-87
Schwebel, M. 390, 415
Search
    for opportunities 339-40
Seasonal careers
    career development activity
      301-3
Self
    responsibility 403
Self-actualization 396
Self-awareness 288
Self-concept development activities
    224-57
Sensitivity
    environment 404
Service providers
    feedback 92
Setting priorities
    self-concept development activity
      246-7
Sexism 375-6
Shearson and Leman Brothers, 350
Shertzer, B. 152
Side effects 96-7
Silhouette activity
    self-concept development activity
      232-3
Simon, B. 216, 284, 258
Skills
    auditory perception 164
    career 294-5
    communication 187
    cooperation 165, 187
    coordination 163
    decision making 188, 23, 294-5
    eye-hand coordination 164
    feeling identification 223
    fine and gross motor 164
    goal setting 188
    goal setting and decision
      making 262

T

White House Statement 7-8
Who are these people 221
    self-concept development activity
      249-50
Who's missing
    physical development activity
      181-2
Who's my partner
    physical development activity
      170-1
Williams, S. 285
Wilmoth, L. 378, 415
Wilt, J. 216
Winter, M.L. 390, 391. 415
Wirth, S. 260, 285
Wishing box
    self-concept development activity
      235-6
Wishing on a birthday cake
    self-concept development activity
      239-40
Wittmer, J.M. 220, 258
Woal, S.T. 325

Woodell, G.D. 332, 370
Workers in our community
    career development activity
      309-10
Working in groups
    social development activity
      203-4
Worzbyt, J.C. 20, 24, 33, 50, 52, 67, 70, 84
Wrenn, C.G. 106, 107, 258
Wuthnow, R. 384, 414

Y

YMCA 142, 146
YWCA 142, 146

Z

Zander, A.F. 414

JOHN C. WORZBYT

Dr. John C. Worzbyt is a professor and coordinator of graduate and doctoral studies in the Counselor Education Department of Indiana University of Pennsylvania (IUP). He earned his doctorate in counselor Education at the University of Rochester, Rochester, New York.

In addition to his administrative responsibilities, Dr. Worzbyt is the coordinator of the elementary school counseling program at IUP; is a Nationally Certified Counselor; and is a consultant to school districts, social service agencies, mental health clinics, professional associations, and hospitals. His areas of expertise are child counseling, self-esteem development through strengths training, decision making, and enhancing organizational work climates.

The author has over twenty years experience as an elementary school teacher, middle school science teacher, elementary school counselor, and counselor educator. He has been an office holder in a number of professional associations, has published articles in national journals and newsletters, and has authored two previous books. Dr. Worzbyt is a 1989 registrant of *The National Distinguished Service Registry: Counseling and Development* and is a 1989 U.S. Department of Education Federal Grant Research recipient in drug and alcohol education.

For the past several years, Dr. Worzbyt has been a keynote speaker and workshop presenter at national, regional, state, and local professional associations and organizations on such topics as Up Your Enthusiasm: How to get High on Life; The Humor Side of Leadership; The ABC Approach to Building Self-Esteem; The Skills Approach to Decision Making; Drug and Alcohol Education: A Wellness Approach; and Life-Style Enhancement: Developing a Happier and Healthier You. He currently manages a small private consulting and workshop business through which he presents programs focusing on human potential and self-improvement to such diverse groups as veterinarian associations, the National 4H Association, The Boy Scouts of America, the National YMCA, The National Association of Extension Home Economists, and the Pennsylvania Department of Occupational Medicine and Health.

Dr. Worzbyt is an avid hiker, swimmer, and boater. He and his wife, Jean, and their two teenagers enjoy spending their summers at their home on Owasco Lake in the Finger Lakes region of New York State.

KATHLEEN O'ROURKE

Dr. O'Rourke is the Guidance Department Chairperson for the Altoona Area School District and is also a part-time Assistant Professor of Counselor Education at Indiana University of Pennsylvania. Her experiences include 25 years as an educator, with 18 of these being served as an elementary school counselor. Currently Dr. O'Rourke is the district coordinator for the Comprehensive Prevention/Intervention Drug and Alcohol Project in the district. This project includes the five major components of Curriculum, Student Assistance Program, Elementary Absenteeism program, Peer Leadership and Parent Education. This program has solidified Dr. O'Rourke's commitment to working in the prevention aspect of guidance and providing as much leadership as possible in assisting students to develop positive self-esteem. She is more convinced than ever that sound elementary school guidance programs are the optimum prevention mechanism.

Prior to becoming involved in the administration facet of guidance, Dr. O'Rourke served as one of five pilot project counselors for the Pennsylvania Elementary School Developmental Guidance Project, coordinated a Career Education Project in the Altoona Area School district, and was involved in a Dropout Prevention project in the 1970's. She also has served as a state consultant to districts involved in implementing developmental guidance programs.

Professionally, Dr. O'Rourke is strongly involved in professional counselor organizations and has been active in the Pennsylvania School Counselors Association since 1973. She has served as President, Chairperson of the Career Education Taskforce, and Chairperson of the Board of Governors. For the past four years, she has been Chairperson of the Elementary/Middle School Committee. In this role, she has presented numerous workshops dealing with elementary school developmental guidance issues. She was also recently elected vice-President of the North Atlantic Region of the American School Counselor Association.

Several awards have been presented to Dr. O'Rourke including the Altoona Area School District CARE Award, the

Distinguished Dissertation Award from Epsilon Chapter of Phi Delta Kappa, and the Pennsylvania Counseling Association Eminent Practitioner Award.